DIALECTIC IN HEGEL'S HISTORY OF PHILOSOPHY

Volume One

Mehmet Tabak

Dialectic in Hegel's *History of Philosophy*: Volume One
© 2013 Mehmet Tabak

Published in New York City by the author.
Printed in the United States

All rights reserved. No part of this book may be reproduced, stored in a retrieval system, or transmitted by any means—electronic or mechanical, including photocopying, recording, or otherwise—without written permission from the publisher, or the author.

First published in 2013

ISBN: 9781939873002

Contents

Preface 3

Dialectic in Hegel's Introduction 9
   1. Introduction to Dialectic 9
   2. The Subject of the History of Philosophy 11
   3. Some Difficulties and Inconsistencies in Lectures 15
   4. The Definition Problem in Hegel 20
   5. Abstract and Concrete in Hegel and Marx 23
   6. Potentiality, Actuality, and Dialectic as Teleological
      Development 26
   7. The Inner Contradiction of the History of Philosophy 33
   8. Conclusion: Looking Forward 38

"Oriental Philosophy" 40
   1. Introduction 40
   2. Chinese Philosophy 42
   3. Indian Philosophy 51
   4. Hegel's Final Verdict on the "Oriental Philosophy" 81

First Greek Period, First Division - Part I: Ionics, Pythagoreans, and
Eleatics 87
   1. Introduction 87
   2. Ionic Philosophy 89
   3. Pythagoras and the Pythagoreans 99
   4. The Eleatic School 106

First Greek Period, First Division - Part II: Heraclitus, the Atomists,
and Empedocles 127
   1. Introduction 127
   2. Heraclitus 127
   3. Leucippus, Democritus, and Empedocles 138

First Greek Period, First Division - Part III: Anaxagoras 153
   1. Introduction 153
   2. The Cosmogony of Anaxagoras 154
   3. The Good and Causality 159
   4. How Mind Rules the World 162

First Greek Period, Second Division - Part I: The Sophists............ 171
  1. Introduction 171
  2. Protagoras.. 175
  3. Gorgias 179

First Greek Period, Second Division - Part II: Socrates 191
  1. Introduction 191
  2. Dialectic Method and Irony in Socrates..................................... 193
  3. The Good as the End of Thought 202
  4. The Shortcomings of Socrates's Dialectic.................................. 206

First Greek Period, Second Division - Part III: The Socratics 213
  1. Introduction 213
  2. The Megarics.. 217
  3. The Cyrenaic School.. 230
  4. The Cynic School 244
  5. A Brief Evaluation of the Progress of Philosophy 249

Bibliography 253

Preface

G. W. F. Hegel treats history in general and the history of philosophy in particular "scientifically." For him, science is necessarily based on a single principle, and it is such a principle that makes any subject a proper system. Seen in this light, the history of philosophy is a whole, and all the philosophical utterances throughout history are the internally related parts of this whole. What makes the whole and its parts internally related is the single, universal principle, which he alternately calls *Being*, Essence, Reason, Mind (a.k.a. Spirit), the Idea, the Notion (a.k.a. the Concept), and God. This principle grounds every relation of the whole, and is said to be the essential *prius* of all. But, the universal principle is not a simple substance. It is an absolute subject, which implicitly entails all of the parts of the whole within itself. For this reason, the historical concretion of the whole is a process of self-realization, a process of externalization if you will, in which the universal principle develops by intensifying and diversifying itself. The history of philosophy exemplifies this teleological development, and is thus thoroughly dialectical in this sense. I will further explain Hegel's unique approach to the history of philosophy, and the dialectical nature of this history, in Chapter 1.

The history of philosophy was obviously very important to Hegel. Indeed, he did not simply think of his own philosophy as the most correct philosophy, or the last stop in the development of philosophy. He also thought his own philosophy represented the philosophical totality in an integrated manner. His account of the history of philosophy was, in a significant sense, an attempt to demonstrate this fact. Because he thought of it to be so important, from 1805 to 1830, he taught this subject nine times, and died, in 1831, before completing the tenth course. His own notes from 1805–1806 suggest that he intended to publish these lectures, though this never materialized.

It was Karl Ludwig Michelet, a close student of Hegel, who first published Hegel's lectures between 1833 and 1836. Michelet used Hegel's notes, mostly written in preparation for the Jena lectures (1805–1806), and his own notes taken from the 1823–1824 lectures, as his framework, and supplemented these with the notes of some other students who attended Hegel's 1825–1826 and 1829–1830 lectures. The first edition published by Michelet proved to be too difficult to follow. Subsequently, Michelet revised, reorganized, and abridged the first edition, and produced the more coherent, less repetitious second edition, which he published between 1840 and 1844. According to some, the second edition was more problematic than the first, since Michelet had actively edited the material he had used. For the first time, between 1892 and 1896, the second Michelet edition, entitled *Lectures on the History of Philosophy* (henceforth, *Lectures*), was translated into English by E. S. Haldane.

German scholar Johannes Hoffmeister accused Michelet of altering the lectures too much and introducing inaccuracies into them. In the 1930s, Hoffmeister used several additional sets of lecture notes, which were not available to Michelet, in a new attempt to reconstruct Hegel's lectures. However, he went no further than reproducing the "Introduction," and a brief segment of Hegel's lecture on Oriental philosophy. In 1971, Quentin Lauer, SJ, a professor of philosophy at Fordham University in New York (1954–1990), published *Hegel's Idea of Philosophy*, which includes a translation of Hegel's *Introduction to History of Philosophy*. As the title of this translation suggests, Lauer also did not go beyond Hegel's "Introduction." In order to avoid too much repetition, he based his translation on Hegel's 1825–1826 lectures. In 1985, another translation of the Hoffmeister edition was published by T. M. Knox and A. V. Miller, which is somewhat lengthier than the Lauer translation and briefer than the original Hoffmeister edition. This translation, too, is basically the translation of Hegel's "Introduction." Beginning in 1990, R. F. Brown and J. M. Stewart began publishing the English translation of the new critical edition of Hegel's lectures, based on five sets of notes taken from the 1825–1826 lectures. While this translation, like the Michelet-Haldane version, is all encompassing, and its translators purport to include material unavailable in other versions, it in fact does not include many of Hegel's comments, some of which are very substantial. In this respect, the Michelet-Haldane version remains unsurpassed. Yet, the Brown-Stewart edition is, on some levels, better. It includes invaluable footnotes, mainly clarifying and correcting Hegel's sources. In contrast to the Michelet-Haldane version, the Brown-Stewart version is also relatively easier to read.

In this work, I mainly use the Michelet-Haldane edition for two reasons: It is the most comprehensive and the most widely available version in English. I have read through the other translations to assure a more accurate interpretation, and occasionally supplemented my commentary with quotations taken from them. In my view, what is sorely missing in the Hegel literature in English is not a new translation or an edition, but a comprehensive interpretation of his lectures on the history of philosophy. While these lectures are widely quoted, some of its specific parts are examined disjointedly, and everyone seems to agree that they are very important; to my knowledge, no one has attempted to give a full account of these lectures. In this work, I try to remedy this shortcoming.

At the same time, despite the rich literature available on this subject, Hegel's dialectic is still little understood. My initial goal was to contribute to this literature by writing a book on Hegel's dialectic. To make a long story short, I found Hegel's *Lectures* to be the most appropriate body of work for this purpose. I first attempted to focus on those passages in which Hegel explicitly deals with dialectic, but this strategy proved to be shortsighted. One reason for this is that dialectic itself has a history. The historicity of dialectic comes across in two distinctive ways, which inform the reasons as to why dialectic had to be dealt with within the context of the entire history of philosophy.

First, in a very general sense, for Hegel the history of philosophy in its entirety represents the historical dialectic of philosophy. For this reason, the demonstration of this general dialectic requires accounting for the entire history of philosophy. In this context, whether or not Hegel explicitly discusses dialectic is not the determining factor. What matters more is the historical process of development in its totality. The historical development of philosophy, in turn, demonstrates what dialectic is and does in a systematic manner. This is because, according to Hegel, the history of philosophy is thoroughly dialectical. For this reason, dialectic has to be demonstrated through the entire history of philosophy, and not disjointedly.

Second, dialectic also is manifest in the history of philosophy in a different sense than the one very briefly outlined above. In this history, there are many different forms of dialectic, explicitly or implicitly found in the thoughts of as many philosophers. What Hegel says of their dialectic individually and collectively is invaluable for any serious attempt to understand Hegel's own dialectic. However, it is not possible to understand the dialectic of these philosophers without accounting for their philosophical ideas. In other words, the dialectic Hegel attributes to Zeno, Heraclitus, the Sophists, Socrates, Plato, the Skeptics, Kant, and so on, is not adequately comprehensible without Hegel's interpretation of their philosophical positions. This, again, requires going through the entire *Lectures*. For these reasons, I have decided to account for Hegel's dialectic within the context of his entire interpretation of the history of philosophy.

Still, one might rightly suspect that the dialectic explored in *Lectures* is insufficient to account for all of what Hegel says on dialectic. This is partially true. While in general the Hegelian dialectic essentially entails a teleological process of development, his description of dialectic comes across somewhat differently in different contexts. These differences have much to do with the nature of what is being considered. For instance, the dialectic of nature is somewhat different than the historical dialectic of philosophy and society, and these two are somewhat different than the dialectic of pure logic. However, this problem is minimized by the fact that *Lectures*, because its scope is so broad, addresses these differences to a large extent. Indeed, in terms of explaining these differences, *Lectures* is the most useful single body of work Hegel produced.

Many scholars treat dialectic strictly as a method. Hegel points out in his analysis of Socrates's philosophy that the Socratic dialectic is closely intertwined with his philosophy, and is not merely a method (see Chapter 7). In Chapter 1, we will observe that Hegel says the same thing about his own dialectic and philosophy. It follows from the identity of dialectic and philosophy that explaining one necessarily involves explaining the other. For this reason, my interpretation of *Lectures* is also an interpretation of Hegel's philosophy, and not simply of his dialectic. Obviously enough, Hegel's other major works can also be studied for the purposes of understanding his dialectical philosophy. What is special about *Lectures* is the fact that it provides a relatively accessible and very comprehensive vantage point for this purpose.

Yet, *Lectures* is not devoid of problems. The most general problem is that, as we have come to know of it today, it is mostly based on the lecture notes of Hegel's students. This problem poses two particular kinds of interpretative issues. The first such issue pertains to the reliability of the notes of his students. This issue is minimized by the fact that *Lectures* is based on some of Hegel's own notes, and the notes of multiple students, all of whom present a largely consistent account. The second such issue emanates from the fact that *Lectures* is based on Hegel's lectures. Hegel's lectures entail the characteristic shortcomings of all course lectures. They do not always engage in what they intend to explain in a sustained and comprehensive manner. As it turns out, there is a common remedy for both of these interpretative issues: Hegel's other works. In interpreting Hegel's *Lectures*, I frequently make use of his other major works. Likewise, *Lectures* provides many useful explanations that help better explain Hegel's other works. Its main "Introduction" is arguably the most important introduction to Hegel's philosophy. Moreover, many of the issues and categories Hegel discusses in his other works, most notably dialectic, find a better articulation in *Lectures*.

My interpretation of *Lectures* is moderately critical. The nature of my criticism has nothing to do with whether or not Hegel's philosophy, or dialectic, is right or wrong. Apart from the ones mentioned above, there are other problems, perhaps more substantial, in *Lectures*. They mainly have to do with the inconsistencies in Hegel's explanations. Hegel is not always accurate about the ideas of the philosophers he deals with. I try to highlight some of these inaccuracies. Also, his interpretations are often too abstruse or insufficient to be of any use. An example of this that caused some uproar is his treatment of what he called "Oriental Philosophy." Since my intention is not to rewrite the history of philosophy, I provide barely enough additional material from external sources to make Hegel's interpretations more comprehensible.

More importantly, Hegel, against his own advice, often attributes his own ideas to the philosophers whose ideas he analyzes. Such attributions are both valuable and problematic. The main problem with them is that his interpretations become confusing, especially to those who are not sufficiently familiar with Hegel's philosophy and with the ideas of the philosophers under his scrutiny. They are valuable because such attributions, once we distinguish them from the ideas of other philosophers, provide us with rich insights into Hegel's own ideas.

Of course, the greatest problem any student of Hegel faces is that all of his writings are notoriously difficult to understand. *Lectures*, though it is relatively easier to follow than some of his other main works, is no great exception in this regard. After all, Hegel presumably once said that "only one of my pupils understood me, and even he unfortunately understood me wrongly." In all likelihood, this is an old urban legend, though one that is likely to have permanent currency for good reasons. I do not think that Hegel can ever be made fully intelligible, unless one oversimplifies his ideas and utterly complicated concepts. For this reason, in reading Hegel, as well as my present interpretation of him, one should not begin with the expectation that many of his key arguments and terms will immediately become clear. One has to stay the course, and develop one's understanding of his philosophy along the way, however frustrating this may appear at first. What is more frustrating and rewarding at the same time is that there does not seem to be an end to what we can learn from, and about, Hegel's philosophy.

My three-volume interpretation of *Lectures* corresponds to the three volumes of the Michelet-Haldane edition. In both cases, this division is based more on the length of the material one can comfortably fit into a single volume than anything else. In other words, our triadic division of *Lectures* is not governed by Hegel's obsession with triads. Hegel himself gives a triadic division to the history of philosophy: the Greek period, the Middle-Ages, and the Modern period. Each period is further divided into three subsections, though these subsections are not always further divided into three parts. It would perhaps be more ideal to present each main period in a separate volume. However, this is practically very difficult to do because roughly two-thirds of Hegel's lectures deals with the Greek period, and the remaining one-third is devoted to the other two main periods (mostly to the Modern period). For this reason, the first two volumes of my work are devoted to the Greek period, and the third volume to the remaining two periods.

More interestingly, the amount of attention devoted to each period clearly indicates the importance Hegel placed upon Greek philosophy. Those readers who are strictly interested in the history of philosophy, however, may be disappointed to discover that some of what we today consider significant philosophers are either dealt with too briefly or not dealt with at all. This disappointment is more likely to emerge from reading Hegel's account of the post-Greek periods. Perhaps, such omissions have to do with Hegel's own prejudices, and with the fact that many philosophers whom we consider to be significant today were not so in Hegel's own times. Relatedly, *Lectures* is not the most scholarly treatment of the history of philosophy, and, despite some limited interventions in this regard, I do not make any substantial effort to improve upon this aspect of *Lectures*. *Lectures* is more suitable for the purpose of understanding Hegel, and should be read primarily for this purpose. My interpretation of *Lectures* is guided by this very purpose. This does not mean that Hegel has nothing to contribute to our understanding of the history of philosophy. Both his method of presenting this history and his interpretation of various philosophers are fruitfully provocative.

Whether we fully agree with him or not, Hegel forces all of us to think differently. He questions and overturns all that is taken by his opponents to be eternally fixed. Reading him encourages us to do the same. In today's world, which is filled with fixed ideas, this cannot be a bad thing. By publishing this work, I am hoping to contribute to our understanding of Hegel and to different ways of thinking about the world as a result.

I wish to thank Akiko Tabak and Shinasi Rama for their support, and Karin van der Tak for her invaluable help with editing. This volume is dedicated to the loving memory of my brother, Cemal Tabak.

Chapter 1

Dialectic in Hegel's Introduction

1. Introduction to Dialectic

In his "Introduction" to *Lectures on the History of Philosophy* (*Lectures*) Hegel, arguably, offers the most accessible introduction to his philosophy and dialectic. As it turns out, explaining what dialectic is and does is the same as explaining Hegel's philosophy. According to Hegel, explaining philosophy involves getting involved in it. Generally speaking, there are two parallel ways of doing philosophy. The first way is to follow, purely logically, the self-development of the universal categories of thought, such as *being, essence,* and *notion/concept*.[1] The second way is to follow thought's development in the spiritual and natural worlds. The spiritual and natural worlds are further divided into various spheres and, consequently, into various "sciences" that study them. The history of philosophy falls into the spiritual realm. It is also the main venue for our present investigation.

Hegel tells us that dialectic "is in general the principle of all motion, of all life, and of all activation in the actual world. Equally, dialectic is also the soul of all genuinely scientific cognition." This is to say, dialectic "asserts itself in all the particular domains and formation of the natural and spiritual world."[2] In this way, philosophy, as the "genuinely scientific cognition," runs parallel to dialectic in "the actual world," natural and spiritual. Indeed, philosophy's aim is to cognize this world by finding itself, its principles and categories, within it. In noticing this parallelism in Hegel, Alexandre Kojéve concludes that the "Hegelian Dialectic is not a *method* of research or of philosophical exposition, but the adequate description of the *structure* of Being, and of the realization and appearance of Being as well."[3]

---

1. Concept or Notion is the translation of *Begriff*, though the former has become the universally accepted translation in recent decades. I use them interchangeably.
2. G. W. F. Hegel, *The Encyclopaedia Logic: Part I of the Encyclopaedia of Philosophical Science with the Zusatze*, trans., with introduction and notes, by T. F. Geraets, W. A. Suchting, and H. S. Harris (Indianapolis: Hackett, 1991), 128–29, 130.
3. Alexandre Kojéve, *Introduction to the Reading of Hegel: Lectures on the Phenomenology of Spirit* (Ithaca: Cornell University Press, 1969), 259; also

However, there is a proviso. According to Hegel, doing philosophy properly requires freeing the mind of all the methodological interventions that are external to its natural rhythm. As John McTaggart puts it, "if it only saw clearly enough," the mind would "see a nature like its own in everything."[4] Since the mind also works dialectically, seeing in everything a "nature like its own" means seeing the presence of dialectic in everything. What Hegel calls "genuinely scientific cognition" is precisely this "seeing" of how everything develops naturally, including cognition. In order to be able to do this, as Quentin Lauer, SJ, adds, ". . . we are to allow human consciousness to show us what it itself is by developing one after the other all the implications of being conscious at all . . ."[5] Thus, the proviso is that we must get rid of any imposition of an external method on the cognitive dialectic. In Hegel's words: "We must abstain from interrupting the immanent rhythm of the movement of conceptual thought; we must refrain from arbitrarily interfering with it, and introducing ideas and reflections that have been obtained elsewhere. Restraint of this sort is itself an essential condition of attending to and getting at the real nature of the notion."[6] This "demands concentrated attention on the notion as such, on simple and ultimate determinations like being-in-itself, being-for-itself, self-identity, and so on, for these are elemental, pure, self-determined functions . . ."[7]

What is found in the history of philosophy is thus the development of the universal Notion, as well as its various determinations, into a complete system. This indicates, too, that philosophy has a history and can only become a complete system through its historical development. This process of development is philosophy's historical dialectic. In this sense, "the study of the history of Philosophy is an introduction to Philosophy itself" (3).[8] Hegel's own philosophy is this philosophy in its final, developed form.

179, 185, 195. Herbert Marcuse also repeats this conclusion. See Herbert Marcuse, *Reason and Revolution: Hegel and the Rise of Social Theory* (New York: Oxford University Press, 1960), 121.
4. John McTaggart, *Studies in the Hegelian Dialectic* (Cambridge: Cambridge University Press, 1896), 143.
5. Quentin Lauer, SJ, *Essays in Hegelian Dialectic* (New York: Fordham University Press, 1977), 2.
6. G. W. F. Hegel, *The Phenomenology of Mind*, trans., with introduction and notes, J. B. Baillie (Mineola: Dover Publications, 2003), 34.
7. Ibid.
8. In this work, all citations within the text, indicated merely by the page number(s), and placed within (. . .), come from G. W. F. Hegel, *Lectures*

It follows that the main, but hidden, task of *Lectures* is to introduce Hegel's own philosophy, which is thoroughly dialectical. The "Introduction" to *Lectures* serves this end in two important ways. First, it tells us how to approach the history of philosophy, and, consequently, philosophy itself. Second, it outlines some of the key terms of the historical dialectic of philosophy. My task is to examine both, and to tease out what the Hegelian dialectic is and does in a more understandable and systematic manner than Hegel describes in the "Introduction" to *Lectures*.

2. The Subject of the History of Philosophy

For Hegel, the history of philosophy is not the mere accumulation of opinions, or isolated systems of thought. As Hegel sees it,

> The possession of self-conscious reason, which belongs to us of the present world, did not arise suddenly, nor did it grow only from the soil of the present. This possession must be regarded as previously present, as an inheritance, and as the result of labor—the labor of all past generations of men . . . [I]n science, and specially in Philosophy, . . . we owe what we [have] to the tradition which, as Herder has put it, like a holy chain, runs through all that was transient, and has therefore passed away. Thus has been preserved and transmitted to us what antiquity produced.
>
> But this tradition is not only a stewardess who simply guards faithfully that which she has received, and

---

on the History of Philosophy, Volumes 1–3, trans. E. S. Haldane (London: Kegan Paul, Trench, Trubner & Co., 1892–1896). All citations that relate to the first volume are represented simply by page number. All citations from the second and third volumes include the volume number in Latin numerical II and III, respectively. Everything else is footnoted, including the other translations of *Lectures on the History of Philosophy*. In all direct quotations, I have changed the British spellings to the American ones. The reason for this alteration is not significant at all. In all direct quotations, the words included in [. . .] are my own additions or modifications, but not the ones bracketed by (. . .). Within the regular text where direct quotation is not involved, everything placed in (. . .) are my own words and phrases.

thus delivers it unchanged to posterity, just as the course of nature in the infinite change and activity of its forms ever remains constant to its original laws and makes no step in advance. Such tradition is no motionless statue, but is alive, and swells like a mighty river, which increases in size the further it advances from its source. The content of this tradition is that which the intellectual world has brought forth, and the universal Mind does not remain stationary . . . [T]he world-spirit [Mind] does not sink into this rest of indifference; this follows from its very nature, for its activity is its life.

In short, "this activity presupposes a material already present, on which it acts, and which it does not merely augment by the addition of new matter, but completely fashions and transforms . . . In this manner that which is received is changed, and the material worked upon is both enriched and preserved at the same time [negation] . . . Philosophy can only arise in connection with previous Philosophy, from which of necessity it has arisen" (2–3). In this sense, what unfolds in the history of philosophy is not pure contingency. It has a continuous inner movement, and, for this reason, is a process of development, and not mere change (11–14).

It follows that dialectic itself is a process of development. According to Hegel, as Lauer explains, "the relation of one philosophy to another is dialectical, which means that a subsequent philosophy does not supplant but rather complements that which preceded it, and that the order of succession is not arbitrary—it is dictated by the necessity of thought in development." This succession, since it involves permanency and change, is a process of negation. Thus, "it is that familiar function of *Aufhebung* [negation] which characterizes every dialectical process; what is *aufgehoben* [negated] is not simply cancelled, even though it is not left as it is; it is retained but at the same time lifted up to higher level."[9]

As Hegel succinctly points out in *Philosophy of Mind*, "This [historical] movement, which philosophy is, finds itself already accomplished, when at the close it seizes its own notion—i.e. only *looks back* on its knowledge."[10] Simply put, when philosophy seizes its

---

9. Quentin Lauer, SJ, *Hegel's Idea of Philosophy*, with a translation of G. W. F. Hegel, *Introduction to History of Philosophy* (New York: Fordham University Press, 1971), 42–43.

10. G. W. F. Hegel, *Philosophy of Mind: Part Three of the Encyclopaedia of the Philosophical Sciences*, trans. A. V. Miller (Oxford: Clarendon Press, 1971), 302.

own Notion at the end, it has reached the cognition of this Notion in its most Absolute form (the Absolute Idea). At this point, it only has to "look back" at its original source. When developed philosophy looks back, it recognizes the Notion of previous philosophies as its own Notion. Thus, Hegel finds his own Notion, in more or less primitive forms, in Thales and all the other philosophers that came after him. What remains to be done is to critically reclaim the primitive Notion, to recognize that, in spite of the shortcomings imposed on it by the previous philosophers, it is the very same universal Notion. A main reason for this looking back, and following the historical development of the Notion is to prove the truth of philosophy. With this proof, Mind finally grasps the totality of its history as its own truth, or "autobiography." To borrow from Jean Hyppolite, this journey is "... the novel of philosophic formation..." Consequently, this philosophical formation, or dialectic, "follows the development of consciousness, which, renouncing [*negating* would be more accurate here!] its first beliefs, reaches through its experiences the properly philosophic point of view, that of the absolute knowledge."[11]

However, neither looking forward from the beginning to the end, nor "looking back" from the vantage point of the end point, should be done in a manner of indifference. The historian of philosophy must get involved in the process as if it were her/his own freely developed thought. In this sense, the historian is also an autobiographer. Hegel provides some important reasons for this need for involvement, or self-immersion in the process. The first is that the doctrine of non-involvement may be impossible to implement in the first place: "Tennemann, for example, conveys this impression of non-involvement. If we look at him more closely, however, we find him completely caught up in the Kantian philosophy, whose main contention is that the true is not to be known." Thus, this non-involvement and indifference strategy is intimately tied to the treatment of the history of philosophy as a heap of opinions in which there reigns the uncertainty, or even the unknowable nature, of the Absolute truth. The gist of Hegel's argument in this context is that "the true," the universal Notion, is knowable, and the history of philosophy, if done correctly, would demonstrate precisely this fact. Consequently, "this *insistence on non-involvement* means for the most part simply that the one who teaches history of philosophy shall act like a dead man in presenting philosophies, that he should treat them as

---

11. Jean Hyppolite, *Genesis and Structure of Hegel's Phenomenology of Spirit* (Evanston: Northwestern University Press, 1974), 12.

something separated from his own spirit, something external, that he should himself be without thought in treating them." This is not simply a moral advice on Hegel's part. Its significance is that "one must be involved in philosophy and not be satisfied with limiting oneself merely to the knowledge of what others have thought." This is because "Truth will be known only when with his spirit one is in it."[12]

When one, "with his spirit," is involved in the historical development of truth, one is also involved in the universal Spirit (Mind). The "successive series" of different philosophies, or philosophers, are actually "interwoven in spirit just as much as in their particular content" (168). The historian, if (s)he is to be effective, has to partake in this universal Spirit, which (s)he is able to do as a spiritual being. Briefly stated, "history does not show us the Becoming of things foreign to us, but the Becoming of ourselves and of our own knowledge" (4). For this reason, says Hegel, "Philosophy is not somnambulism, but is [one] developed consciousness . . ." in which the individual consciousness (finite spirit) is "interwoven" with the universal Spirit (39).

However, ultimately the Absolute subjects of the history of philosophy are not the philosophers. Spirit marches forward through the philosophical ages and minds, impelled by its inner necessity. "What the history of philosophy shows us," says Hegel, "is a succession of noble minds, a gallery of heroes of thought, who, by the power of Reason, have penetrated into the being of things, of nature and of spirit, into the Being of God, and have won for us by their labors the highest treasure, the treasure of reasoned knowledge" (1). As it turns out, the real task of the philosopher is to cognize the Spirit as it manifests itself in and through history.

This last remark calls to mind Hegel's view of "World-historical men—the heroes of an epoch."[13] The similarity between world-historical persons, such as Alexander and Napoleon, and the "heroes of thought" (i.e., philosophers), is that they both do the bidding of the eternal Mind. Instead of unconsciously doing the work of the universal Mind, as the world-historical persons do with their deeds, philosophers seek to become conscious of the Mind as well as its deeds. What matters more in the history of philosophy is not the individual and her/his deeds, but the development of Spirit. As Hegel further describes it,

---

12. Lauer, *Hegel's Idea of Philosophy*, 91–92.
13. G. W. F. Hegel, *The Philosophy of History*, trans. J. Sibree (New York: Dover Publications Inc., 1956), 30–31.

The events and actions of this history are therefore such that personality and individual character do not enter to any large degree into its content and matter. In this respect the history of Philosophy contrasts with political history, in which the individual, according to the peculiarity of his disposition, talents, affections, the strength or weakness of his character, and in general, according to that through which he is this individual, is the subject of actions and events. In Philosophy, the less deserts and merits are accorded to the particular individual, the better is the history; and the more it deals with thought as free, with the universal character of man as man, the more this thought, which is devoid of special [individual] characteristic, is itself shown to be the producing subject (1–2).

3. Some Difficulties and Inconsistencies in Lectures

Lauer observes that the "task Hegel had set himself at the outset of his course of lectures was that of observing philosophical thought, beginning with its first abstract attempts to find in reason the explanation of reality and proceeding to the systematic realization that, concretely, reason finds all reality in itself." Moreover, Hegel also wanted to "show that the development of pure thought so elaborately worked out in his *Science of Logic* has its exact counterpart in the empirically verifiable development of philosophy from the first faltering steps of Thales to the elaboration of Hegel's own system."[14] In conformity with Lauer's point regarding the parallelism between the purely logical and temporal dialectic of philosophy, Hegel says, in *Encyclopaedia Logic*, that the "starting point of the Logic is the same as the starting point of the history of philosophy in the proper sense of the word. This starting point is to be found in Eleatic philosophy, and, more precisely, in the philosophy of Parmenides, who apprehends the Absolute as being."[15] However, several complications arise in this regard when we turn to the pages of *Lectures*.

One complication of lesser importance is that Parmenides is here taken to be the first philosopher, whereas Hegel also gives Thales the same credit in *Lectures*. We may overlook this problem to some extent

---

14. Lauer, *Essays in Hegelian Dialectic*, 67, 72.
15. Hegel, *The Encyclopaedia Logic*, 138.

for Hegel says in the above passage that Parmenides is the starting point in the "proper sense," because he was the first to consider the Absolute *being* as "pure thought."[16] In *Lectures*, to complicate things further, Hegel also asserts that "it was in Zeno that Philosophy first attained to a purer expression of itself" (241). Hegel also gives, when his turn comes, a similar credit to Anaxagoras. This lesser complication, then, in a way endorses the claim of parallel dialectic of logic and the history of philosophy. They both begin with pure thought, that is, abstract *being*, or the abstract Notion. What is unclear is to whom this beginning precisely belongs.

Closely related to this complication is the sequencing of the philosophers in *Lectures*. For instance, several philosophers are introduced before Anaxagoras, who was born before them. One reason for this is that Hegel treats the philosophers who belong to the same school of thought together. However, Hegel also somewhat manipulates the chronological sequencing of the philosophers in order to more closely match their logical sequencing in *Logic*. Even so, some mismatches are still present. For instance, abstract *being* is the first category in *Logic*, and the category of *quantity* comes later. In historical terms, the category of quantity, which is associated with the Pythagoreans, comes before pure *being*. Indeed, Hegel at times downplays this parallelism himself: "Though the development of Philosophy in history must correspond to the development of logical philosophy, there will still be passages in it which are absent in historical development" (302).[17] Or, more mildly put, "I maintain that the sequence in the systems of Philosophy in History is *similar* to the sequence in the logical deduction of the Notion-determinations in the Idea" (30, italics added).

Hegel goes on to suggest that this similarity holds especially true if the "fundamental conceptions appearing in the history of Philosophy be entirely divested of what regards their outward form . . ." (ibid.). The "outward form" is the way philosophers express their concepts. To use one example, the outward form of Thales's Notion, or *being*, is water. The inward form of his Notion is the abstract, universal *being*. Water thus signifies such a *being*. However, this clarification poses an interpretative complication. It is not Thales who explicitly posits water as an abstract *being*, but Hegel. Without the awareness of this Hegelian intervention, understanding Hegel's interpretation of various philosophers becomes extremely difficult.

---

16. Ibid.
17. Also see, G.W.F. Hegel, *Elements of the Philosophy of Right*, trans. H. B. Nisbet (Cambridge: Cambridge University Press, 1991), 61.

Often, Hegel discusses the concepts of philosophers in such a manner that suggests they themselves were aware of the *inner form* of their Notion.

Another complication pertains to the beginning and the end of the categories in dialectic. This complication arises especially when we compare the historical dialectic of philosophy proposed in *Lectures* to the one presented in *Logic*. In one very plausible reading of Hegel, dialectic is precisely the concretion, or development, of the abstract Notion. Yet, it is also said to be the reverse. In *Logic*, for instance, the concrete and actual is considered to be the *real* beginning point, as opposed to the beginning point of presentation and demonstration, which is always an abstraction from the concrete. Ascending from the abstract to the concrete is simply a way of proving the concretely true. This strategy is also repeated in *The Philosophy of Right*, where Hegel explains why he does not "begin with the highest instance, that is, with the concretely true." He goes on to say, "we wish to see the truth precisely in the form of a result, and it is essential for this purpose that we should comprehend the abstract concept itself [first]."[18]

Indeed, in *Logic* Hegel struggles with the question of "With What the Science Must Begin." After explaining why we must begin with the purely abstract Notion (*being-in-itself*), even though the concrete comes first in actuality, he proposes yet another explanation: dialectic is ultimately circular. He thus adds, "The essential requirement for the science of logic is not so much that the beginning be a pure [abstract] immediacy, but rather that the whole of the science be within itself a circle in which the first is also the last and the last is also the first."[19] Hegel offers a similar view elsewhere when he says philosophy "forms a circle." It does not begin immediately, but is rather "rounded off within itself." Nevertheless, it "has an initial or immediate point—for it must begin somewhere—a point which is not demonstrated and is not a result. But the starting point of philosophy is immediately relative, for it must appear at another endpoint as a result."[20]

However, this logical sequencing of the categories from the abstract to the concrete, or circularity, cannot be neatly applied to the history of philosophy. In *Lectures*, Hegel consistently says that in the history of philosophy the abstract is the real beginning point: "that

---

18. Ibid., 61–62.
19. G. W. F. Hegel, *Hegel's Science of Logic*, trans. A. V. Miller (New York: Humanity Books, 1989), 71.
20. Hegel, *Elements of the Philosophy of Right*, 26.

which commences is implicit, immediate, abstract, general—it is what has not yet advanced; the more concrete and richer comes later . . ." Here, Hegel categorically rejects the view that "what must come first is the concrete." As for the history of philosophy, "the earliest philosophies are the poorest and the most abstract. In them the Idea is the least determined; they keep merely to generalities [abstractions] not yet realized." Hegel goes on to repeat that "the original philosophy is the most abstract, because it is the original and has *not as yet* [italics added] made any movement forward; the last, which proceeds from this forward and impelling influence," of the abstract "is the most concrete" (40–42). In short, all that is concrete and actual emerges out of the impelling influence and development of the abstract.

What is particularly difficult to understand in this context is this: According to Hegel, the abstract *being* cannot exist on its own, which is the view expressed in *Logic*. Yet, everything evolves out of the abstract *being* in the history of philosophy. In *Logic*, this is an easier complication to resolve. The abstract is abstracted out of the concrete in the first place. On the other hand, in the dialectic of nature, there is a perfect cycle in which the concrete and abstract constantly supplement and replace each other, or even coexist. A seed becomes a plant, and the latter reproduces itself in the seed. However, in the history of philosophy and of civilizations, in evolutionary spiritual dialectic that is, abstract always precedes the concrete. It is not meaningful, for instance, to say that Parmenides's *being* is an abstraction from the concrete Absolute Idea entertained by Hegel. The beginning of historical philosophy is the abstract and not an abstraction. The only way out of this dilemma is to show that the abstract *being* of the early philosophers is also the concretely Absolute in some sense. As we will see next, Hegel argues that the abstract *being* of the early philosophers implicitly entails the concrete within itself, even if these philosophers were not aware of this point.

The last point is related to yet another complication. Hegel insists that "we must not expect to find the questions of our consciousness and the interests of the present world responded by the ancients; such questions presuppose a certain development, or concreteness, in thought. Therefore, every philosophy belongs to its own time . . ."; and, "every philosophy is the philosophy of its own day, a link in the whole chain of spiritual development, and thus it can only find satisfaction for the interests belonging to its particular time" (45). Certain aspects of what he says here are understandable. We should not attribute to past philosophers and philosophies conclusions and interests that they themselves could not have entertained. For instance, we should not attribute to Aristotle the conclusions reached by Hegel himself. What Hegel means in this context is that the degree of actuality obtained in Aristotle's society prevented the actualization of his philosophy beyond the level he was able to develop. This claim, of course, somewhat falls apart when Hegel says Aristotle's logic has not seen any improvement until Hegel's time. Indeed, one of the main purposes of Hegel's *Logic* was to quicken "the dead bones of [this modern] logic" inherited from Aristotle.[21]

Another related complication is that Hegel also says the "scientific products of reason form the content of this history, and these are not past." They are "true always and for every time" (39). In the previous paragraph, he gives the impression that each philosophy belongs to its own time. These two statements appear contradictory. However, a hopeful reconciliation of these divergent points is possible, since Hegel also says "all philosophies ever live and are present in their principles, but Philosophy no longer has the particular form and aspect possessed by that of Plato and Aristotle" (46). In this reconciliation, we find an important dialectical contradiction. The Notion of philosophy is both eternal-unchanging-universal (permanent), and transient-diverse (subject to variation and change). Hegel calls this the "inner contradiction" of philosophy and history (see Section 7).

The main task of philosophy is to cognize the universal Notion in its development, and to arrive at its Absolute form at the end (56). If philosophy cognizes the infinite universal Notion as its principle, then we should expect this principle to be timeless. The dilemma that arises from this expectation is that philosophy itself is time-bound in Hegel's view. According to Hegel, "philosophy . . . makes its appearance at a time when Mind of a people has worked its way out of the indifference and the stolidity of the first life of nature . . . ," and that it begins when the necessities of life are adequately supplied. Philosophy "may thus be called a kind of luxury" (46). Hegel even imposes geographical and cultural conditions on the emergence of philosophy in *Lectures* and, especially so, in *The Philosophy of History*. Without considering these points sufficiently, or demonstrating their validity, Hegel goes on to assert that the first philosophy is to be found in the ancient Greek world. Consequently, he declares "Oriental Philosophy" a pseudo-philosophy. I will discuss the specific reasons for this last declaration in the next chapter. Whether or not we deem the Hegelian arguments for beginning philosophy with Thales sound, it cannot be denied that he, in doing so, ends up

---

21. Hegel, *Science of Logic*, 51–53; and *The Encyclopaedia Logic*, 53.

making the dialectic of philosophy time-bound and thus finite. Philosophy, he often says, is 2,500 years old, and ends with his times (with him really). But he also says, as seen earlier, that the Notion of philosophy is eternal. He would have been more consistent with himself, I suggest, had he begun philosophy with Adam and Eve and in every geographical region.

4. The Definition Problem in Hegel

There is yet another type of inconsistency in Hegel's writings. This one is deliberate, but even more consequential than the ones enumerated above. It has to do with Hegel's usage of the key philosophical terms. It is not possible, of course, to go through all of the key terms Hegel uses in this chapter. In this section, I consider some of them to illustrate the complexity involved in the Hegelian definition problem.

The Notion is one of these terms that *Lectures* utilizes very frequently. The German equivalent of the Notion is *Begriff*. However, all of the more recent translations of Hegel's works into English translate *Begriff* as the Concept. By *Begriff*, Hegel usually means self-determining, concrete thought, or thought as the subject (agent) of its own processes and history (see below). However, and herein lies the crux of the matter, clarity and consistent use of terms is certainly not one of Hegel's strong suits.

Definitions for Hegel are too limited, and are thus unstable. Whatever definition we choose to attach to the Notion/Concept, or other popular Hegelian terms, at some point it becomes unsatisfactory. For instance, if we say that the Concept is a more appropriate translation because it denotes a more *concrete* comprehension, we have to explain what the *concrete* means in Hegelian terms. If we attempt to do this, we soon come to the recognition that the *concrete* is, in some sense, also the *abstract*. In short, it was Hegel who once said that definitions are "dangerous," especially since they cannot account for the contradictions present in what they intend to define.[22] The Concept, *Begriff*, itself entails a contradiction since it is at once the concrete and the abstract (see Section 5).

The definition problem is compounded by the fact that Hegel hardly ever sticks to a single use of his important terms. In *Science of Logic*, he treats the Notion/Concept as the third, and hence the most

---

22. Hegel, *Elements of the Philosophy of Right*, 26–27.

concrete category of thought. The first category, *being*, develops into the category of *essence*, and then into to the Notion. However, one would be completely lost while reading Hegel if one were to think that these were all mutually exclusive categories. Just to give an example, Hegel says, "Being is the Concept" though only "in-itself."[23] Here, at least a distinction is made in the sense that *being* is the abstract Concept. In *Lectures*, on the other hand, he introduces the Notion/Concept from the outset, and often equates it with such categories as *being* and *essence*, and even with the types of *being* that he deems utterly abstract. At times, he uses the Notion and the Idea as synonyms, even though, as we will see below, he says the Idea is the further determination of the Notion/Concept.

The Idea, in turn, is often called the Absolute Idea, and is used interchangeably with *being*, Spirit, and even God. For instance, he says "the absolute Idea alone is *being*, imperishable *life*, *self-knowing truth*, and is *all truth*." It encompasses both "Nature and spirit," which are "in general different modes of presenting" the "*existence*" of the Absolute Idea, and "art and religion its different modes of apprehending itself and giving itself an adequate existence." Hence, the Absolute Idea "embraces those shapes of real and ideal finitude, as well as of infinitude . . ." The "business of philosophy is to cognize [the Absolute Idea] in these manifold manifestations of itself."[24] Here, the Absolute Idea seems to be more concrete than Spirit, since the former encompasses the latter. In *Encyclopaedia Logic*, he also says "the Idea of the universal essence of appearances . . ." is "the Absolute, God."[25] Two pages later, he adds, "Free and genuine thought is inwardly *concrete*; hence is Idea," though he adds that the Idea is the unity of both inwardly and outwardly concrete form. This unity makes the Idea "Absolute."[26] In his *Philosophy of Right*, he calls the Idea ". . . the reason within an object," thus, here too, giving the Idea an outwardly concrete form.[27] As if to complicate things further, in *The Philosophy of History*, Hegel says that Spirit operates in *time*, and that the "Nature is the development of the Idea in Space."[28] This distinction between Spirit and the Idea is not always sustained by Hegel, since both Spirit and the Idea have temporal and spatial extensions. Despite the common uses of Spirit and the Idea, Spirit at times comes across as more concrete than the Idea. For this reason,

---

23. Hegel, *The Encyclopaedia Logic*, 135.
24. Hegel, *Science of Logic*, 824–26.
25. Hegel, *The Encyclopaedia Logic*, 36.
26. Ibid., 28.
27. Hegel, *Elements of the Philosophy of Right*, 26.
28. Hegel, *The Philosophy of History*, 72.

McTaggart says, "Spirit . . . is the most concrete of all things . . . and the Idea . . . is only imperfectly concrete, even in its highest form."[29] In this sense, Spirit encompasses the Idea as one of its attributes.

To these complications, we can add that his logic, says Hegel, is the "science of the Idea in and for itself." *"The Philosophy of Nature,"* on the other hand, seeks to comprehend the Idea "in its otherness," and *"The Philosophy of Spirit* [Mind]" is the science of "the Idea that returns into itself out of its otherness."[30] These differentiations are useful insofar as one tries to understand the different philosophical sciences of Hegel. But, one should not go so far as to think that these terms are also not of one piece. Indeed, in *Philosophy of Mind*, which Hegel says above is "the Idea that returns into itself out of its otherness [nature]," we are told more explicitly that Mind, or Spirit, is "a type of the absolute idea."[31] Spirit, on the other hand, has multiple meanings. Mind is just one of them, and *soul* is another. We are thus left with a host of technical terms that are sometimes used interchangeably and sometimes for different ends. There is no ready-made remedy for this problem. What we can hope for is that the context in which these terms are used clarifies their meaning, which is not always the case.

Yet, we must seek some clarity in the way Hegel uses his main terms before we can begin to understand him. Fortunately, the complicated use of his terms is not entirely arbitrary. We have two standards with which we can manage them to some extent. First, as J. N. Findlay points out, "Hegel does indeed say that his various categories" are all "determinations of thought," and can be seen as successive definitions of "the Absolute." [32] This explains the interchangeability of different categories. Second, the variation in the meaning given to each category is guided by two other terms, which also have complicated meanings: the *abstract* and the *concrete*. This explains, to some extent, the different uses of the same term, since being more abstract or concrete signifies different stages of *being*.

---

29. McTaggart, *Studies in the Hegelian Dialectic*, 75.
30. Hegel, *The Encylopaedia Logic*, 42.
31. Hegel, *Philosophy of Mind*, 1.
32. J. N. Findlay, *Hegel: A Re-Examination* (New York: Collier Books, 1958), 151.

5. Abstract and Concrete in Hegel and Marx

The Hegelian dialectic would be very difficult to grasp if we were to approach it with the common definitions of the abstract and the concrete one finds in dictionaries, or in non-dialectical thinking. The concrete is often said to be anything that exists in a tangible, material, or physical form; or to things that are real or solid. In analytical philosophies, it is customary to say, as E. V. Ilyenkov points out, that "the concrete is that which is immediately given in individual experience as an 'individual thing,' an individual experience . . ."[33] The concrete is hence usually treated merely as a matter of sense perception, the perception of a thing in its individualized existence. The abstract, on the other hand, is often treated as the antonym of the concrete, and is associated with general thought, with abstruse ideas, or with ideas that lack factuality.

On the other hand, in much of the literature on the Hegelian-Marxist dialectic, the concrete is taken to mean, via Marx, "a synthesis of many determinations, thus a unity of the diverse."[34] Hegel also often uses the same definition of the concrete (II, 13). This definition of the concrete is based on the internal relations of the specific determinations of a thing or a phenomenon. When taken individually, each determination is considered to be an abstract. The concrete is the synthetic unity of many determinations that are abstracts on their own. This view of the concrete, however, needs to be further complicated.

Marx, for instance, says society ("population," "community," "State," etc.) is "an already existing concrete whole." But, this totality, "regarded as a mental *concretum*, is in FACT a product of thinking."[35] It is in the same sense that Hegel says, in referring to the totality of human needs, "it is that concretum *of representational thought* which we call *the human being.*"[36] It follows that there is a distinction between a concrete existent and the concrete as a mental representation of such an existent. In the latter sense, the concrete becomes what we

---

33. E. V. Ilyenkov attributes this view to John Stuart Mill. For a valuable critique of this "nondialectical" view of the concrete, and the latter's dialectical understanding, see E. V. Ilyenkov, *The Dialectics of the Abstract and the Concrete in Marx's Capital* (Delhi: Aakar Books, 2008), 31–38.
34. Karl Marx, "Introduction" to *Outlines of the Critique of Political Economy*, in *Karl Marx and Frederick Engels Collected Works*, Vol. 28 (New York: International Publishers, 1986), 38.
35. Ibid.
36. G. W. F. Hegel, *Elements of the Philosophy of Right*, 228.

ordinarily think is an abstract, since thought in ordinary usage is equated with the abstract.

But, when Marx says in *Capital*, and elsewhere, that his method of presentation, as opposed to the method of inquiry, ascends from the abstract to the concrete, the ambiguities involved in the meaning of the abstract and the concrete make it difficult to understand what he means. We may give different accounts of what Marx actually takes as his abstract beginning point (commodity, value, and labor process are all plausible candidates), though having this debate here is not necessary for our present purposes. For the sake of illustrating the complication involved in the meaning of the abstract, let us use one of Marx's own accounts. He says, "What I proceed from is the simplest social form [abstract] in which the product of labor presents itself in contemporary society, and this is the '*commodity*.'" Hegel, too, often calls the abstract the simple form of *being*. Marx continues, "This I analyze initially in the *form in which it appears*. Here I find that on the one hand in its natural form it is a *thing for use*, alias a *use-value*; on the other hand, a *bearer of exchange-value*, and from this point of view it is itself an 'exchange-value.'"[37] Marx is here referring to the appearance of commodity in bourgeois society, and not to its essence, which is alienated labor power. Nevertheless, the simplicity of commodity has disappeared in its appearance, since Marx says that commodity is a bearer of both use and exchange value. When we read *Capital* beyond the chapter on commodity, we find that commodity entails two kinds of labor: abstract labor (attached to exchange value) and concrete labor (attached to use value). Commodity also entails the existing legal, property relations, as well as fetishistic ideology. All these are the moments of the commodity form of the product, and since they are its manifold determinations, commodity is a concrete, "a unity of the diverse" in this sense. (The reference to only one side of labor as "concrete labor" further complicates the meaning of both the concrete and the abstract Marx utilizes here.) Yet, from another vantage point, commodity is an abstract because it is a particular part of the whole system, the capitalist society, even though commodity entails all of the relations of this system within itself. It is also an abstract in the sense that it is a mental *concretum*.

In some sense, Marx's understanding of commodity also mimics what Hegel says of the particulars: all "particulars are but mirrors and copies" of the system and "have their actuality only" in the "unity" of

---

37. Karl Marx, "Marginal Notes on Adolph Wagner's Lehrbuch der politischen Oekonomie," in *Karl Marx and Frederick Engels Collected Works*, Vol. 24 (New York: International Publishers, 1989), 544–45.

the whole (28). Here, we realize that the abstract entails within itself the concrete, many-sided determinations. This is especially true of the universal categories of thought. Thus, Hegel repeatedly refers to the abstract Idea (pure *being*) as the "concrete." He says, for instance, that "the Idea is in its content concrete within itself, and this in two ways: first it is concrete potentiality, and that it is its interest that what is in itself should be there for it." This formulation says in effect that the abstract *being*, or Idea, is implicitly, or potentially, a concrete. Here, we see a useful distinction between the abstract as the implicit concrete in-itself, and the concrete which develops necessarily and explicitly out of the abstract *being*. Hegel goes on to add,

> Since the implicit [abstract] is already concrete within itself, and we only set forth what is implicitly there, the new form which now looks different, and which was formerly shut up in the original unity, is merely distinguished. The concrete must become for itself or explicit; as implicit or potential it is only differentiated within itself, not as yet explicitly set forth, but still in a state of unity. The concrete is thus simple [abstract], and yet at the same time differentiated [actual and concrete]. This, its inward contradiction, which is indeed the impelling force in development, brings distinction into being.

It is precisely this inner, or "inward," contradiction between the abstract and the concrete that makes dialectical development possible and necessary. In its abstract state, *being* is the undifferentiated unity of many implicit determinations. In its process of development (actualization or concretion), it faces self-differentiation or "distinction," that is, explicit negativity and contradiction. But, this is neither where dialectic begins nor where it terminates. *Being*'s "right to be taken back and reinstated extends beyond the difference; for its truth is only to be found in unity" (24–25). As we will see, for Hegel, this unity is *actuality*.

The Hegelian definition of Notion/Concept, for instance, entails the dialectical tension (the inner contradiction) between the concrete and the abstract. Hegel says, "Thought is not something empty and abstract, but is determining, self-determining indeed; in other words thought is essentially concrete. This Concrete thought is what we call the 'Concept.' Thought must be a concept, no matter how abstract it may seem; it must be concrete in itself." Thus, "the Concept is different than bare thought," or a specific thought. "The Concept is genuine knowledge . . ." Hegel also adds that the "Concept is the universal which particularizes itself . . . ," and, "still further determined, is the Idea. The Idea is the Concept's self-realization."[38] Elsewhere, Hegel calls the further determination of the Concept, that is, its self-particularization dialectic: "The moving principle of the concept, which not only dissolves the particularizations of the universal but also produces [the particulars,] is what I call *dialectic*."[39] Thus, dialectical process both produces and dissolves the particulars entailed within the universal Concept. This process occurs of necessity because the concrete is implicitly entailed in the abstract *being* as its potentiality.

6. Potentiality, Actuality, and Dialectic as Teleological Development

It has become necessary at this stage of our progression to treat the abstract as *potentiality* and the concrete as *actuality*. In *Logic*, potentiality and actuality are called *being-in-itself* and *being-for-itself*, though *being-there* is also considered as their mediating moment. In the "Introduction" to *Lectures*, unlike in *Logic*, these two couplets are discussed together. In *Logic*, Hegel equates the abstract *being* (i.e., *being-in-itself*) with nothing. I suggest that Hegel's *being-in-itself* should be equated with potentiality from the outset, instead of *nothing*. More importantly for our present purposes, the potentiality-actuality couplet is more suggestive of Hegel's dialectical intentions than is the abstract-concrete couplet. What I mean here is that the term "potentiality" signifies dynamism, that is, the "pregnancy" of *being-in-itself*—the possibility of its development as in giving birth—more readily to us than does the term "abstract." The focus on *potentiality-actuality* in this section also reinforces the view that Hegel's dialectic is teleological, since potentiality implies the presence of the end goal within that which develops.

In order for development to occur, two "principles" have to be in place, says Hegel. "The first is what is known as capacity, power, what I call *being-in-itself (potentia)*; the second principle is that of *being-for-itself*, actuality *(actus)*" (20). In between the two, logically, is *being-there*. Hence, we have the usual triadic structure of Hegel's dialectic. Before I proceed any further, I should clarify one more complication

---

38. G. W. F. Hegel, *Hegel's Introduction to the Lectures on History of Philosophy*, trans. T. M. Knox and A. V. Miller (Oxford: Oxford University Press, 1985), 68–69.
39. Hegel, *Elements of the Philosophy of Right*, 60.

involving these categories. *For-itself* is translated from the German *für-sich*. Hegel sometimes refers to *being-for-itself* also as *being-in-and-for-itself*, and sometimes he uses *for-itself* to mean *by-itself*. *Being-in-and-for-itself* is more suggestive of Hegel's intentions in describing the most concrete form of *being*, that is, its *actuality*. For instance, elsewhere Hegel says, "Eternal Being, in-and-for-itself, is something which unfolds itself, differentiates itself, posits itself as its own difference, again, is at the same time eternally done away with and absorbed; what has essential Being, Being-in-and-for-itself, eternally returns to itself in this, and only in so far as it does this is it Spirit."[40] When he uses *being-for-itself* to mean *by-itself*, his intentions become blurry. This tends to be the case when Hegel has in mind the non-synthetic conceptions of existents. To add to these, he sometimes also refers to any one of these categories simply as *being*. Throughout the present book, I try to clarify what I think he means when such complications arise.

Let us begin with Hegel's description of these categories in the "Introduction" to *Lectures*:

> *Being-in-itself.* With regard to development, what immediately comes to our attention is that there must be something there that develops, which is to say something hidden—the seed, the tendency, the capacity, what Aristotle calls *dunamis*, i.e., possibility (not some superficial possibility as such, but real possibility), or, as it is called, the in-itself, that which is in itself and at first merely that . . . What is in itself, however, is not yet the true but only the abstract; it is the seed of what truly is, the tendency, the being-in-itself of the true. It is something simple, something which, of course, contains in itself multiple qualities [and is thus concrete within itself], but in the form of simplicity—a content which is still hidden.
>
> An example of this is the seed. The seed is simple . . . This simple thing, however, is pregnant with all the qualities of the tree. In the seed is contained the whole tree, its trunk, branches, leaves, its color, odor, taste, etc. Nevertheless, this simple thing is the seed, not the tree itself; the fully articulated tree does not yet exist. It is essential to know that there is something utterly

---

40. G. W. F. Hegel, *Lectures on the Philosophy of Religion*, Vol. 3, trans. Rev. E. B. Spiers and J. Burdon Sanderson (New York: The Humanities Press Inc., 1962), 35.

simple, which in itself contains a manifold, which latter, however, does not yet exist for itself [in actuality].

Thus, "With Aristotle," we can say that "*all* that develops is contained" in the simple, which is "in-itself," or "the dunamis, *potentia*," or "the tendency." Consequently, "in development no more comes out than what is already there in itself."[41] Another way to say this in Hegelian terms is that potentiality is the "negative actuality."[42]

Simply put, "*being-there*" (*Dasein*) is mere existence. Thus, "What follows is that the in-itself, the simple, the hidden, develops and unfolds." This means that the in-itself develops by positing itself into "something distinct," or particular. In this manner, what is in-itself enters "into existence." Existence is the inherent necessity of *being-in-itself*. It follows that *being-there* is "existential separateness" of a thing, as this or that particular existence.[43] This stage is the mediating moment of *being-in-itself*, and is the same as what Hegel calls the particularization of the abstract universal above.

This is to say, the abstract Concept becomes, for instance, the concept of table. It is the copula *is* in the statement, *this is a table*. In ordinary thinking, we do not usually consider the meaning of *is*, and think of the table as *this* table before us. In speculative philosophy, the table is essentially the concept of the table, its table-ness. In other words, the Concept is the essence of the table we experience. Without this category, the philosophical truth of the table in question cannot be ascertained. It remains a mere appearance, or a mere *being-there*. For this reason, the triadic transition of the Concept, or *being*, is the transition of the essence into existence. The following, says Hegel, are the triadic determinations of *being*, which is here conceived as essence: "(I) As *simple* essence, essence in itself, which in its determinations remains within itself; (II) As emerging into determinate being, or in accordance with its Existence and *Appearance*; and (III) As essence that is one with Appearance, as *actuality*."[44]

In *Lectures*, Hegel asserts that to think of the particular determination without the universal Notion is a "delusive mode of reasoning," which "from doubt of, or aversion to, the particular form in which a Universal finds its actuality, will not grasp or even allow this universal nature . . ." To illustrate the delusiveness of this aversion with some humor, Hegel likens it to "an invalid

---

41. Lauer, *Hegel's Idea of Philosophy*, 76–77.
42. Hegel, *Elements of the Philosophy of Right*, 67.
43. Lauer, *Hegel's Idea of Philosophy*, 77.
44. Hegel, *Science of Logic*, 391.

recommended by the doctor to eat fruit, and who has cherries, plums or grapes, before him, but who pedantically refuses to take anything because no part of what is offered him is fruit, some of it being cherries, and the rest plums or grapes" (18–19).

Thus, through self-mediation the *being-in-itself*, which we have now identified with the abstract Concept and the simple essence, acquires determinacy. However, to use the language of *Logic*, "The being that is kept firmly distinct from the determinacy, *being-in-itself*, would be only the empty abstraction of being. In being-there, the determinacy is one with being and is at the same time posited as negation; this determinacy is *limit, restriction*." In other words, the determinacy of *being* is precisely its particularization into something specific, which is limited and thus finite, such as a table; whereas the abstract *being-in-itself* is indeterminate and infinite potentiality (universal). In this process of self-determination, *being-in-itself* undergoes negation and reproduces itself as the *other* of itself. But, since its otherness is already its implicit potentiality, "otherness is not something indifferent outside, but its own moment." In order to be actual, *being-in-itself* "must be there," that is, it must acquire a limited, but real existence.[45]

Another helpful passage to clarify all this is given in Hegel's *Elements of the Philosophy of Right*. "The concept and its existence (Existenz) are two aspects (of the same thing), separate and united, like soul and body." The latter, when separated, is existence as *being-there* only (*Existenz*). The "concept," when separated, is *being-in-itself* only. However, even though we may perceive them separately, neither one can have any life or development on its own. "The body is the same life as the soul, and yet the two can be said to lie outside one another. A soul without a body would not be a living thing, and vice versa. Thus the existence (*Dasein*) of the concept is its body, just as the latter obeys the soul which produced it." As for the Idea, we are now told, it is the "unity of existence (*Dasein*)," of *being-there*, and the Concept entailed in what is there. Hegel adds that this unity is not a mere harmony, but a "complete interpenetration" of the body by the soul.[46] The Idea is thus the unity of the Concept (soul) and mere *being-there* (body), which has now become, through this interpenetrative unity, *being-for-itself*. This unity is the *actuality*.

In short, Hegel argues that "it is essentially in the nature of the Idea to develop, and only through development to arrive at comprehension of itself, or to become what it is," that is, concrete

---

45. Hegel, *The Encyclopedia Logic*, 148.
46. Hegel, *Elements of the Philosophy of Right*, 25–26.

and actual (20). This also means that the actual becomes the actual when the Idea self-comprehends itself as the essence of the object. He further adds to this that "this is the first absolute condition for comprehension: what is not implicitly there cannot come within [the result] or be for it . . ." (70). Thus, *being-in-itself* becomes *being-for-itself* in actuality. This suggests the equivalency of the Idea with *being-for-itself*. This equivalency further suggests that the Idea is more concrete than the Concept, though Hegel does not always maintain this difference.

Of *being-for-itself*, Hegel further says the following:

> *Being-for-itself*. The third determination is that what is in itself and what exists and is for itself are one and the same. This is precisely what is meant by development. If the in-itself were no longer the in-itself, then something else would be there, and a complete change would have taken place. In this case there is something and it becomes something else. In regard to development, it is true, we can also speak of change, but the change must be such that the other which results is nevertheless still identical with the first, such that the simple, the in-itself, is not annihilated. It is something concrete, something differentiated, but still maintained in the unity of the original in-itself.[47]

Here, we have arrived at a very crucial inner contradiction of dialectical development: permanency in change. In other words, change does not annihilate the original, simple *being*, which is retained as the identity, or essence, of that which changes, or becomes. It is this self-preservation that makes change development, for development is precisely the movement of the same subject. This inner contradiction of permanency and change is one of the most essential principles of the Hegelian dialectic. According to Hegel, the history of philosophy entails this inner contradiction (see Section 7), as do nature and logic.

We must, at this point, make an important distinction between the dialectic of Mind and of nature. In nature, "the subject which commenced and the matter which forms the end are two separate units, as in the case of seed and fruit . . ." Similarly, "in animal life the parent and the young are different individuals although their nature [essence] is the same." Thus, this "doubling process" in nature

---

47. Lauer, *Hegel's Idea of Philosophy*, 78.

produces two separate things, even though their "content is the same" (22–23). This is not the case with Mind, which is "consciousness and therefore it is free, uniting in itself the beginning and the end."

> As with the germ in nature, Mind indeed resolves itself back into unity after constituting itself [as other]. But what is in itself becomes for Mind and thus arrives at being for-itself. The fruit and seed newly contained within it on the other hand, do not become for the original germ, but for us alone; in the case of Mind both factors not only are implicitly the same in character, but there is a being for the other and at the same time a being for self. That for which the "other" is, is the same as that "other;" and thus alone Mind is at home with itself in its "other." The development of Mind lies in the fact that its going forth and separation [that is, its "going without itself,"] constitutes its [own] coming to itself (22–23).

Hegel describes this "coming-to-self of Mind . . . as its complete and highest end . . ." This process of "going without itself" and "coming to itself" is completed at the end of the history of philosophy. For this reason, dialectic also assumes its most developed form at the end of history (i.e., with Hegel's philosophy). It must be reiterated here that this process is an all-encompassing development in which the truth is established in its totality. Hegel says that the final development of Mind encompasses,

> Everything that from eternity has happened in heaven and earth . . . ; the life of God and all the deeds of time simply are the struggles for Mind to know itself, to make itself objective to itself, to find itself, be for itself, and finally unite itself to itself; it is alienated and divided, but only so as to be able thus to find itself and return to itself. Only in this manner does Mind attain its freedom, for that is free which is not connected with or dependent on another (23).

In short, the potentiality of Mind is infinite, and, unlike nature, Mind knowingly wills its own dialectic and unites its beginning with its result. This willing is its freedom, and is a unique inherent capacity, or power, of Mind.

Hegel says in *The Philosophy of History* that "the principle of *Development* involves also the existence of a latent germ of being—a capacity or potentiality striving to realize itself. This formal conception finds actual existence in Spirit; which has the History of the World for its theatre, its possession, and the sphere of its realization." This point brings us to another distinction. While the dialectic of nature repeats itself endlessly (Hegel lived before Charles Darwin!), historical-spiritual dialectic can in general be characterized as "an advance to something better, more perfect."[48] Here, the notion of *perfectibility* makes its way into the vocabulary of dialectic. While potentiality is a characteristic of all types of *being*, perfectibility belongs only to the spiritual being. Thus, according to Hegel,

> The changes that take place in Nature—how infinitely manifold so ever they may be—exhibit only a perpetually self-repeating cycle; in Nature there happens "nothing new under the sun," and the multiform play of its phenomena so far induces a feeling of ennui; only in those changes which take place in the region of Spirit does anything new arise. This peculiarity in the world of Mind has indicated in the case of man an altogether different destiny from that of merely natural objects—in which we find always one and the same stable character, to which all change reverts;—namely, a real capacity for change . . . for the better—an impulse of *perfectibility*.[49]

Perfectibility, in turn, implies a destiny that is already implicit in the spiritual, abstract being as its potentiality. The achievement of this destiny is inevitable, and what is achieved in the process is progressively more perfect. This is no less true of the history of philosophy, according to Hegel. Of this, he says, "The whole of the history of Philosophy is a progression impelled by an inherent necessity, and one which is implicitly rational and *a priori* determined through its Idea; and this the history of Philosophy has to exemplify. Contingency must vanish on the appearance of Philosophy. Its history is just as absolutely determined as the development of Notions, and the impelling force is the inner dialectic of the forms [Notions]" (37).Once again, in this last passage we find a hint at the aforementioned inner contradiction between permanency and change

---

48. Hegel, *The Philosophy of History*, 54.
49. Ibid.

in the historical dialectic of philosophy. Change as contingency "vanishes on the appearance of (the absolute) Philosophy."

7. The Inner Contradiction of the History of Philosophy

In *The Philosophy of History*, Hegel says in history there "are many considerable periods . . . in which . . . development seems to have been intermitted; in which . . . the whole enormous gain of previous culture appears to have been entirely lost . . ." But, this should not lead to the conclusion that history is simply filled with "external contingencies," of mere relativity, lacking an internal and permanent principle of development. In the final analysis, "Universal History," that is, history considered as a totality from the viewpoint of Spirit's development, "exhibits the *gradation* in the development of that principle whose substantial *purport* is the consciousness of Freedom."[50]

In other words, even though new things do come about in history, none of its products are *essentially* new. A similar inner contradiction is also expressed in *Elements of the Philosophy of Right* with respect to logical development of categories.

> The idea must continually determine itself further within itself, for it is initially no more than an abstract concept. But this initial concept [the abstract Idea] is never abandoned. On the contrary, it merely becomes continually richer in itself, so that the last determination is also the richest [most concrete]. Those determinations which previously only existed in themselves thereby attain their free self-sufficiency, but in such a way that the concept remains the soul which holds everything together and which arrives at its own differentiation only through an immanent process. One cannot therefore say that the concept arrives at anything [essentially] new; on the contrary, the last determination coincides in unity with the first. Thus, even if the concept appears to be fragmented in its existence, this is merely a semblance, as is subsequently confirmed when all its details finally return in the concept of the universal.[51]

---

50. Ibid.
51. Hegel, *Elements of the Philosophy of Right*, 61.

One of Hegel's favorite examples, the "germ," or the seed, and the plant comes to our aid here as an analogy, even though the dialectic it describes is not a mere analogy.

> From the germ much is produced when at first nothing was to be seen but the whole of what is brought forth, if not developed, is yet hidden and ideally contained within itself. The principle of this projection into existence is that the germ cannot remain merely implicit, but is impelled towards development, since it presents the contradiction of being only implicit and yet not desiring so to be. But this coming without itself [actualization] has an end in view; its completion fully reached, and its previously determined end [telos] is the fruit or produce of the germ, which causes a return to the first condition.

The point that needs to be further highlighted here is that "the plant . . . does not lose itself in mere indefinite change . . ." (22–23). That which develops, or changes, is retained in the concrete end result. This is a significantly different view of dialectic than the one often attributed to Hegel, namely, that dialectic is nothing but negativity in which only change reigns. For Hegel, dialectic as change is also a positive development. This is because "the negative side must indeed contain within it the positive, for all change, all the process of life is founded on this" (90).

The dialectic in the history of philosophy has the same inner contradiction described above. Hegel posits this contradiction in general terms as follows: "The thought which may first occur to us in the history of Philosophy is that the subject itself contains an inner contradiction. For Philosophy aims at understanding what is unchangeable, eternal, in and for itself: its end is Truth. But history tells us of that which has at one time existed, at another time has vanished, having been expelled by something else." The following dilemma arises from the juxtaposition of philosophy's central principle and aim with its own history: "Truth is eternal; it does not fall within the sphere of the transient, and has no history. But if it has a history, and as this history is only the representation of a succession of past forms of knowledge, the truth is not to be found in it, for the truth cannot be what has passed away" (7–8). Thus, when each is taken in isolation, philosophy's principle-aim and its history are utterly contradictory.

Dialectic in Hegel's *History of Philosophy*

In spite of this apparent contradiction, Hegel maintains that the eternal principle, that which is permanently present, is retained in the historical dialectic of philosophy. The truth remains one. But, this needs to be explained.

> The . . . statement, that the Truth is only one, is still abstract and formal. In the deeper sense it is our starting point. But the aim of Philosophy is to know this one Truth as the immediate source from which all else proceeds, both all the laws of nature and all the manifestations of life and consciousness of which they are mere rejections, or to lead these laws and manifestations in ways apparently contrary, back to that single source, and from that source to comprehend them, which is to understand their derivation. Thus what is most essential is to know that the single truth [the Notion] is not merely a solitary, empty thought, but one determined within itself (19–20).

This important paragraph, in a nutshell, not only says that the truth is one, which is manifested in apparently manifold and contradictory ways, but also that the One is "the source from which all else proceeds."

Consistently with the above thoughts, Hegel outlines four general principles of the historical dialectic of philosophy. These principles are introduced a priori as the conclusions of the entire course of this history, which the ensuing lectures intend to prove. The first main principle has two parts: First, "the whole of the history of Philosophy is a progression impelled by an inherent necessity, and one which is implicitly rational and *a priori* determined through its Idea; and this the history of Philosophy has to exemplify . . ." What this history exemplifies is the teleological development of the Notion from its "implicit rationality" to its explicit and absolutely concrete manifestation, which is the explicitly rational. The implicitly rational is necessarily infinite for what is truly rational, *the truth*, cannot be finite. This leads to the second part of the first principle: "The finite is not true, nor is it what it is to be—its determinate nature is bound up with its existence." The implicit infinite potentiality existing in finitude is bound to shatter the fetters established by the limits of the finite existence. Thus, and necessarily so, "the inward Idea abolishes [negates] these finite forms . . ." in the course of its development. Hegel goes on to conclude that "a philosophy, which has not the absolute form identical with the content, must pass away because its form is not that of truth" (36–37).

The second main principle is a clarification of the last sentence. If all of the past philosophies could completely "pass away," so would the Notion of philosophy. In such a scenario, the permanency of the Notion in dialectical development would be severely undermined, if not completely annihilated. This is not the case because "every philosophy has been and still is necessary. Thus none have passed away, but all are affirmatively contained as elements in a whole." For this reason, "the most recent philosophy," that is, Hegel's own philosophy, is "the result of all preceding [philosophies]," and retains the abstract philosophical principle in it (37–38).

In one sense, if the Notion of philosophy persists and abides in many different, finite forms of philosophy, "no philosophy has ever been refuted." However, since the history of philosophy proves otherwise, this last statement sounds odd and needs clarification. Hegel provides one: "What has been refuted is not the principle of . . . philosophy, but merely the fact that the principle [of each given philosophy] should be considered final and absolute in character." What Hegel is telling us here is that all philosophies hold their principle to be the universal truth. What is refutable, and refuted, is whether or not the principle each philosophy upholds is truly "absolute in character." The third principle is an elaboration of the second, basically telling us how certain philosophical principles in the past have been, and remained, one-sided, and thus failed to capture the whole truth (ibid.).

The fourth principle obtained from the history of philosophy is that "we must not regard the history of Philosophy as dealing [strictly] with the past, even though it is history. The scientific products of reason form the content of this history, and these are not past. What is obtained in this field of labor [of Mind] is the True, and, as such, the Eternal; it is not what exists now, and not then; it is true not only today or tomorrow, but beyond all time, and in as far as it is in time, it is true always and for every time." In short, "the history of Philosophy has not [simply] to do with what is gone, but with the living present." The media used to obtain its results may be finite and thus "transient," and have perished over time. But, the "effects produced and work performed are not again destroyed or interrupted by what succeeds . . ." (38–39).

In the final analysis, the developed state of philosophy entails, ". . . one Idea in its totality and in all its individual parts, like one life in a living being, one pulse throbs throughout all its members. All the parts represented in it, and their systematization, emanate from the one Idea . . ." (28). Thus, the members of the whole are not merely tied together externally. Spirit (Mind), says Hegel, "permeates through everything," and is "the unity of itself and of a semblance [appearance] of its 'other,' as of the subjective and the particular. As universal, it is object to itself, and thus determined as a particular, it is this individual: but as universal it reaches over this its 'other,' so that its 'other' and itself are comprised in one" (72).

Said differently, dialectic is not reducible to a merely negative change. In *Elements of the Philosophy of Right*, Hegel emphasizes the point that dialectic "consists not merely in producing and apprehending the determination as an opposite and limiting factor," which pertains to the particular *other*, "but [also] in producing and apprehending the *positive* content and result which it contains . . ." As importantly, adds Hegel, "it is this [positive] alone which makes [dialectic] a *development* and immanent progression."[52] "That is to say," in dialectical development, "the universal Idea continues to remain at the foundation and is still the all-embracing and unchangeable." In this sense, "development is not a change" as in "becoming 'another,' but really is a going within itself, a self-immersion, the progress forward makes the Idea which was previously general and undetermined, determined within itself" (28). Thus, dialectic is the passing of the Idea into its own other, and not the becoming of *another*—as in the subject becoming something altogether different. Dialectic as negation, then, is precisely this process of "self-immersion" within the particularized *others* of the Idea, which are its own diversified determinations. For this reason, dialectical development is at once a process of "expansion," and "contraction" (35), or intensification and extension. These are correlative couplets, "the most extensive is also the most intensive." It follows that "the more intensive is Mind [or its Notion], the more extensive it is, hence the larger is its embrace." However, to repeat, "Extension as development is not dispersion or falling asunder, but a uniting bond which is the more powerful and intense as the expanse of that embraced is greater in extent and richer" (28). In short, "the diversity and number of philosophies not only does not prejudice Philosophy itself, that is to say the possibility of a [universal] philosophy, but that such diversity is, and has been, absolutely necessary to the existence of a science of Philosophy and that it is essential to it" (19).

---

52. Ibid., 60.

8. Conclusion: Looking Forward

In the remainder of this volume, we will cover, after a brief encounter with "Oriental Philosophy," the Greek philosophy from Thales to the Socratics. This volume thus coincides with the first volume of the Michelet edition, and includes Hegel's interpretation of several "Oriental" and twenty-six early Greek philosophers, some of who are grouped into various philosophical schools. The second volume deals with the rest of the Greek philosophy, and the third encompasses the philosophy of the Middle Ages and the modern philosophy up to Hegel. As indicated above, Hegel sees his philosophy as the culmination of all philosophy, which he summarizes at the very end of the third volume merely in terms of the results obtained from the history of philosophy.

To anticipate, "the present point is the highest stage reached." Since his is the truly Absolute philosophy, it contains and synthesizes the specific principles of the previous, more abstract philosophies. This is precisely the conclusion Hegel arrives at at the end of *Lectures*: "To this point the World spirit has come, and each stage has its own form in the true system of Philosophy; nothing has been lost, all principles are preserved, since Philosophy in its final aspect [form] is the totality of forms. The concrete idea is the result of the strivings of spirit during almost twenty-five centuries of earnest work to become objective to itself, to know itself." Hegel goes on to add that "all the various philosophies are no mere fashionable theories of the time . . . ; they are neither chance products nor the blaze of a fire of straw, nor casual eruptions here and there, but a spiritual, reasonable, forward advance; they are of necessity of one Philosophy in its development" (III, 546–47).

In short, Hegel at the very end of the third and final volume of *Lectures* claims to have obtained the following final results of the history of philosophy: First, "that throughout all time there has been only one Philosophy, the contemporary differences of which constitute the necessary aspects of the one principle." Second, "that the succession of philosophic systems is not due to chance, but represents the necessary succession of stages in the development of this science." The necessity of development is based on the claim that the succession of the philosophical stages is teleological. Third, "that the final philosophy of a [given] period is the result of this development, and is truth in the highest form, which the self-consciousness of spirit affords of itself. The latest philosophy contains therefore those which went before; it embraces in itself all the different stages thereof; it is the product and result of those that preceded it." (In a nutshell, this passage also answers the difficult question: What is Hegel's philosophy?) It follows that "this series . . . is not a multiplicity, nor does it even remain a series, if we understand thereby that one of its members merely follows on another; but in the very process of coming to the knowledge of itself it is transformed into the moments of the one Spirit, or the one self-present Spirit" (III, 552–53). Thus, the multiplicity of spirits, or philosophical minds and Notions, must be understood as the *moments* of One Spirit, which is "self-present" in these moments as their *prius*. Dialectic thus understood is a teleological process of development and change in which Spirit permanently abides. Our task now is to demonstrate how this had happened in 2,500 years, from Thales to Hegel, though, beforehand, we must also account for "Oriental Philosophy," which Hegel calls "preliminary."

CHAPTER 2

"Oriental Philosophy"

1. Introduction

Hegel's lecture on Eastern philosophy cannot be taken as a serious, scholarly analysis. It is based on insufficient information, and smacks of prejudice. Yet, it is an important lecture, which sheds light on what he considers "true," or proper, philosophy. This point is revealed in his opening statement: "The first Philosophy in order is the so-called Oriental, which, however, does not enter into the substance or range of our subject as represented here. Its position is preliminary, and we only deal with it at all in order to account for not treating of it at greater length, and to show in what relation it stands to Thought and to true Philosophy" (117).

In other words, "Oriental Philosophy" is used as a yardstick to illustrate what true philosophy is, and is not. However, his illustration also presupposes a yardstick of "true" philosophy against which Eastern philosophy stands short. This taller yardstick is implicitly derived from his own philosophy; from what he considers to be the most developed philosophical system. Since Eastern philosophy fails to match the scope and depth of Hegel's philosophy, it also fails to count as true philosophy. All of its shortcomings then furnish decisive evidence that Eastern philosophy is not properly philosophical. However, this way of measuring philosophies is inverted when Hegel begins the assessment of early Greek philosophers. The shortcomings of their ideas are seen as evidence that they represent the undeveloped seeds of true philosophy, and thus belong to it as its necessary initial building blocks.

The psychological basis of Hegel's ill-treatment of Eastern philosophy falls beyond the scope of my interest. We may, however, detect a theoretical reason that highlights Hegel's way of thinking well. For him, the history of philosophy constitutes a living organic whole. Since he assumes that every such whole has a point of origination, a kind of a seed out of which the whole develops, he has to find this seed in the ancient Greek world itself. In other words, he has to show that the early Greek philosophy had developed organically without any direct influence from the East. To this end, he makes the debatable claim that the "great Oriental ideas penetrate[d] into Italy," only during the "first centuries of Christendom." In particular, they influenced "the Gnostic philosophy" by forcing "the idea of the illimitable into the Western mind, until in the Church the latter again succeeded in obtaining the ascendency and hence in firmly establishing the Divine" (126).

In this claim, we begin to detect some ambivalence on Hegel's part. As we will see below, "the idea of the illimitable" is a significant philosophical thought, according to Hegel. This ambivalence was already signaled in his "Introduction" to *Lectures* where he says, in the East, "we are able to . . . find thoughts about life and death and of the transition of Being into passing away; from life comes death and from death comes life; even in Being, in what is positive, the negation is already present. The negative side must indeed contain within itself the positive, for all change, all the process of life is found on this [contradiction]." Yet, Hegel insists that these Eastern thoughts are not properly philosophical. Hegel's first explanation for this is that these reflections "only occasionally come forth" (90). In Hegel's account of it, this assertion holds true of Chinese philosophy only because Hegel makes short work of it. He handles it all in but six pages! His treatment of Indian philosophy is more generous, and contains more than occasional philosophical reflections.

His second excuse is more reasonable, though in principle only. He adds that "Philosophy is only present when thought, as such, is made the absolute ground and root of everything else . . ." The first "content" of philosophy is just "universal thought" (ibid.). This is not to be found in the Eastern reflections, says Hegel. Yet, in describing Indian philosophy, he says "the idea of the Indians . . . is that there is one universal substance which may be laid hold of in the abstract or in the concrete, and out of which everything takes its origin" (127). His final verdict, explored in the last section of this chapter, is that Indian philosophy is defective because its philosophical idea lacks individual subjectivity. However, he also finds "intellectual substantiality" in it, which, in some sense of the philosophical yardstick, is philosophically the superior of much of the Western thought, according to Hegel himself.

Because Hegel's treatment of Eastern philosophy is based on insufficient information, it becomes necessary to provide additional information on the specific philosophies Hegel discusses below. The reader should note beforehand that what I add is not an authoritative and exhaustive account of these philosophies by any serious standard. My purpose is to supplement Hegel's comments so that they can be better understood. What emerges even from my rudimentary exposition of these traditions is that the ancient Chinese and Indian philosophies were far more developed than Hegel had presumed. A secondary effect of this exposition, I am hoping, will be a useful introduction to, or familiarization with, many salient philosophical ideas we will encounter in the ensuing chapters.

2. Chinese Philosophy

2.1 Confucius

Confucius is the first Chinese philosopher considered in this section. What Hegel says of his teachings is very brief, and basically amounts to the following: "We have conversations between Confucius and his followers in which there is nothing definite further than a commonplace moral put in the form of good, sound doctrine, which may be found as well expressed and better, in every place and amongst every people. Cicero gives us *De Officiis*, a book of moral teaching more comprehensive and better than all the books of Confucius. He is hence only a man who has a certain amount of practical and worldly wisdom—one with whom there is no speculative philosophy" (121). To get a better sense of Hegel's evaluation of Confucius, we have to remember that he did not think very highly of Cicero, whom he disparages throughout *Lectures*. There is, of course, more to Confucius's teachings than the reduction by Hegel described above. I will mention several important philosophical ideas that are found therein.

First is what is known as "the rectification of names." In *Analects*, Confucius says of this that "if names are not rectified, then words are not appropriate. If words are not appropriate, then deeds are not accomplished."[1] Fung Yu-Lan usefully summarizes this principle as follows: "Things in actual fact should be made to accord with the implications attached to them by names." In other words, "every name contains certain implications which constitute the essence of that class of things to which this name applies. Such things should therefore agree with this ideal essence." For instance, "the essence of the ruler is what the ruler ideally ought to be . . ." In Chinese philosophy, this is called "'the way of the ruler.'"[2] Accordingly, Confucius says, "Let a ruler be a ruler, a subject a subject, a father a

---

1. Confucius, *The Analects*, trans. Raymond Dawson (Oxford: Oxford University Press, 2008), 49.
2. Fung Yu-Lan, *A Short History of Chinese Philosophy* (New York, The Free Press, 1966), 41–42.

father, and a son a son."³ Thus, the proper function of persons is to act in accordance with the universal, ideal Notion, that is, the Name.

Another relevant teaching of Confucius pertains to individual virtues. Here, we find the important concepts of *Yi* and *Li*. The former is "a categorical imperative," indicating the "oughtness" or "righteousness" of a situation or action. *Li*, on the other hand, is associated with the customs and rules of proper conduct. *Yi* is the formal, universal expression of the moral. Its practical equivalent is called *Jen* ("human-heartedness"). In Confucius's words, this means "'loving others.'" This practical expression seems to derive from the doctrine of Names. What ought to be done derives from the proper function indicated by the Name so that, for instance, "the father acts the way a father should act who loves his son," and so on.⁴ At times, the proper action is expressed as obedience to authority, though the ruler should also act with virtue and love, following the proper *end* indicated by the Name *ruler*. For instance, "A public servant who on confronting danger is prepared to lay down his life, who on confronting gain concentrates on what is right, who when sacrificing concentrates on reverence, who when mourning concentrates on grief should definitely be all right."⁵ We also find in the Confucian moral teachings such universal "Western" maxims as "'. . . do not do to others what you do not wish yourself . . .'"⁶

Clearly, what is lacking in Confucius's teachings is not universal thought, or the principle of the Good entailed in the Name, which we also find in Socrates, but the kind of reasoning, or a Socratic dialectic, which seeks to establish its principles on firm, universally accepted grounds. In Confucius's teachings, this step of reasoning is missing. However, such dialectic is explicitly present in the teachings of the Mohists, founded by Mo Tzu at the beginning of the fifth century BC. In the *Mo-Tzu*, as Fung directly quotes from it, we find the following remark:

> "Dialectic serves to make clear the distinction between right and wrong, to discriminate between order and disorder, to make evident points of similarity and difference, to examine the principles of names and actualities, to differentiate what is beneficial and what is

---

3. Confucius, *The Analects*, 46.
4. Fung, *A Short History of Chinese Philosophy*, 42. See Confucius, *Analects*, 47–48.
5. Confucius, *Analects*, 77.
6. Fung, *A Short History of Chinese Philosophy*, 42. See Confucius, *Analects*, 44.

harmful and to remove doubts and uncertainties. It observes the happenings of all things, and investigates the order and relation between the various judgments. It uses names to designate actualities, propositions to express ideas, statements to set forth causes, and taking and giving according to classes."[7]

While it is assumed that Mo Tzu was aware of Confucianism, whether or not he was directly influenced by it is not clear (to me). What is more clearly established is that Mohism significantly influenced the further development of Confucianism. This indicates, too, that Chinese philosophical ideas are not as barren and arid as Hegel suggests.

Confucius's teachings also depend on thought and knowledge. Knowledge itself is obtained through thoughtful learning. He says, "If one studies but does not think, one is caught in a trap. If one thinks but does not study, one is in peril."[8] Also, knowledge for Confucius is continuous, and implies, in a Hegelian fashion, that the philosopher is a medium of knowledge. Of his own knowledge, Confucius says, "I transmit but do not create. Being fond of the truth, I am an admirer of antiquity."[9]

As interestingly, Confucius also has a theory of the soul or spirit, *chi* or *qi*, which is a vital power, or energy, governing the body. The virtuous man guards himself against three things, which seems to require reason, or, at least, the knowledge of how *qi* works: "In the time of his youth, when his vital powers have not yet settled down, he is on guard in matters of sex; when he reaches the prime of life and his vital powers have just attained consistency, he is on his guard in matters of contention; and when he becomes old and his vital powers have declined, he is on his guard in matters of acquisition."[10] In Plato's *Republic*, these thoughts *roughly* translate into the virtues of moderation, courage, and wisdom. However, the main point is that knowledge is crucial to happiness, which comes from the knowledge of virtues. This idea is very prominent in many philosophical traditions from the East to the West, including the Socratic tradition.

---

7. Fung, *A Short History of Chinese Philosophy*, 120. For a very useful comparison of this Mohist dialectic to that of Socrates, see Benjamin Isadore Schwartz, *The World of Thought in Ancient China* (Cambridge, MA: Belknap Press 1985), 162–66.
8. Confucius, *Analects*, 7.
9. Ibid., 24.
10. Ibid., 67.

The knowledge of *Ming* is also important. *Ming* is often translated as "Fate, Destiny, or Decree." To Confucius, *Ming* means "the decree of heaven," and is thus "perceived as a purposeful force" that governs the world beyond our control. However, the knowledge of *Ming* does not translate into "doing nothing." It rather requires "doing for nothing." In the context of *Ming*, this means doing what we ought to do "without caring [whether] in the process we succeed or fail."[11] While this suggests that our actions should be guided by what is a priori given, the good, or virtuous, it also lends itself to another moral-philosophical position. Awareness of *Ming* brings about stability and happiness: "The wise are not perplexed; the humane do not worry, and the courageous do not feel fear."[12] Happiness thus boils down to doing what is inherently good, in and for itself.

These are some of the salient thoughts of Confucius. Whether or not they amount to a proper philosophy depends on the yardstick we use. However, it is clear that Confucius's philosophy in not devoid of the speculative, universal Notion.

2.2 The Philosophy of the I Ching

Hegel is somewhat more generous with the philosophy of the *I Ching*. What Hegel focuses on in this section is the theory of the *Yang* and *Yin*. Originally, *Yang* meant light, and *Ying* meant darkness. Later on, these came to signify two opposite cosmic principles, "respectively representing masculinity, activity, heat, brightness, dryness, hardness, etc., for the *Yang*," and the opposites of these for the *Yin*.[13] To speak the Hegelian language here, with these concepts we have the core dialectical principle of the unity of opposites. *Yang* and *Yin* represent the principles of the universe, and the qualities and quantities enumerated above are their particular determinations. Like Hegel's dialectic, it is the unity, or identity of opposites, that is of primary importance in a contradiction. Noticing this similarity, Tsung-I Dow goes so far as to suggest that "there is strong evidence that the formation of the trilogy by Hegel was influenced by the Yin-Yang concept in the *Book of Changes* with which Hegel was familiar when he taught the history of eastern ideas at the University of Heidelberg. For it is difficult to differentiate the concept of the unity

---

11. Fung, *A Short History of Chinese Philosophy*, 45.
12. Confucius, *Analects*, 34.
13. Fung, *A Short History of Chinese Philosophy*, 45.

of Yin-Yang from the concept of the unity of opposites or the synthesis of thesis and antithesis [found in Hegel]."[14] Even though the claim that Hegel was directly influenced by the Yin-Yang concept might be a difficult pill to swallow, the close similarity of this concept and Hegel's theory of contradiction is unmistakable. Why Hegel ignores this similarity in *Lectures* is not something we can firmly establish.

Instead, Hegel focuses on the symbolic representation of these principles, and how they are used to produce various tables and symbols. Before presenting the derivation of tables from the lines representing *Yang* and *Yin*, Hegel warns us that

> these symbols are quite abstract categories, and consequently the most superficial determinations of the understanding. It must certainly be considered that pure thoughts are brought to consciousness, but in this case we make no advance, merely remaining stationary so far as they are concerned. The concrete is not conceived of speculatively [strictly as thought products], but is simply taken from ordinary ideas, inasmuch as it is expressed in accordance with their forms of representation and of perception. Hence in this collection of concrete principles there is not to be found in one single instance a . . . conception of universal natural or spiritual powers (121–22).

As we are about to see, what Hegel says here is flatly untrue, even though his comment is useful in the sense that it indicates what Hegel expects from a "proper" philosophy.

As for the symbols representing *Yang* and *Yin*, "the two fundamental figures are a horizontal line (—, Yang) and the one which is broken into two equal parts (--, Yin). The first which is the perfect, the father, the manlike, the unity, such as is represented by the Pythagoreans, represents the affirmative; the second is the imperfect, the mother, the womanly, the duality and the negation." Instead of explaining the dialectical implications of these thoughts, Hegel dismissively concludes that "these signs are held in high esteem,

---

14. Tsung-I Dow, "Yin-Yang Dialectical Monism: A New Attempt to Explore the Symbiotic Relationship of Man and Nature through Reformulation of the Confucian-Taoist Metaphysical System," accessed January 22, 2013, Source:
http://thomehfang.com/suncrates/7Dow.html.

for they are considered to be the Principles of things" (122). He thus unduly reduces the principles of *Yang* and *Yin* to "these signs," or lines.

Next, Hegel proceeds to explain how these lines are used to generate various figures and tables. Basically, two *Yang* lines, when placed above each other, constitute a figure that represents the great *Yang*; a *Yang* line above the broken *Yin* line represents the little *Yang*; a *Yin* line above another *Yin* line represents the great *Yin*; and the *Yin* line above the *Yang* line represents the little *Yin*. "The signification of these four representations is matter as perfect and imperfect. The two Yangs are perfect matter: the first is in the category of youth and power; the second is the same matter, but as old and powerless. The third and fourth images, where Yin constitutes the basis, are imperfect matter, which has again the two determinations of youth and age, strength and weakness." These lines are further formulated into eight trigrams, and these trigrams are combined to produce sixty-four hexagrams. The eight trigrams, or figures, "are called Kua." Hegel first positively concludes from this summary that "all symbols have the advantage of indicating thoughts and of calling up significations, and in this way such are likewise present there." Thought "thus forms the first beginning." However, afterwards "it goes into the clouds, and Philosophy does likewise." Hegel adds that "if Windischmann in his commentary recognizes in this system . . . a 'thorough interconnection between all Kua, in the whole series,' it should be remembered that not a particle of the Notion is to be found in it" (122–23). For Hegel, the Notion is the universal that provides the "thorough interconnection between" the particular determinations in nature, represented by *kua* in the *I Ching*.

Hegel arrives at this conclusion haphazardly, however. Young Kun Kim observes in this regard that "while Hegel knew that what he called Oneness (*Einheit*) created two and many, he did not see their connections clearly. He does not seem to have read the following important sentence in the I Ching: 'In the *I* there is the Great Ultimate (*t'ai chi*), which produced the two Forms (i). These two Forms produced the four emblems (*hsiang*) and these four emblems produced the eight trigrams [*kua*].'"[15] In the book of *Explanation*, as Fung quotes it, we read the following: "The Supreme [or Great] Ultimate through movement produces the *Yang*. This Movement, having reached its limit, is followed by Quiescence, and by this Quiescence it produces the *Yin*. When Quiescence has reached its

---

15. Young Kun Kim, "Hegel's Criticism of Chinese Philosophy," *Philosophy East and West* 28, no. 2 (1978), pp. 173–80, 176.

limit, there is a return to Movement. Thus the Movement and Quiescence [and, consequently, *Yang* and *Yin*], in alteration, each become the source of the other. The distinction between the *Yin* and *Yang* is determined and the Two Forms (i.e., the *Yin* and *Yang*) stand revealed."[16] It seems that when considering the *kua*, Hegel ignores the One, and thus begins with the determinate many, or eight *kua*, even though he notices Oneness separately. He does, however, ignore the Great Ultimate entirely. *T'ai chi*, the Great or Supreme Ultimate, is precisely the universal Notion Hegel thinks is missing in the philosophy of the *I Ching*.

Following the implications of these thoughts further falls beyond the scope of our investigation, though I think the shortcomings of Hegel's interpretation of it has been made amply clear. It seems that the philosophy of *I Ching* satisfies Hegel's requirements for proper philosophy more thoroughly than he thought.

2.3 The Philosophy of Lao Tzu

Hegel says Lao Tzu's book, "Tao-King [*Tao Te Ching*] . . . is an important work amongst the Taoists or the followers of reason, who call their rule in life Tao-Tao, which means the observation of the dictates or the laws of reason." Hegel only hints at what this means by quoting "one special passage," which says the following: "Without a name Tao is the beginning of Heaven and Earth, and with a name she is the Mother of the Universe. It is only in her imperfect state that she is considered with affection; who desires to know her must be devoid of passions" (124). Thus, knowing *Tao* requires pure reason. Hegel has very little to say on this important Taoist principle.

According to Fung, the doctrine of Names before Lao Tzu "succeeded in discovering 'that which lies beyond shapes and features,'" that is, that which lies beyond the sensible things. Even though non-philosophical, ordinary consciousness gives the sense-objects names, it does not distinguish names (concepts) from the objects themselves. The "philosophers of the School of Names" thought about the names themselves. As if he were borrowing the language of Hegel, Fung describes this thinking of names as follows: "To think of names is to think about thinking. It is thought about thought and therefore is thought on a higher level" than ordinary

---

16. Fung, *A Short History of Chinese Philosophy*, 269–70.

consciousness.[17] In this sense, this school establishes concepts (names) as the truth, or as the essence, of objects.

Lao Tzu goes beyond the doctrine of names as described above, and speaks of the unnamable. This is where his philosophy becomes truly speculative. Names are the universals that derive from something eternal, which is the *Tao*. *Tao Te Ching* states that "'the *Tao* that can be comprised in words is not the eternal *Tao*; the name that can be named is not the abiding name.'" In a sense, then, the *Tao* is the abstract, essence of names, the eternal, abiding, absolute universal, though it is itself unnamable. As such, the *Tao* is "'the beginning'" and the "'Mother'" of "'Heaven and Earth.'" Analogously speaking, "'the *Tao* is . . . the Uncarved Block . . . Once the block is carved, there are names.'"[18] This makes the *Tao* very akin to Hegel's abstract Notion, though, erroneously, Hegel treats *Tao* as absolutely *empty* nothingness, as we will see below.

There seems to be a tension involved in calling the unnamable "*Tao*" for calling it as such is also to name it. This tension is acknowledged by Lao Tzu, who says "*Tao* existed before word and names, before heaven and earth, before the ten thousand things. It is the unlimited father and mother of all limited things." But, "I do not know its name, so I call it by an alias: *Tao*. Forced to describe it, I only say 'It is great.'" As importantly, this abstractly Absolute Notion (i.e., *Tao*) "is the beginning of all understanding"[19] The philosophical significance of this explanation is that it, in effect, designates the *Tao* as a pure category, which, to speak anachronistically, smacks of Hegelian idealism.

The *Tao* simply *is*. Any predication of it is contradictory in the sense that any predicate attached to the *Tao* forces what is infinite and indeterminate into a particular, finite determination. Calling the *Tao* "*Tao*" does not have the same signification as calling a table "table," or giving a table object the name of table. "When we call a table a table we mean that it has some attributes by which it can be named. But when we call the *Tao Tao*, we do not mean that it has such namable attributes." Thus, "all we can say is that *Tao*, since it is that through which all things come to be, is necessarily not a mere thing among these other things . . . If it were such a thing, it could not at the same time be that through which *all* things . . . come to be." With

---

17. Ibid., 94.
18. Ibid., 94–95.
19. *Lao Tzu, The Tao Te Ching of Lao Tzu*, trans. Brian Browne Walker (New York: St. Martin's Press, 1995), 1 and 25. In reference to this work, numbers indicate the section and not the page number.

this thought, we enter directly into the realm of ontology. The logic of this ontology is basically as follows: "Anything that comes to be is a being, and there are many beings. The coming to be of things implies that first of all there is Being." In short, in the words of Lao Tzu, "'All things in the world come into being from Being (*Yu*); and Being comes into being from Non-being (*Wu*).'"[20]

After skipping the steps outlined above almost entirely, Hegel concludes that "to the Chinese what is highest and the origin of things is nothing, emptiness, the altogether undetermined, the abstract universal, and this is also called Tao or reason." Similarly, "When the Greeks say that the absolute is one, or when men in modern times say that it is the highest existence, all determinations are abolished, and by the merely abstract Being nothing has been expressed excepting this same negation, only in an affirmative form." Hegel asserts at this point that if philosophy fails to go beyond such an abstract expression, "it still stands on its most elementary stage." Rhetorically asking, "What is there to be found in all this learning?" (125).

Two points need to be added here in response to Hegel's conclusion. First, as we have seen above, Lao Tzu's *Tao*, the abstract absolute (*Tao*), does not stand still, but, rather, unfolds into further determinations of itself, much like Hegel's abstract *being* in *Logic*, which, remarkably, he also equates with "nothing." In *Tao Te Ching* we read, "the great *Tao* flows in every direction. Everything in existence depends on it . . ."[21] Second, and following from the first, it would be more plausible to think of *Tao* as a potentiality rather than as total "emptiness," as Hegel asserts above. At least, this is the more plausible way Thomas Watters treats *Tao*.[22]

Tao, more properly speaking, is called "nonbeing" in the sense that it is not a material, tangible, sensible existent. It gives "birth to oneness" which is the undifferentiated nature in its unity. "Oneness gives birth to yin and yang," which are dialectical opposites. These two "give birth to heaven, earth and beings [existents]." It follows that everything in existence entails opposites, or "carries within itself both yin and yang." The stability and harmony of the existents depends on the proportional "blending together" of "these vital breaths [*chi*]."[23] In this way, there is always a return to *Tao* in so far as

---

20. Fung, *A Short History of Chinese Philosophy*, 96.
21. *Lao Tzu, The Tao Te Ching*, 34.
22. Thomas Watters, *Lao-Tzu: A Study in Chinese Philosophy* (London: Williams & Norgate, 1870), 47.
23. *Lao Tzu, The Tao Te Ching*, 42.

the blending is proportional.[24] No existent can abide if it does not entail or follow *Tao*. Contradiction thus occupies a significant position in *Tao Te Ching*. Its significance also spills into guidance for happy life and even governance. What is important here is to find the center.

At the same time, and this is also important in Hegel, contradictory terms find their meaning through each other, that is, through their identity, which is derived from *Tao*. For instance, "when people find one thing beautiful, another consequently becomes ugly. When one man is held up as good, another is judged deficient." Likewise,

> ... being and nonbeing balance each other;
> difficult and easy define each other;
> long and short illustrate each other;
> high and low rest upon one another ... ;
> what is to come follows upon what has been.[25]

By going into Chinese philosophy slightly deeper than Hegel had done, I sought to show that his demotion of the Chinese philosophy to the status of pre-philosophy is not based on sufficient evidence. Even a cursory presentation of topics discussed here indicates otherwise. More importantly, I also tried to tease out some foundational information from the three Chinese philosophical traditions discussed here to identify what is also important to Hegel.

3. Indian Philosophy

3.1 Introduction

Moses I. Findlay notes in passim that "Hegel ... held a singularly ill-informed and unsympathetic view of one of the most Hegelian of peoples and religions," namely, the Indian people and religion.[26] This comment captures the popular view of Hegel well, and is true to a large extent. However, Hegel did not hold a "singularly . . .

---

24. Ibid., 51.
25. Ibid., 2.
26. J. N. Findlay, *Hegel: A Re-Examination*, 133.

unsympathetic" view of the Indians. As it will become clear below, he was rather ambivalent in his assessment of them.[27]

Hegel's demotion of the Indian philosophy begins with its identification with religion. Even though the "Indian culture is developed to a high degree, and it is imposing," says Hegel, its "Philosophy is identical with its Religion . . . Hence the holy books or Vedas . . . form the general groundwork for Philosophy . . . Indian Philosophy thus stands within Religion . . ." The religious basis of the Indian philosophy provides this philosophy with the idea of the "illimitable," and this idea is precisely what makes Indian thought appear on the margins of proper philosophy. Because of "the idea of the illimitable," on the one hand, and because of the relationship of this idea to "the Divine," on the other, the Eastern philosophy is a mixture of philosophy and religion (126–27).

Western religions—the Roman, Greek, Jewish, and Christian—are based on "the principle of individual freedom." This principle influences their conceptions of gods, which appear "immediately as the explicit, personal forms" (117). For this reason, these religions are non-philosophical for they lack the illimitable idea. In contrast, Eastern religion "much more directly" reminds us of "the philosophic conception." This holds true despite the fact that "the Orientals certainly have also individual forms [of gods], such as Brahma, Vishnu and Civa . . ." (117). These gods, obviously, are of Indian origin, which leads us to the conclusion that Hegel takes the Indian religion-philosophy as the general representative of the East.

Because "in the East the element of [individual] subjectivity has not come forth, religious ideas are not individualized, and we have predominating universal ideas, which hence present the appearance of being philosophic ideas and thoughts." The reason for the absence of individual subjectivity is that individual "freedom is wanting" amongst the Easterners, and thus their "individuality is not real, but

---

27. Hegel's main source in his treatment of the Indian philosophy is Henry Thomas Colebrooke, *Essays on the Religion and Philosophy of the Hindus* (London: Williams & Norgate, 1858).
One of the most detailed accounts of Hegel's approach to the Indian philosophy can be found in Ignatius Viyagappa, *G.W.F. Hegel's Concept of Indian Philosophy* (Rome: Universita Gregoriana Editrice, 1980). This book is a great resource of information, though it is mainly descriptive.
Another similarly useful and historical-descriptive, but much shorter, work is Robert Bernaconi, "With What the History of Philosophy Begin? Hegel's Role in the Debate on the Place of India within the History of Philosophy," in *Hegel's History of Philosophy: New Interpretations*, ed. David A. Duquette (New York: State University of New York, 2003), Ch. 2.

merely superficial." Consequently, the Gods of the Easterners "appear to be universal principles which thus seem to bear a relationship to Philosophy or even seem to be themselves philosophic" (117–18.) Here, Hegel also argues that free individuality is a necessary condition of philosophical thought, and such individuality first arises explicitly with the Greeks. In other words, what gives the Eastern religion-philosophy its philosophical advantage over Western religions, namely the absence of individual subjectivity, is also what, in part, makes the former *only* apparently philosophical.

Along similar lines, in *Philosophy of Mind* Hegel says that "the Hindus . . . regard a human being, the Brahmin, as god, and the withdrawal of the human spirit into its indeterminate universality is held to be divine, to be the immediate identity with God." Even though we find here the "awakening of the mind," still the "mind does not as yet grasp itself in its absolute freedom," which means that it does not "know itself as the concrete universal which is for itself." This means it has not as yet made its "Notion into an object for itself in the form of thought."[28] Thus, the contemplation of the universal substance, the infinite and eternal Idea, is a precondition of being philosophical, though such contemplation is not by itself sufficient.

Another related precondition of philosophy is the "negation of the finite," which is also present in Eastern philosophy, "but in such a manner that the individual [i.e., the finite spirit] only reaches to its freedom in this unity with the substantial." This unity thus is purely negative. The individual and the particular determinations either completely vanish in the illimitable substance, or they are kept completely apart from it. Consequently, the "destruction of all that is particular either is an illimitable, the exaltitude of the East, or, in so far as that which is posited and determined for itself is known, it is a dry, dead understanding, which cannot take up the speculative Notion into itself." In short, Hegel asserts that, because of the separation—or externalization—of the particular from the universal, we "find only dry understanding amongst the Easterners, a mere enumeration of determinations [finites], a logic like the Wolffian of old" (119). As we will see in the third volume of the present work, Hegel does not think much of the Wolffian logic, which is influenced by Leibniz's atomism.

Remarkably, in the same context, Hegel reverses his assessment of Indian philosophy in the very same context, and says, "The idea of the Indians more appropriately expressed, is that there is one universal substance which may be laid hold of in the abstract or in the

---

28. G. W. F. Hegel, *Philosophy of Mind*, 43–44.

concrete, and out of which everything takes its origin" (ibid.). This contradicts the view that the idea of the Indians is abstract emptiness into which everything vanishes, and the view that the finite determinations in Indian philosophy are disconnected in an atomistic manner. As we will see, some Indian philosophical schools are ambivalently atomistic. But, as Hegel acknowledges, their logic is not to be dismissed as pure nonsense. For instance, he says of the Nyaya that it is "the most developed" Indian philosophy, because "it more particularly gives the rules for reasoning, and may be compared to the logic of Aristotle" (128). A kind of reasoning that "may be compared to the logic of Aristotle" is no small feat of achievement, especially since the Nyaya chronologically preceded Aristotle.

Hegel's final verdict, presented at the end of this chapter, reduces the Indian philosophy to the "idea of the illimitable" in which the individual and the particular presumably vanish. It may well be the case that this verdict is derived from the philosophical-religious teachings of the Indians. What is remarkable is that, without a significant stretch of imagination, such a verdict cannot be related to the three specific Indian philosophical traditions Hegel discusses. For this reason, we should anticipate that Hegel's final verdict, which mimics the introductory comments presented above, has little direct bearing on the evidence he presents.

The three philosophical traditions Hegel considers are the Sanc'hya, the Vaiseshica, and the Nyaya. He considers the latter two together and very briefly, and devotes most of his attention to the Sanc'hya. In presenting Hegel's analysis we face the dual dilemma of his ambivalence on the status of Indian philosophy and the insufficient information on which his analysis is based. In order to remedy these dilemmas to some extent, I supplement Hegel's account with brief introductions to these philosophies.

3.2   The Sanc'hya

3.2.1   A Brief Introduction to the Sanc'hya

The Sanc'hya (Saṃkhya, Sankhya) is one of the oldest philosophical schools of India. It is said that Kapila was its founder. Some estimate that he may have lived during the sixth century BCE. The original text of this philosophy is the *Saṃkhya Karika*. It consists of seventy-two brief Karikas (verses), which are attributed to Isvarakrsna (circa 200 CE), who presumably penned down the teachings of Kapila. The Sanc'hya is a dualistic philosophy, based on two fundamental principles: *prakriti* and *purusha*.

According to Swami Bawra, the Sanc'hya "establishes both an underlying cause that is unchanging and a visible reality filled with forms that are constantly changing." The ultimate cause of "all these diverse forms" is "one invisible source," which is *prakriti*. This source is "beyond our vision and perception and is described by negative adjectives such as formless, colorless and weightless." Everything in nature is a "projection of this single cause." For this reason, the Sanc'hya declares that "every effect has a quality similar to its cause but not the same form of its cause." There is thus a supersensible, "underlying" cause for everything, without which existence is not possible.[29] Because of the single source of origination, nature is first considered as one "formless" entity. However, the dialectic of *prakriti* involves its further concretion into three other stages, which are "causal, subtle and gross."[30] It is in and through these stages that the knowledge of *prakriti* becomes possible through various methods, which I will discuss below.

Each stage is shaped by the specific relationship of the three *gunas*. *Gunas* are the constituent powers of *prakriti*. This means that these powers are inherent in *prakriti*, which further means that each stage of development, or concretion, represents the self-development of *prakriti*. The first *guna* is called *rajas*. This *guna* is responsible for the activation of the other powers. For this reason, this *guna* is also translated to mean the power to change or move things. The second *guna* is called *sattva*, which is considered to be the power to illuminate things, or make them manifest. This *guna* is also associated with stability and order. The third *guna* is called *tamas*, which is the power of destruction.[31] These *gunas* account for the dynamic formation and destruction of Nature. They are also responsible for sensation, through which the knowledge of Nature and its primal origin (i.e., *prakriti*) becomes possible.

The Sanc'hya provides a five-step reasoning to prove *prakriti*. First, "the finite cannot be the cause of the universe. Logically we have to proceed from the finite to the infinite, from the limited to the unlimited . . . , from the temporary to the permanent, from the many to the one," that is, to *prakriti*. Second, since the worldly, finite things

---

29. *Samkhya Karika: with Gaudapadacarya Bhasya*, commentator Brahmrishi Vishvatma Bawra (USA: Brahmrishi Yoga Publications, 2012), 25. All quotations from Bawra below are from this work.
30. *Samkhya Karika*, 1.
31. Theos Bernard, *Hindu Philosophy* (New Delhi: Motilal Banarsidass, 1999), 74–75.

"possess certain common characteristics" in that they can all produce three sensations ("pleasure, pain, indifference"), they must have "a common source composed of three Gunas," which produce these sensations. Third, *guna*s are also effects. Since cause and effect can be distinguished through observation, and since "all effects arise from the activity of the potent [efficient] cause," *gunas* also have a cause, which is *prakriti*. Thus, and fourth, a *guna*, which is also a "limited effect . . . cannot be regarded as its own cause." It must have a cause other than itself. Therefore, fifth, all effects "point to a world-cause where they are potentially contained," since the diverse merge into a unity in evolution.[32]

The theory of causality in Sanc'hya is called *Satkaryavada*. *Satkaryavada* opposes the *Asatkaryavada*, which is another theory of causality. The latter believes that the effect does not pre-exist in the cause, whereas *Satkaryavada* holds the opposite view. Thus, *Samkhya Karika* succinctly posits, in a five-step argument, that "the effect is existent (in its cause), since nonexistent cannot be produced, since the material (cause) is selected, since everything cannot be produced (from anything), since a potent cause produces that of which it is capable, and since (effect is) of the same nature as the cause."[33]

Chandradhar Sharma usefully reformulates these five arguments as follows. First, "if the effect does not pre-exist in the cause, it becomes a mere nonentity . . ." It follows that that which is a nonentity cannot be produced. Out of nothing comes nothing. Second, "the effect is only a manifestation of its material cause, because it is invariably connected with it." Third, "everything cannot be produced out of everything." Were it so, then, say, one could produce cheese out of water. This reasoning assumes two related things: a material cause entails a limited number of possible effects, and the cause of everything is a multiplicity of materials. This further means that "the effect, before its manifestation, is potentially contained in its material cause. Production is only an actualization of the potential." Fourth, since finite matter, of itself, is not an agent of production there must be an "efficient cause" that induces matter to produce its effects. Fifth, "the effect is the essence of its material cause and as such identical with it."[34]

---

32. Chandradhar Sharma, *A Critical Survey of Indian Philosophy* (New Delhi: Motilal Banarsidass, 1960), 151–52. See also, *Samkhya Karika*, 30–31 (Karika XV).
33. *Samkhya Karika*, 18 (Karika IX).
34. Sharma, *A Critical Survey of Indian Philosophy*. I took the liberty of revising Sharma's summary, especially the fourth argument, which he conflates with the third.

The causal theory of Sanc'hya leads to "the concept of *prakriti* as the root cause of the world of objects." It is "the potentiality of nature, 'the receptacle and nurse of all generation.'" Because infinite "regress is to be avoided," *prakriti* is defined as the "uncaused cause."[35] When it is treated as the first principle of the universe, *prakriti* is called "*Pradhana*," or "Primal Nature," which is the ultimate "evolvent" of the seven subtle evolvents in Nature and the sixteen evolutes that they produce.[36] The seven evolvents are also evolutes, since they are produced by the Primal Nature. With *prakriti* and *purusha* added, the seven subtle categories and the sixteen evolutes amount to the twenty-five categories of the Sanc'hya. I name and discuss these categories later through Hegel's analysis of the Sanc'hya.

Purusha, as indicated above, is the second main principle of the dualistic Sanc'hya. In *Samkhya Karika*, *purusha*, or "Spirit," is treated as the antithesis of nature. Nature is devoid of consciousness, "and from that contrast it follows that Spirit is endowed with the characteristics of witnessing, isolation, indifference, perception and inactivity."[37] However, Bawra, in his interpretation of this particular Karika (XIX), adds to it that "*purusha* is not the doer, but only observer, seer, or knower. It witnesses the action and activities of Nature. The attributes [*gunas*] of Nature are the cause of activities, not *purusha*. Movement is a quality of Nature."[38]

It is difficult to understand how *purusha* sees, witnesses, etc., without having the quality of movement. It makes sense to say that it is not the cause of movement in Nature. But Bawra also tells us in his explanation of Karika XVII that "Nature is used and enjoyed by Spirit. Nature has no consciousness and without knowledge objects cannot be appreciated. Sweetness cannot taste its own sweetness. There must be a knower or enjoyer capable of determining the quality of sweetness. Nature is insentient, without knowledge or consciousness, so there must be another capable of enjoying, knowing and seeing. That other is called *purusha*. Additionally, there must be a master, ruler or controller for whom nature creates . . ."[39] These thoughts indicate that *purusha* has the quality of movement within itself. They also suggest that nature exists for the sake of *purusha*, which, in turn, lends itself to the conclusion that *purusha* is the final cause of nature. Along similar lines, as Karika XVII directly

---

35. Ibid., 152.
36. *Samkhya Karika*, 6 (Karika III).
37. Ibid., 40 (Karika XIX).
38. *Samkhya Karika*, 41.
39. Ibid., 38.

states, "The Spirit exists since composite objects exist for one another; since the reverse of that which has three attributes and the rest; since there must be control; since there must be someone who enjoys; and since there is activity for release."[40] In short, the relationship of *purusha* and Nature remains ambivalent in the Sanc'hya, as does the meaning of *purusha*.

Hence, the dualism of the Sanc'hya is not clearly maintained. For instance, according to Bawra, "*purusha* is described as that which makes life perfect. *Purusha* is pure consciousness . . . Pure consciousness is the soul [or spirit] . . . , the indweller. This indwelling presence animates the causal essence or seed of each being, and everything in existence."[41] If it animates the "causal seed" of "everything in existence," or "makes life perfect," then it is involved in the evolution of nature. But, we are also told that *purusha* neither produces nor is produced. In the words of Sharma,

> [*Purusha*] is the soul, the self, the spirit, the subject, the knower. It is neither body nor senses nor brain nor mind (manas) nor ego (ahankāra) nor intellect. It is not a substance which possesses the quality of Consciousness. Consciousness is its essence. It is itself pure and transcendental consciousness. It is the ultimate knower which is the foundation of all knowledge. It is the pure subject which can never become an object of knowledge. It is the silent witness, the emancipated alone, the neutral seer, the peaceful eternal. It is beyond time and space, beyond change activity. It is self-luminous and self-proved. It is uncaused, eternal and all pervading. It is the indubitable real, the postulate of knowledge, and all doubts and denials presuppose its existence.[42]

Sharma, who ascribes certain attributes to *purusha* in the above context, also says that "it is inactive, indifferent, and possesses no attributes."[43] These contradictory descriptions are also present in Colebrooke's essay on the Sanc'hya. He says that "*purusha* is neither produced nor productive," but also adds that "by the union of the soul and nature, creation . . . is effected," and "the soul's wish is

---

40. Ibid., 36.
41. *Samkhya Karika*, 1.
42. Sharma, *A Critical Survey of Indian Philosophy*, 155–56.
43. Ibid., 163.

fruition or liberation."⁴⁴ Indeed, Sharma confirms the presence of these complications in his concluding remarks on the Sanc'hya.⁴⁵ Hegel also picks up on these contradictions, as discussed below.

3.2.2 Hegel on the Sanc'hya

According to Hegel, the Sanc'hya teaches that "through Thought, the true Science, . . . freedom can be accomplished; the temporal and worldly means of procuring enjoyment and keeping off spiritual or bodily evil are insufficient; even the methods advocated by the Vedas are not effectual for the purpose, and these are found in the revealed form of worship, or in the performance of religious ceremonies as directed in the Vedas." "Such a retreat into Thought takes place in the Religion as well as in the Philosophy of the Indians, and they assert with reference to this state of bliss that it is what is highest of all, and that even the gods do not attain to it" (129).

Yet, the Sanc'hya, says Hegel, also "differs from Religion in that it has a complete system of thought or logic." Moreover, "the abstraction" of thought "is not made a reduction to what is empty, but is raised up into the significance of a determinate thought." In other words, the "retreat into Thought," on the one hand, is a method of attaining happiness, and requires "a reduction to what is empty." On the other hand, there is also a scientific aspect to the Sanc'hya, which involves "the correct knowledge of the principles . . . of the material and of the immaterial world" (130). To anticipate Hegel's final verdict on the Sanc'hya at the end of this chapter, he ignores this latter aspect of the Sanc'hya and reduces it to "empty" thought.

The epistemology of the *Sanc'hya* is divided into three parts: "the method of knowledge, the object of knowledge, and the determinate form of the knowledge of principles" (ibid.). These epistemological components are, in turn, driven by ontological considerations on *being* and causality. The method of knowledge refers to the three possible ways knowledge can be obtained: perception, inference, and affirmation ("valid testimony"). The Sanc'hya defines perception as "the application (of senses) to (their special) objects."⁴⁶ Hegel adds to this that "perception is said to require no explanation" (130). We return to perception below since it is the basis of inference.

---

44. Colebrooke, *Essays on the Religion and Philosophy of the Hindus*, 154–55.
45. Sharma, *A Critical Survey of Indian Philosophy*, 162, 165–68.
46. *Samkhya Karika*, 10 (Karika V).

As for *inference*, the *Samkhya Karika* holds that it is of various kinds, "preceded by the (knowledge of) *linga* (the middle term) and the *lignin* (the major term). *Linga* is a mark or sign of something. Inference is preceded by the knowledge of the middle term, where a major term is inferred by means of a middle term. For example, upon seeing a staff in hand, the possessor is inferred to be a mendicant. When preceded by a major term, a middle term can be inferred by the observation of the major term. Using the same example, upon seeing a mendicant, one can infer that the staff belongs to him."[47]

Hegel says that the Sanc'hya version of inference is "a conclusion arrived at from the operation of cause and effect, by which one determination merely passes over into a second." Three forms of inferences are said to exist in the Sanc'hya "because inferences are made either from cause to effect, from effect to cause, or in accordance with different relations of cause and effect." Some examples Hegel provides are as follows: "Rain, we may say, is foretold when a cloud is seen to be gathering; fire, when a hill is seen to be smoking; or the movement of the moon is inferred when, at different times, it is observed to be in different places." For Hegel, these "are simple, dry relations, originating from the understanding," which he often relates to knowledge obtained from mere sense-perception (ibid.). What Hegel means here, but does not explain, is that obtaining the truth of a phenomenon through observation leads to mere understanding, which, for Hegel, is a limited form of cognition. Inference through perception and observation, as he tells us elsewhere, is the hallmark of "the general point of view taken by ordinary consciousness, and more or less by the [natural] sciences."[48]

Indeed, much of Hegel's *Phenomenology of Mind* is devoted to superseding this limited form of cognition ("the understanding," "ordinary consciousness," etc.). In a nutshell, Hegel holds the view that observation cannot lead to absolute (properly philosophical) knowledge, which must be of the speculative kind. In ordinary consciousness, the truth is not found in the subject but only in the object of sense-perception. In sense-perception, "the I does not contain or imply a manifold of ideas, the I here does not think: nor does the thing mean what has a multiplicity of qualities. Rather, the thing, the fact, *is*; and it *is* merely because it *is*." Thus, the understanding too readily separates the subject from the object of knowledge, and makes their relationship purely external. [49]

---

47. *Samkhya Karika*, 10–11 (Karika V, and Bhasya V).
48. Hegel, *Philosophy of Mind*, 161–62.
49. Hegel, *Phenomenology of Mind*, 55.

Consequently, the essence (the universal truth) of the object, which, for Hegel, ultimately lies in the consciousness of the subject, is merely attributed to the object as it appears to the senses. From this results the inability to see the complexity of the truth of the object. As Hegel further explains it,

> Sense-certainty itself has thus to be asked: What is the *This*? If we take it in the two-fold form of its existence, as the *Now* and as the *Here*, the dialectic it has in it will take a form as intelligible as the This itself. To the question, What is the Now? we reply, for example, the Now is night-time. To test the truth of this certainty of sense, a simple experiment is all we need: write that truth down. A truth cannot lose anything by being written down, and just as little by our preserving and keeping it. If we look again at the truth we have written down, look at it *now*, *at this* noon-time, we will have to say it has turned stale and become out of date.
>
> The Now that is night is kept fixed [in sense-certainty], i.e. it is treated as what it is given out to be, as something which *is*; but it proves to be rather a something which is [also] *not*. The Now itself no doubt maintains itself, but as what is *not* night; similarly in its relation to the day which the Now is at present, it maintains itself as something that is also not day, or as altogether something negative. This self-maintaining Now is therefore not something immediate but something mediated; for, *qua* something that remains and preserves itself, it is determined through and *by means* of the fact that something else, namely day and night, is *not*. Thereby it is just as much as ever it was before, Now, and in being this simple fact, it is indifferent to what is still associated with it; just as little as night or day is its being, it is just as truly *also* day and night; it is not in the least affected by this otherness through which it is what it is. A simple entity of this sort, which is by and through negation, which is neither this nor that, which is a *not-this*, and with equal indifference this as well as that—a thing of this kind we call a Universal. The Universal is therefore in point of fact the

truth of sense-certainty, the true content of sense—experience.[50]

These thoughts also explain why Hegel is initially dismissive of the method of inference advocated by the Sanc'hya. He links the Sanc'hya's method of inference to "ordinary consciousness," which he says is based on sense-perception, and does not recognize the Universal as "the truth of sense-certainty." For Hegel, the Universal Notion is the "true content," the essence and substance of knowledge obtained from experience, and must be recognized as such.

Hegel's negative evaluation of the Sanc'hya above ignores the theory of causation this philosophy proposes. However, he gives a more positive evaluation of its method of inference when he considers the theory of causation in the Sanc'hya. He says that "of the various kinds of knowledge already given, that of reasoning," which establishes "the connection existing with the conclusion through the relation of cause and effect," is the "chief" aspect of the Sanc'hya, and of more philosophical interest (138). In the system of Kapila, "the understanding and all other principles derived from it are . . . effects, and from these they reason to their causes." For Hegel, this is both similar to and different from "our [Hegel's] inference." Accordingly, Hegel highlights the fact that in this system of thought, "'effects [implicitly] exist even before the operation of the causes; for what does not exist cannot be made explicit in existence through causality.'" Thus, and in agreement with Colebrooke, "'this means that effects are educts rather than products.'" To educe is to bring out something that already exists potentially, or implicitly. This approach assumes that "the effect is already contained in the cause . . ." For example, "oil is already existent in the seeds of sesamum before it is pressed out; rice is in the husk before it is thrashed; milk is in the udder of the cow before it is milked." Thus, "cause and effect are in reality the same; a piece of a dress is not really different from the yarn from which it is woven, for the material is the same." A conclusion drawn from this understanding of causality is "the eternity of the world . . ." This principle is in agreement with the saying that "'Out of nothing there comes nothing,'" and "is opposed to the belief in a creation of the world from nothing in our religious sense." Hegel continues,

---

50. Ibid., 55–56.

As a matter of fact, it must also be said, "God creates the world not out of nothing, but out of Himself; it is His own determination, by Him brought into existence." The distinction between cause and effect is only a formal distinction; it is the understanding that keeps them separate, and not reason. Moisture is the same as rain; or again we speak in mechanics of different movements, whereas motion has the same velocity before as after impact. The ordinary consciousness cannot comprehend the fact that there is no real distinction between cause and effect (138–39).

Even though Hegel generally acknowledges different forms of causality, the form of causality described above is crucial to his dialectic.[51] What Hegel fails to mention in this context is that the Sanc'hya method of inference from causality leads knowledge back to *prakriti*, which is the original, Universal cause of the objects of sense-perception. For this reason, the Sanc'hya attempts to prove the supersensible Universal, the *thing-in-itself* of phenomena, and thus cannot be reduced to the "ordinary consciousness" of the phenomenalism of various stripes, Kantian or otherwise.

Thirdly, in the Sanc'hya affirmation means "tradition or revelation," and derives from "the orthodox Vedas." Affirmation can take two forms: "in a wider sense," it is the "immediate certainty . . . in my consciousness, and in a less wide sense, an assurance through verbal communication or through tradition" (ibid.). Affirmation as a form of knowledge does not concern Hegel here at all.

As for the objects of knowledge, Hegel notes that there are twenty-five objects, or principles, of knowledge in the Sanc'hya. These objects also represent the developmental dialectic of *prakriti*. They are as follows:

> 1. Nature [*prakriti*], as the origin of everything, is said to be the universal, the material cause, eternal matter, undistinguished and undistinguishable, without parts, productive but without production [that is, it is not produced], absolute substance.

---

51. For instance, in *Logic*, he says that "effect contains nothing whatever that cause does not contain. Conversely, cause contains nothing which is not in its effect . . . Cause as such implies its effect, and effect implies its cause . . . In this *identity* of cause and effect, the form through which they are distinguished as implicit determinations and as positedness is sublated [negated]." Hegel, *Hegel's Science of Logic*, 559–60.

2. Intelligence is the first production of Nature and [produces] . . . other principles, distinguishable as three gods through the efficacy of three qualities, which are Goodness, Foulness and Darkness [*gunas*] . . .

3. Consciousness, personality, the belief that in all perceptions and meditations I am present, that the objects of sense, as well as of intelligence, concern me, in short that I am I. It issues from the power of intelligence, and itself brings forth the following principles.

4–8. Five very subtle particles, rudiments or atoms, which are only perceptible to an existence of a higher order, and not through the senses of men; these proceed from the principle of consciousness, and bring forth on their own account the five elements—space and the first origination of earth, water, fire, and air.

9–19. The eleven succeeding principles [objects of knowledge] are the organs of feeling, which are produced by the personality. There are ten external organs, comprising the five senses and five active organs—the organs of the voice, hands and feet, the excretory and genital organs. The eleventh organ is that of the inward sense.

20–24. These principles are the five elements brought forth from the earlier-named rudiments—the ether which takes possession of space, air, fire, water, and earth.

25. The soul [*purusha*].

What is not entirely clear in Hegel's presentation is whether or not the soul is the last product of nature. If we ignore the ambivalence involved in the Sanc'hya's treatment of the relationship between *prakriti* and *purusha*, the latter is generally said to be "neither a cause nor an effect." [52] As stated earlier, the Sanc'hya often gives the impression that *purusha* is some kind of a cause. However, it is never stated that it is also an effect. *Purusha* is by and large excluded from the development of nature. To this effect *Samkhya Karika* states that "Spirit is neither an evolute nor an evolvent."[53]

Hegel passes a harsh judgment on this (non)system: "In this very unsystematic form we see only the first beginnings of reflection,

---

52. Sharma, *A Critical Survey of Indian Philosophy*, 162.
53. *Samkhya Karika*, 6 (Karika III).

which seem to be put together as a universal. But this arrangement is, to say nothing of being unsystematic, not even intelligent." He offers the following reasoning for this harsh judgment. On the one hand, it is stated that these principles are "outside of and successive to one another," but also that "their unity is found in the Soul." Moreover, it is said that the soul neither produces nor is produced. Yet, it seems to emerge out of the processes of nature. It is also said that the soul is one, but also that "there are many souls," and that the soul is "sentient, eternal, immaterial and unchangeable" (131).

Hegel's objections here are largely valid. While it is claimed that *prakriti* is solely responsible for the production of the twenty-three categories, which include the senses and organs, we also find that the latter are the plural manifestations of the soul. To this effect, Karika XVIII states that "the plurality of the spirits is established because birth, death, and organs are allotted separately; because there is no activity at one time; and because there are modifications of the three attributes [*gunas*]." It thus follows that there are many *purushas* through which the universal *purusha* manifests itself in (human) nature, or psyche. The further proof of the plurality of the soul (a.k.a. "Spirit") is as follows:

> Is Spirit one—controlling all the bodies like a string passing through a chain of jewels—or are there many spirits controlling each body? . . . If there were one Spirit then when one was born all would be born; or when one was to die all would die; likewise if one were to have any organic defect in the shape of deafness, blindness, dumbness, mutilation or lameness, then all would be deaf, blind mutilated or lame. But it does not happen so. Therefore, because birth, death and the organs are allotted separately, the plurality of Spirits is established.

Moreover, "There is no dominance of one activity at one time, all people are not engaged in one virtue all at one and the same time . . . , [and] there are different modifications of the three attributes [*gunas*]," which produce different personalities: the happy, unhappy, and delusional persons.[54] Bawra briefly comments that the one and many *purushas* are two different stages of Spirit.[55]

---

54. Ibid., 38–39 (Karika XVIII, and Bhasya XVIII).
55. Ibid., 39–40.

We must note that the Sanc'hya does not explicitly reject that Spirit is also one. The above "proof" of the plurality of Spirit does nothing of this sort. In fact, in many instances, the Sanc'hya affirms that Spirit is one. What is lacking is the acknowledgement, and consequently and explanation for, the contradiction between one and many souls, or *purushas*. More importantly for our present purposes, these contradictory positions are not altogether alien to Hegel's own dialectic. However, instead of engaging with this contradiction, Hegel merely suggests that these unresolved contradictions may be due to the distinction "between the theistic and atheistic systems of the Sanc'hya." Without considering this distinction any further, Hegel emphasizes the common ground of these two traditions, which is that the "knowledge of the soul still remains the principal point" for both (132). This conclusion is severely limited, since, as we have seen above, the knowledge of *prakriti* is also of crucial importance in the Sanc'hya. Hegel does not show any awareness of the fact that the system of the Sanc'hya is largely built upon *prakriti*, which is the One, absolute substance of Nature. Instead, he is entangled in the complications involved in the conception of *purusha*.

After this conclusion, Hegel suddenly adopts a more positive evaluation of the Sanc'hya in particular and the Eastern philosophy in general. He says that the abstraction mentioned above "is at the same time an important consideration," namely that "the negation of the object which is contained in thought, is necessary in order to comprehend" (ibid.). In other words, its abstraction from nature distinguishes the soul from the object (nature), instead of making thought strictly dependent on the object-world. In considering the syllogism of the Sanc'hya above, Hegel gave us the opposite impression of the Sanc'hya. This abstraction is an important point for Hegel, which he does not explain in this context. What he means by "comprehension" here is philosophical knowledge beyond mere perception. In *Logic*, he gives us the following explanation.

> The need for philosophy can be determined more precisely in the following manner. As feeling and intuition the spirit [mind] has what is sensible for its object; as fantasy, it has images; and as will, purposes, etc. But the spirit needs also, in *antithesis to*, or merely in *distinction from these forms* of its thereness and of its objects [hence its plural manifestations], to give satisfaction to its highest inwardness, *to thinking*, and to make thinking into its object. In this way, spirit comes *to itself* in the deepest sense of the word [and cognizes itself as the

object of its own thinking]; for its principle, its unadulterated selfhood, is thinking. But when it goes about its business in this way, what happens is that thinking [as understanding] gets entangled in contradictions; that is to say, it loses itself in the fixed nonidentity between thoughts, and therefore it does not reach itself [as the identity of the thought objects], but rather stays stuck in its counterpart [that is, in the world of objects]. The higher need goes against this result reached by a thinking that belongs to the understanding alone; it is grounded in the fact that thinking will not give up, but remains faithful to itself even in this conscious loss of its being at home with itself, "*so that it may overcome*," and may accomplish in thinking itself the resolution of its own contradictions.[56]

Of course, Hegel does not find all of these thoughts in the Sanc'hya. What he detects in it is the necessary negation of the object by the thinking subject, which brings out the latter in its "unadulterated selfhood." Because of the presence of this purification through the negation of the object, the Sanc'hya "has far more depth than the ordinary talk about immediate consciousness" (132). Immediate consciousness refers to sense perception and to the inferences that arise from it as forms of immediate knowledge. After the lengthy passage from *Logic* above, Hegel goes on to reject the assertion that "immediate knowing" is the "*exclusive* form of the consciousness of truth."[57]

Now, Hegel is ready to challenge the "superficial and perverted" view, which holds that "the Easterners . . . have lived in [complete] unity with nature," and hence did not raise the soul above it. He says that even though it is true that with the Indians "the soul in its activity, mind, is indeed undoubtedly in relation with nature and in unity with the truth of nature . . . , this true unity [nevertheless] essentially contains the moment of the negation of nature as it is in its immediacy." Thus, in "the idea which is present to the Indians . . . the spiritual is only one with nature in so far as it is within itself, and at the same time manifests the natural as [its own] negative." This interpretation also undermines the rigidly dualistic reading of the Sanc'hya. Hegel goes even further, and depicts the soul in the Sanc'hya in teleological terms, which becomes evident, he says, in the

---

56. Hegel, *The Encyclopaedia Logic*, 35.
57. Ibid.

Sanc'hya's approach to creation. "The soul's desire and end is for satisfaction and freedom, and with this view it is endowed with a subtle environment, in which all the above-mentioned principles are contained, but only in their elementary development." This point closely resembles the Aristotle-inspired Hegelian theory of potentiality discussed in the previous chapter. Hegel himself makes this connection when he says, "something of our ideal, or of the implicit is present in this idea; it is like the blossom which is ideally in the bud, and yet is not actual and real. The expression for this is *Lingam*, the generative power of nature, which holds a high place in the estimation of all Indians." This implicit form, then, "assumes a coarse bodily shape, and clothes itself in several garbs." In this way, the soul sinks back into the "coarse materiality," and "inhabits" it in the same way "immediate knowledge" does. The Sanc'hya, however, does not leave the soul in this state of affairs. In order to prevent "the descent" of the soul "into a coarse materiality," it recommends "philosophic contemplation . . . ," which repeats the process of negation and brings the soul back to its pure self by means of abstraction (132–33).

Here, Hegel presents the Sanc'hya as if it had a complete dialectical process, with a triadic structure. This becomes more evident when Hegel goes on to say that "it is noteworthy that in the observing consciousness of the Indians it struck them that what is true and in and for itself contains three determinations, and the Notion of the Idea is perfected in three moments." Hegel likens these three moments to the triadic structure of his own dialectic, and favorably calls it "this sublime consciousness of the trinity." Hegel points out, again favorably, that we find this trinity "in Plato and others," before it "went astray in the region of thinking contemplation," and retained "its place only in Religion" later, though merely "as a Beyond." Afterwards, "the understanding [Empiricism]" declared "it to be senseless." It was "Kant who broke open the road once more to its comprehension." As Hegel succinctly puts it, "the reality and totality of the Notion of everything, considered in its substance, is absorbed by the triad of determinations; and it has become the business of our times to bring this to consciousness" (134–35).

However, Hegel now says, with the Indians, the triadic structure of "the Notion of everything" remained undeveloped because their "consciousness proceeded from sensuous observation merely." He concludes that the main problem with this trinity of the Sanc'hya is, "as far as we are [Hegel is] concerned," that "the third principle is not the return to the first which Mind and Idea demand, and which is effected by the removal of the negation in order to effect a reconciliation with itself and to go back within itself. With the Indians the third is still change and negation" (135–36).

Next, Hegel considers the "further determinations of the intelligence . . ." in the Sanc'hya. There are "eight kinds of intelligence," though Hegel briefly considers four, which pertain to the Good (associated with *sattva*), and then considers eight kinds that fall under the fourth moment of the Good, which is power. The first three are "virtue . . . , science and knowledge . . . , [and] freedom from passion." These three follow from one another and lead to the fourth, which is "power." Ultimately, the intelligence that brings about power gives the mind unlimited power to separate itself from the body, and the external world, and achieve what we might consider supernatural powers. Power is said to be "eight-fold, and hence eight special qualities are given as being present" in it. These are:

> [1] the power to contract oneself into a . . . [very] small form, for which everything shall be penetrable; [2] the power to expand into a gigantic body; [3] the power to become light enough to be able to mount to the sun on a sunbeam; [4] the possession of unlimited power of action in the organs, so that with the finger-tips the moon may be touched; [5] irresistible will, so that, for instance, one may dive into the earth as easily as in the water; [6] mastery over all living and lifeless existence; [7] the power to change the course of nature; [8] and the power to perform everything that is wished (136–37).

Hegel concludes that these "transcendent" powers bring the Sanc'hya to produce the complete independence of the mind. This suggests something altogether different than the conclusion he offers above, which we have called "the-lack-of-return from the coarse reality." Now, he concludes, "sensuous evidence is of no account as opposed to this [transcendent powers], for with the Indian, perception of the senses is, generally speaking, absent; everything adopts the form of imaginary images, every dream is esteemed just as much as truth and actuality. The Sanc'hya ascribes this power to man, in so far as he elevates himself through the working of his thought into inward subjectivity" (137). Informed by this thought, in the last section of his lecture on the Sanc'hya, Hegel returns to the already tired idea that, in the final analysis, ". . . personality and self-consciousness disappear for the Indian" (140), which, in the interest of brevity, I skip here—

since Hegel returns to it once again after briefly dealing with two additional Indian philosophical schools.

3.3 The Nyaya and the Vaiseshica

3.3.1 A Brief Introduction to the Vaiseshica

The Vaiseshica (Vaisheshika) is closely related to the Nyaya. Canade (Kanãda) is the founder of the Vaiseshica, which is thought by some to be older than Buddhism. The main emphasis of the Vaiseshica is to identify and catalog the plural categories of the universe. "A category is called *padartha* and the entire universe is reduced to six or seven *padarthas*." *Padartha* "literally means 'the meaning of a word' . . ." The Vaiseshica holds that all objects "can be thought and named." For this reason, the Vaiseshica is described as, or criticized for, being "a mere catalogue of the knowables, an enumeration of the diverse reals without any attempts to synthesize them." This philosophy can also be described as "pluralistic realism" because it holds that the universe consists of a plurality of atoms and individual souls.[58] Thus, the Vaiseshica is also described as an atomistic philosophy.

The seven categories of the Vaiseshica are divided into two groups, designating *being* and *non-being*. The six categories of *being* are "substance," "quality," "action," "generality," "particularity," and "inherence." The seventh category is "negation," or "privation," which is said to be a later addition to this philosophy. This category, by itself, falls under *non-being*, and signifies the possible contradictions of *being*.[59]

Substance is the first category. There are nine original, "ultimate" substances, which are both material and spiritual. They are earth, water, fire, air, ether, time, space, spirit, and mind. From these ultimate, absolute substances arise all the compound substances, that is, the material and spiritual objects in nature. The ultimate material substances are said to be the simple essences of the compounds. The "compound substances are necessarily transient . . . ," whereas the ultimate substances are not. Even the ultimate material substances, such as earth, water, and air, are conceived as "supra-sensible, eternal, partless, unique atoms . . ." Ether is also a material, or "physical substance," but not atomic in structure. Each of these five elements

---

58. Sharma, *A Critical Survey of Indian Philosophy*, 175–76.
59. Ibid., 176.

"possesses a peculiar quality that distinguishes [it] from the rest." The "peculiar qualities of earth, water, fire, air, and ether are smell, taste, color, touch, and sound respectively, which are sensed by the five external senses." The external senses are of the same nature as the five sensible qualities. For instance, "sense of smell is constituted by the element of earth." Time and space, like ether, are continuous (indivisible, and partless), or "one each, eternal and all-pervading." They are also imperceptible, though, unlike ether and the other material substances, time and space are non-physical. It is us who think of them as having parts. "Time is the cause of our cognitions of past, present, and future," as well as such qualities as "young" and "old" we attribute to things. Space is the "cause of our cognitions of 'east' and 'west,' 'here' and 'there,' 'near' and 'far.'" Ether is the "substratum of the quality of sound." The soul (spirit) is also of an atomic substance. There exist an infinite number of individual souls. These souls are the substrata of the quality of consciousness. "Consciousness is not the essence of the self." It is "adventitious," and merely resides in the self. The self contains other qualities as well. Among them are "desire and volition." The essential relationship of the self to consciousness, desire, and volition is confirmed by such statements as "'I know,' 'I am happy,' 'I want to do this,' etc.'" The last substance is mind, which is "regarded as the internal sense." There are many individual minds that exit independently of each other in each selfhood. It is the organ through which the self comes to cognize objects and their distinct qualities. Thus, an important function of mind is to discriminate the qualities of the external senses. For instance, "we do not perceive color, touch, taste, smell and sound simultaneously, even though all the external senses may be in contact with their objects [simultaneously]."[60] It also follows from this that understanding (perception) is a function of discrimination of what is being sensed by the soul.

Now that we have already spoken of various qualities, a more general articulation of the category of quality is necessary. Quality, the second category, even though it is treated as an independent category, because it can be perceived, thought, and named, cannot exist without substance. Quality is passive. Thus, it does not engage in action, production, causality, etc. Canade describes quality as "that which inheres in a substance, which does not possess quality or action, which does not produce any composite thing, and which is not the cause of conjunction and disjunction like an action."[61]

---

60. Ibid., 177–78.
61. Ibid., 178–79.

Karma, or action, is the third category. Like quality, action too must inhere in a substance. Action is "the cause of conjunction and disjunction." It is because of this category that compound substances are formed and unformed. Action is also said to be of five kinds: "upward and downward movements," "contraction," "expansion," and "locomotion."[62] It appears that these five kinds of action all pertain to the temporal and spatial movement of substances, whereas conjunction pertains to the formation of the atomic substances into compound objects, and disjunction to their dissolution thereafter.

The fourth category, *samanya*, or generality, is similar to the categories of "universal," or "genus." The *samanya* designates the commonality of individuals. There is one *samanya* for each class of things, which resides in many individuals of a class as their essence. For instance, "there is the class-essence of the universal of man, called 'man-ness' or 'humanity,' which inheres in all [particular] individual men." Thus, an individual, such as Canade, is a particular man who shares with all other such individuals the universal attribute of "man-ness." One important thing to note about this otherwise familiar category in Western thought is that it is materialistic. Even though thought confirms the relationship of the universal and the particular, they both "are objective realities." In this sense, the existence of the universal and the particular does not strictly depend on thought, which is the case with idealism. There are many *samanyas*, which correspond to as many classes of things. It is said that "a universal cannot subsist in another universal." Thus, man-ness and cow-ness are never mixed in the same individual. Each universal constitutes the "being" of the individual. It appears that a lower level of *samanya* also exists, as suggested by Sharma.[63] This explanation of *samanya*, of course, leaves out many questions that we might wish to raise. For instance, a human individual and a cow partake in other universals, such as animal, etc. It seems that the universal "man" is the particularizing, and thus distinguishing, characteristic of the human individuals, even if they may also bear other, secondary universal characteristics.

This brings us to the fifth category *vishesa*, or particularity. The Vaiseshica, also spelled as Vaisheshika, derives its name from the word *vishesa*. Sharma points out that "the composite objects of this world, which we generally call 'particular' objects, are not real 'particulars' according to Nyaya-Vaisheishika." For example, "one atom is similar to another atom of the same element and one soul is similar to

---

62. Ibid., 179.
63. Ibid., 179–80.

another soul." Atom and soul are thus generals. *Vishesa* "is the differentium of ultimate eternal substances which are otherwise alike."[64] This point requires us to think of *vishesa* also as quality, though this is not explicitly stated.

The sixth category is *samavaya,* or inherence. Canade calls it "the relation between cause and effect." Prashastabada, who wrote the classical *bhasya,* or commentary, on Canade's philosophy, says that *samavaya* is "the relationship subsisting among things that are inseparable, standing to one another in the relation of the container and the contained, and being the basis of the idea, 'this is in that.'" The things that are inseparably related are the following: "the part and the whole, the quality and the substance, the action and the substance, the particular and the universal, the *vishesa* and the eternal substance." Each part of these couplets are said to inhere in each other. Inherence is not perceptible. It is inferred from the essential relationship of the parts of each couplet.[65] The category of inherence somewhat contradicts the theory of causality upheld by the Vaiseshica. As we will see below, this philosophy also claims that the cause and effect are separate, or do not inhere in each other.

The seventh category is *abhava,* or non-existence. This is the only negative category. Sharma says that the six other categories are absolute, whereas *abhava* is "relative in its conception." Thus, absolute negation is a non-category because of its "impossibility." It follows that negation involves some sense of positive affirmation. However, he also says *abhava* is of four different kinds, one of which is absolute. These are: "antecedent," "subsequent," "mutual," and the "absolute" forms of non-existence (*abhava*). The first kind refers to the *abhava* of a "thing before its production." The second refers to the *abhava* of a thing "after its destruction." The third is the *abhava* "of a thing as another thing which is different from it." These three kinds of *abhava* are obviously relative. The fourth "refers to the absence of a relation between two things in the past, the present and the future." Sharma provides further reasoning for these four kinds of *abhava,* which can all be detected in the following propositions: "A pot does not exist before its production; nor after its destruction; nor as a cloth; nor is there a 'liquid pot.'"

---

64. Ibid., 180–81.
65. Ibid., 181–82.

Antecedent negation has no beginning, but it has an end. It ends when the thing [a pot] is produced. Subsequent negation has a beginning, but has no end. It begins when the [pot] is destroyed and has no end since the same [pot] cannot be produced again. Mutual negation is exclusion and is opposed to identity. [A pot does not exist as a cloth, which implies that it exists as a non-cloth]. [Mutual negation] is both beginning-less and endless. Absolute negation is . . . [also] beginning-less and endless.

This last form of negation basically refers to an absurd idea or proposition in which the subject and predicate contradict each other. For instance, *this pot* is made of liquid. Sharma provides other examples: "Hare's horn, barren woman's child, sky-flower, etc." Mutual negation, on the other hand, is logical and relational. It establishes the truth of something negatively, as in "S is not P."[66] The category of *abhava*, in short, is an important category of the logic of the Vaiseshica.

Lastly, we need to consider the theory of causality and atomism of the Vaiseshica. The Vaiseshica and the Nyaya subscribe to the same theory of causality, which is the *Asatkaryavada*. This theory opposes the Sanc'hya theory of causality (*Satkaryavada*). As explained in the context of the Sanc'hya, the *Asatkaryavada* holds that "the effect does not pre-exist in its cause." Every effect is thus "a fresh beginning, a fresh creation." However, this does not mean that things, or objects, are created out of nothing. Rather, it means that the material cause (atoms) of compound objects does not entail within itself the forms of these objects. Thus, the creation of objects appears to be contingent rather than strictly teleological.

In order to better understand this theory of causality, we would do well to examine the atomism of the Vaiseshica, albeit briefly. As Sharma explains it, "we find that the material objects of the world are composed of parts and are subject to production and destruction. They are divisible into smaller parts and the latter are further divisible into still smaller parts. By this logic we have to accept the minutest particle of matter which may not be further divisible." Actually, it is not self-evident to me as to why, "by this logic," the indivisibility of the minutest particle would necessarily follow. Rather, it should be more the case that the possibility of infinite divisibility makes it self-evident that a particle's existence is eternal for the division never

---

66. Ibid., 182.

completely annihilates the part, and that the atomic part always remains potentially many parts. At any rate, the Vaiseshica holds that the "invisible, partless, and eternal particle" is the atom (*paramāṇu*). All physical objects are "produced by the combinations of atoms," in "different [quantitative and qualitative] combinations." That this is a contingent process can be obtained from the claim that "these combinations do not form the essential nature of the atoms nor do they pre-exist in them."[67]

The combinations come about from the admixture of different types of atoms, which are of four kinds: "earth, water, fire, and air." Ether is the "medium" through which these atoms are combined into perceptible objects. Each atom type has a specific quality, which makes possible different kinds of sensation (see above). Thus, depending on the specific quality and quantity of atoms in a combination, we perceive each object differently. The atoms are motionless "in themselves." "Motion is imparted to them by the Unseen Power of merit (*dharma*) and demerit (*adharma*), which resides in the individual souls and wants to fructify in the form of enjoyment and suffering." For this reason, the Vaiseshica atomism "is not [strictly] materialistic . . . because it admits the reality of spiritual substances—souls and God—and . . . the law of *Karma*." Atoms are merely the material cause of "this world of which God, assisted by the Unseen Power, is the efficient cause."[68]

However, the relationship between God and the individual souls is not clearly stated, and it is thus not clear if some objects in nature are directly caused by God, without the assistance of the Unseen Power residing in the individual souls. For instance, the creation of a stone or an animal in nature has nothing to do with the Unseen Power of merit and demerit, though they may serve the purposes of enjoyment and suffering. At any rate, we are here interested in outlining the basic tenets of an ancient philosophy, and not in criticizing it. We leave this task to Hegel.

3.3.2 A Brief Introduction to the Nyaya

Gotama is the founder of this philosophical school, and its first articulation is collected in *Nyaya Sutra*. This work consists of five books, each containing two chapters. Satis Chandra Vidyabhusana, in his introduction to *Nyaya Sutra*, comments that Gotama, perhaps, did

---

67. Ibid., 183.
68. Ibid., 183–84.

not author all of the ten chapters.[69] The Nyaya is very closely related to the Vaiseshica. One of the main distinguishing characteristics of the former from the latter is its emphasis on logic and epistemology. As Sharma points out, there are some other points of difference. For instance, the Nyaya establishes sixteen categories, or objects to be known. The seven "real" categories of the Vaiseshica are contained in one, the second of the sixteen categories of the Nyaya. For instance, "the first category [of the Nyaya] is Pramana or the valid means of knowledge." This highlights the primacy of the logical and epistemological character of the Nyaya. Second, the Nyaya has a more complex theory of valid means of knowledge than the Vaiseshica and the Sanc'hya. It subscribes to four such means of knowledge: "perception, inference, comparison, and verbal authority."[70] We should also add that the Nyaya, even though it subscribes to the same theory of causality as Vaiseshica, offers a more complex articulation of this theory than the latter.

The Nyaya, like many other Indian philosophies, connects happiness to knowledge. As the first Sutra of *Nyaya Sutra* states, "Supreme felicity is attained by the knowledge about the true nature of sixteen categories . . ." These categories are: "means of right knowledge, objects of right knowledge [including the seven categories of the Vaiseshica], doubt, purpose, familiar instance, established tenet, members [of a syllogism], confutation, ascertainment, discussion, wrangling, cavil, fallacy, quibble, futility, and occasion for rebuke." We should note that "confutation" is translated from the word *tarka*, which can also mean "argumentation," "*reductio ad absurdum*," or "hypothetical reasoning."[71]

If we examine these categories, they designate various forms of knowledge ranging from true knowledge to falsity. Not all of them provide valid knowledge, though knowing them all is required for discerning what is valid and what is not. Thus, various methods are needed to sort them out. Happiness comes from the release of pain through true knowledge, which allows us to negate "pain" by negating "birth, activity, faults, and misapprehension" successively in "the reverse order." This negation process is called "release."[72] The

---

69. Gotama, *The Nyaya Sutras of Gotam*, ed. Satis Chandra Vidyabhusana, *The Sacred Books of the Hindus*, Vol. 3 (Allababad: Sudhindranatha Vasu, 1913), x. henceforth, I refer to this work simply as *Nyaya Sutra*.
70. Sharma, *A Critical Survey of Indian Philosophy*, 191–92.
71. *Nyaya Sutra*, 1, (Bk. 1, Ch. 1, Sutra 1—henceforth, I.1.1, etc.).
72. Ibid., 2 (I.1.2).

four methods of release are, as already indicated, "perception, inference, comparison, and word [authoritative testimony.]"⁷³

"Perception is that knowledge which arises from the contact of a sense with its object and which is determinate, unnameable and non-erratic."⁷⁴ This definition of perception is restated by Sharma as "non-erroneous cognition which produced by the intercourse of the sense-organs with the objects, which is not [before the intercourse] associated with a name and which is well-defined."⁷⁵ This Sutra on perception is supplemented by the following additional three comments: First, perception must be "determinate," that is, one must clearly sense the object. An example of an indeterminate perception is when "a man looking from a distance cannot ascertain whether there is smoke or dust." Second, true knowledge requires the correspondence of the object and its name. If the senses produce the perception of an unnamable, it is not conducive to knowledge. Third, true perception must be non-erratic. For instance, "in summer the sun's rays coming in contact with earthly heat quiver and appear to the eyes of men as water. The knowledge of water derived in this way is not perception. To eliminate such cases the epithet non-erratic has been used."⁷⁶ As Sharma further notes, the Nyaya approach to obtaining knowledge through perception calls to mind Kant's theory, which holds that "'precepts without concepts are blind and concepts without precepts are empty.'" Thus, true perception in the Nyaya requires matching the perceived object with a well-defined name, that is, its proper concept.⁷⁷

In *Nyaya Sutra*, Gotama says, "Inference is knowledge which is preceded by perception, and is of three kinds: a priori, a posteriori, and 'commonly seen.'" The following self-explanatory commentary is attached to this Sutra:

> A priori is the knowledge of effect derived from the perception of its cause, e. g., one, seeing clouds, infers that there will be rain. A posteriori is the knowledge of cause derived from the perception of its effect, e. g., one, seeing a river swollen, infers that there was rain. "Commonly seen" is the knowledge of one thing derived from the perception of another thing with

---

73. Ibid., 2 (I.1.3).
74. Ibid., 3 (I.1.4).
75. Sharma, *A Critical Survey of Indian Philosophy*, 193.
76. *Nyaya Sutra*, 3 (I.1.4).
77. Sharma, *A Critical Survey of Indian Philosophy*, 194.

which it is commonly seen, e. g., one seeing a beast possessing horns, infers that it possesses also a tail, or one seeing smoke on a hill infers that there is (fire on it).[78]

"Comparison is the knowledge of a thing through its similarity to another thing previously well known." If one sees an animal that looks like a cow, and has heard previously that "a *bos gavaeus* is like a cow," one concludes, by comparison, that the animal must be a *bos gavaeus*. Similarity is derived logically from the name, and not from perception. The Nyaya rejects the view that comparison is not a distinct method of knowledge, and says the following in this regard:

> Some hold that comparison is not a separate means of knowledge, for when one notices the likeness of a cow in a strange animal one really performs an act of perception. In reply it is urged that we cannot deny comparison as a separate means of knowledge, for how does otherwise the name *bos gavaeus* signify the general notion of the animal called *bos gavaeus*. That the name *bos gavaeus* signifies one and all members of the *bos gavaeus* class is not a result of perception but the consequence of a distinct knowledge called comparison.[79]

"Word (verbal testimony) is the instructive assertion of a reliable person." There are two kinds of testimony, perceptible and non-perceptible. A doctor's advice to take "butter" for strength is of the first, and a religious teacher's assertion that horse sacrifice helps one "conquer heaven" is of the second kind. The first kind is verifiable the second is not, though it too counts as valid knowledge.[80]

The method of inference is of particular interest to philosophers, and is closely associated with the category of *members*. Indeed, most interpretations of the Nyaya discuss inference within the context of members. This means that inference in the Nyaya is essentially syllogism. This becomes obvious when we consider the category of members further. In the first instance, "members" refers to the parts of a syllogism. As Gotama states, "The members (of a syllogism) are proposition, reason, example, application, and conclusion."[81] In this

---

78. *Nyaya Sutra*, 3 (I.1.5).
79. Ibid., 3–4 (I.1.6).
80. Ibid., 4 (I.1.7–8).
81. Ibid., 10 (I.1.32).

way, the Nyaya employs a five-step syllogistic inference, as opposed to the typically three-step syllogism of the Western logic influenced by Aristotle.

These five steps operate in the following way.

1. Proposition: This hill is fiery.
2. Reason: Because it is smoky.
3. Example: Whatever is smoky is fiery, as a kitchen.
4. Application: So is this hill (smoky).
5. Conclusion: Therefore this hill is fiery.[82]

The syllogistic inference of the Nyaya stated above closely resembles the Aristotelian syllogism. As Sharma notes, "like the Aristotelian syllogism, the Indian inference has three terms. The major, the minor and the middle . . ." In the syllogism quoted earlier, hill is the minor, the fire the major, and smoke the middle term. However, the logic of the Nyaya "does not separate deduction from induction." The Aristotelian syllogism, on the other hand, is only deductive and formal. From this difference arises the need to establish the conclusion in the former in five steps and in the latter in three. Nevertheless, the main terms of a syllogism, as already indicated, remain three in both. Obviously, there is some redundancy in the five-member syllogism of the Nyaya. Thus, "we can easily leave out the first two or the last two which are essentially the same." We achieve the most well-known of the Aristotelian syllogisms if we exclude the first two. Thus, this five-step syllogism becomes: (1) Whatever is smoky is fiery, as a kitchen; (2) So is this hill (smoky); (3) Therefore this hill is fiery. If we edit this shorter reasoning, as Sharma does, we get the following: "(1) All things which have smoke have fire (Major premise); (2) This hill has smoke (Minor premise); (3) Therefore this hill has fire (Conclusion)." Sharma adds that "the Nyaya rightly regards deduction and induction as inseparably related, as two aspects of the same process—the truth now realized in western logic."[83]

As noted earlier, the theory of causality in the Nyaya is essentially the same as the one held by the Vaiseshica. However, the former has a more elaborate articulation of this theory. The Nyaya defines a cause "as an unconditional and invariable antecedent of an effect and an effect as an invariable consequent of a cause. The same cause produces the same effect and the same effect is produced by the same

---

82. Ibid.
83. Sharma, *A Critical Survey of Indian Philosophy*, 198–99.

cause. Plurality of causes is ruled out." From "its antecedence" and "invariability," results the "unconditionality, or necessity" of the cause. "Unconditional antecedence is immediate and direct antecedence and excludes the fallacy or remote cause." In this exclusion, pertinent evidence that may be considered a cause is excluded if it undermines an inductive argument. In short, the Nyaya "definition of a cause is the same as that in western inductive logic" proposed by David Hume, J. S. Mill, and others.[84]

The Nyaya also "recognizes five kinds of accidental antecedents which are not real causes."

> Firstly, the qualities of a cause are mere accidental antecedents. The color of a potter's staff is not the cause of a pot. Secondly, the cause of a cause or a remote cause is not unconditional. The potter's father is not the cause of a pot. Thirdly, the co-effects of a cause are themselves not causally related. The sound produced by the potter's staff is not the cause of a pot, though it may invariably precede the pot. Night and day are not causally related. Fourthly, eternal substances like space are not unconditional antecedents. Fifthly, unnecessary things like the potter's ass are not unconditional antecedents; though the potter's ass may be invariably present when the potter is making a pot, yet it is not the cause of the pot. A cause must be an unconditional and necessary antecedent.

It also follows from the above discussion that an effect does not ". . . pre-exist in its cause. It is a fresh beginning, a new creation." Sharma includes more detailed discussion of the Nyaya theory of causation, which, for the sake of brevity, we must omit.[85]

3.3.3 Hegel on the Nyaya and the Vaiseshica

"The philosophy of Gotama and that of Canade belong to one another. The philosophy of Gotama is called (reasoning), and that of Canade, Vaiseshica (particular). The first is an especially perfect dialectic, and the second, on the other hand, occupies itself with physics, that is, with particular or sensuous objects" (141). Hegel thus

---

84. Ibid., 205.
85. Ibid., 205–7.

combines the two, like Colebrooke, though he mostly discusses the Nyaya. Of interest here is also Hegel's reference to the Nyaya as "an especially perfect dialectic." It seems that he borrows this epithet from Colebrooke, who uses it to mean syllogistic logic of the Aristotelian kind.

Most of Hegel's commentary in this section is merely descriptive, and consists of roughly four pages. He describes in some detail the theory of names, and its triadic structure (enunciation-definition-investigation), and the methods and objects of investigation, which we have enumerated above, and will not repeat here. He becomes somewhat more analytical with the syllogism of the Nyaya. Of this, Hegel says that these "syllogisms are with us." However, the manner of adopting them (in five steps indicated by the fire, hill, smoke case) propounds "the matter . . . first." Instead, "we should . . . begin with the general" (144). What Hegel has in mind is the fact that the logic of Nyaya begins with the material evidence of observation and moves to the formal validity of the proof. For Hegel, all valid inferences are triadic in nature, as is syllogism. Hegel is suggesting here that the above syllogism should move from the third member to the fifth in an Aristotelian manner. For the record, we should point out that, as Colebrooke argues, the followers of another Indian philosophical tradition, the Mimansa, "combine the syllogism to three members, either the first three or last three."[86]

Because of the almost complete absence of philosophical engagement with the Nyaya and the Vaiseshica, Hegel fails to prove his claim that these are not properly philosophical schools of thought. Instead, in order to prove his claim, he abruptly proceeds with a commentary on the issue of individuality again.

4. Hegel's Final Verdict on the "Oriental Philosophy"

Hegel begins his extremely difficult concluding commentary with the following remark: "We have seen that in India the point of main importance is the soul's drawing itself within itself, raising itself up into liberty, or thought, which constitutes itself for itself. This becoming explicit of soul in the most abstract mode may be called intellectual substantiality . . ." This "intellectual substantiality," so defined, is one of the virtues of the Indians. However, instead of "the unity of mind and nature" (he equates soul with mind here), what we find in the Indian philosophy is their separation. Hegel, repeating

---

86. Colebrooke, *Essays on the Religion and Philosophy of the Hindus*, 186–87.

some his own key arguments, points out that "to mind, the consideration of nature is only the vehicle of thought or its exercise, which has as its aim the liberation of mind" (144–45). The Indian "intellectual substantiality" lacks this dialectic in which Spirit obtains its freedom, according to Hegel. We must note that Hegel here reduces the entire Indian philosophy to one particular aspect of the Sanc'hya, namely, the transcendent powers of mind to completely free itself from Nature by a process of abstraction.

However, according to Hegel, intellectual substantiality is not an altogether useless endeavor. The problem with the Indian mode of thinking in this regard is that it uses intellectual substantiality merely as the end. To obtain this end, it purges the soul/mind of all that is objective and natural. In proper philosophy, says Hegel, intellectual substantiality "is in general the true commencement." It follows that "to philosophize is the idealism of making thought, in its own right, the principle of truth" (145). Thus, philosophizing must begin with its own universal thought, the Notion, and establish it as the *prius* of reality, and not simply as the end of dialectic, which is presumably the case with the Indians.

Intellectual substantiality also has much to do with the absence of individuality. Here, Hegel generalizes his argument to include the entire Eastern thought. The Eastern "intellectual substantiality is the opposite of the reflection, understanding, and the subjective individuality of the European." With the European "subjective individuality," the *I* is of crucial importance: "With us [Europeans] it is of importance that I will, know, believe, think this particular thing according to the grounds that I have for so doing, and in accordance with my own free will; and upon this an infinite value is set." The Indians consider this individual subjectivity "vanity." Thus, "the point of interest is to reach intellectual substantiality in order to drown in it that subjective vanity with all its cleverness and reflection. This is the advantage of arriving at this point of view." In short, "intellectual substantiality is the other extreme form of this [vanity]; it is that in which all the subjectivity of the 'I' is lost" (ibid.).

While Hegel's critics often emphasize his critical approach to the Indian philosophy, it is clear that Hegel here finds both the Indian intellectual substantiality and the Western subjective individuality defective. The "defect" of the first, he says, is that while intellectual substantiality is ". . . represented as end and aim for the subject, as a condition that has to be produced in the interest of the subject, even though it be most objective, is yet only quite abstractly objective; and hence the essential form of objectivity is wanting to it." Such an intellectual substantiality "thus remaining in abstraction, has as its existence the subjective soul alone." Thus, it lacks the objectivity of soul, which can only be realized in and through nature. In the "empty vanity," on the other hand, only "the subjective power of negation alone remains . . ." This is to say subjective individuality rejects the substantive universal thought (which Hegel also calls "objective thought"). What we have here is pure vanity, which ironically declares the knowledge of the substantive idea vanity. For subjective individuality, "this abstraction of intellectual substantiality only signifies an escape into what is empty and without determination, wherein everything vanishes" (ibid.). For Hegel, in subjective individuality, there are only particular determinations. Without their substantive *prius*, that is, the illimitable, Absolute Idea, such determinations also vanish for they are only appearances without essence, or ground.

The solution, says Hegel,

> is to force forward the real ground of the inwardly self-forming and determining objectivity—the eternal form within itself, which is what men call Thought. Just as this Thought in the first place, as subjective, is mine, because I think, but in the second place is universality which comprehends intellectual substantiality, it is likewise in the third place forming activity, the principle of determination. This higher kind of objectivity that unfolds itself, alone gives a place to the particular content, allows it to have free scope and receives it into itself.

In contrast, the "Eastern ideas tend to destroy [the particular]," which can only be "preserved active in the soil of thought; it cannot exist when regarded as independent, but must exist only as a moment in the whole system." Consequently, Eastern philosophy, despite having intellectual substantiality, or "a definite content," is "destitute of thought or system because [in it, thought] comes from [without] and is outside of the unity [with nature]." Hence,

> On that side there stands intellectual substantiality, on this side it appears dry and barren; the particular thus only has the dead form of simple reason and conclusion, such as we find in the Scholastics. Based on the ground of thought, on the other hand, the particular may receive its dues; it may be regarded and grasped as a moment in the whole organization. The Idea has not

become objective in the Indian Philosophy; hence the external and objective has not been comprehended in accordance with the Idea. This is the deficiency in Orientalism (145–46).

Hegel links this "deficiency" to lack of real individual freedom, as mentioned above. In other words, "the true, objective ground of thought finds its basis in the real freedom of the subject; the universal or substantial must itself have objectivity." This can only occur when the individual becomes the medium of universal thought and gives it concrete, "immediate existence and actual presence" (146). We are to find this "principle . . . in the Greek world." In the philosophical history of this world, "the universal first appears as quite abstract, and as such it confronts the concrete world; but its value is both for the ground of the concrete world and for that which is implicit. It is not a beyond; for the value of the present lies in the fact that it exists in the implicit; or that which is implicit, the universal, is the truth of present objects" (147).

However, Hegel is not able to find either this complete philosophy, which establishes the universal as the truth of existence and the existence as the implicitness of the universal, or its prerequisite individual freedom, until much later in the historical development of philosophy. What we first find in the pre-Socratic Greek world is a struggle to purify thought, not unlike the Indian philosophy, and subsequently achieve intellectual substantiality, which Hegel has defined above as "the soul's drawing itself within itself, raising itself up into liberty, or thought, which constitutes itself for itself." The issue of subjective individuality will first come up in the context of the Sophists and the Socratics in a manner unsatisfactory to Hegel. Thus, Hegel's final verdict on the "Oriental Philosophy" is both unfair and problematic. It is unfair for the simple reason that what he demands is a complete system that resembles his own. True, he finds shortcomings in the Western philosophical traditions also. However, he regards them as the necessary components of the complete philosophical system, instead of designating them as insufficiently "philosophical utterances."

As he told us in the introduction to his lecture on "Oriental Philosophy," the Eastern philosophies are not properly philosophical on account of proposing too few such utterances. This turns out not to be the case. The falsity of this claim is all the more obvious when we go, as I have tried to do, slightly beyond the information on these traditions that was available to Hegel. Indeed, what we have observed above are rich philosophical traditions that, I now claim, surpass the depth and scope of much of the early Greek philosophical traditions. Hegel's verdict is also highly problematic because it has little bearing on the philosophical traditions he discusses. Besides several pertinent but abstractly stated points, the "immersion" of consciousness in the substantive Absolute has not been demonstrated y Hegel.

Still, it was necessary to consider Hegel's treatment of "Oriental Philosophy" to illustrate, at least partially, what Hegel is looking for in a proper philosophy. In doing so, I went beyond Hegel to find more philosophically relevant information in two of the Eastern philosophies, the Chinese and Indian. I am hoping that the additional information provided above proves useful as an introduction to the many topics we are about to encounter in the early Greek philosophy, covered in this volume, and beyond, as we move through the later Greek period to the Middle Ages and modernity in the subsequent two volumes.

CHAPTER 3

First Greek Period, First Division - Part I: Ionics, Pythagoreans, and Eleatics

1. Introduction

In one of his materialist moments in *Lectures*, Hegel argues that "we find the greatest activity in Greek life on the coasts of Asia Minor, in the Greek islands, and then towards the west of Magna Graecia; we see amongst these people, through their internal political activity and their intercourse with foreigners, the existence of a diversity and variety in their relations, whereby narrowness of vision is done away with, and the universal rises in its place." Here, Hegel partly attributes the rise of the universal, philosophical Notion in Greece to their cosmopolitanism. This thought opens the way for external influences on Greek thought, which Hegel denied in the previous chapter. He also ties the variations in the philosophical outlooks among the early Greeks to their geographical location when he says that such variations "partake of the character of the geographical distinction." More generally speaking, "the geographical distinction makes its appearance in the manifestation of Thought, in the fact that, with the Orientals a sensuous, material side is dominant, and in the west, Thought, on the contrary, prevails, because it is constituted into the principle in the form of thought." This East and West distinction is not simply a divide between "the Orientals" and the Greeks. It is also reflected within Greek philosophy itself. Within the early Greek philosophy, says Hegel, "Those philosophers who turned to the east knew the absolute in a real determination of nature, while towards Italy there is the ideal determination of the absolute" (169–70). This distinction represents the materialism of the Ionians and the idealism of the Eleatics and the Pythagoreans.

Remarkably, also, Hegel's depiction of "the Orientals" here is the opposite of what he says of them in his lecture on "Oriental Philosophy." There, at the end of the lecture, their philosophy is reduced to abstract idealism, to complete immersion of the individual into substantive consciousness. In the same lecture, as we have seen, Hegel also explicitly rejects the "perverted" idea that the Easterners are immersed in the sensuous world of nature. Here, he says, with them the "sensuous, material side is dominant," and that this has something to do with their geography.

What Hegel considers to be the first period of Greek philosophy includes: (a) The Ionians (Thales, Anaximander, and Anaximenes); (b) Pythagoras and the Pythagoreans; (c) the Eleatics (Xenophanes, Parmenides, Melissus, and Zeno); (d) Heraclitus; (e) Empedocles, Leucippus, and Democritus; and (f) Anaxagoras. Hegel tells us that his main task is to "trace and point out the progression of . . . philosophy . . ." in this period. This task is also the main task of *Lectures* in its entirety. This "progression" is dialectical, and signifies the development of the philosophical Notion, that is, its movement from the abstract to the concrete cognition of the Notion. As indicated in Chapter 1, the concretion of the abstract Notion generally takes two forms: intensification and diversification. This also means that Hegel sees all the variations in philosophies as the necessary moments of the whole system of philosophy, and, because they are moments of the same system, as continuous links of a single chain.

I have divided the first Greek period into three chapters (Chapters 3–5). This division is somewhat arbitrarily based on the length of my presentation, and somewhat on the philosophical grounds given by Hegel. I discuss the Ionians, the Pythagoreans, and the Eleatics in Chapter 3. In Hegel's estimation, these three philosophical schools constitute a triadic attempt to purify and intensify the philosophical Notion. With the Ionians, "we find wholly abstract characterizations such as water, air, and 'the infinite [matter],' which nonetheless take a particular shape." This is the first step the Greek philosophical thought takes. "Pythagoras marks step (2)." This second step constitutes a double movement. First, whereas with the Ionians "the absolute was defined in a natural mode as water and the like, the form of the determination . . . [of the absolute] is now the unit or number." Number is a non-sensible sensuous thought. For this reason, it is closer to the properly philosophical idea, or the Notion, than the Ionic sensuous principles. Second, the universal is "what is in and for itself." Number as a universal unit "fragments into 1, 2, 3, and so on." In its fragmentation, the universal "proceeds to something concrete." This is precisely what dialectic is and does: the progression from the One to many. The many is implicitly present within the One. However, even though the Pythagorean principle captures the rhythm of dialectical development well, it is still based on a limited absolute, that is, Number, precisely because this universal still carries the birth-pangs of sensuousness. "The Eleatics constitute step (3). Here, thought is forcibly torn free from sensuous shape, and from the form of number too." The principle of the Eleatics is "pure being," which, according to Hegel, is pure thought. With this step, the Eleatics assert that only the One is true, "not the many" (170).[1] Total negation of the many—of what is particular and finite, of what is in motion and changing—is the hallmark of the Eleatic dialectic. However, this dialectic suspends the One in mid-air by denying the rational truth of anything that contradicts the unity of the One, including the categories of motion and *becoming*.

I discuss Heraclitus and the Atomists (Empedocles, Leucippus, and Democritus) in Chapter 4, and Anaxagoras in Chapter 5.

2. Ionic Philosophy

2.1 Introduction

As mentioned above, the Absolute of the Ionics is a definite, sensuous thought, derived from natural elements, such as water, air, and fire. Indeed, early Greek philosophical works were mainly concerned with nature, and they saw these natural elements as the essence of the whole nature. For this reason, "the thought contained in [the Ionic philosophy] is very abstract and barren" (171). In other words, "the Absolute" of the Ionics "is not yet the self-determining, the Notion turned back into itself, but only a dead abstraction" from nature (193, 208). In what follows, Hegel attempts to vindicate the Ionic Notion to some extent, and place it within the annals of the history of proper philosophy.

2.2 Thales

Diogenes Laërtius comments that "according to some [Thales] left nothing in writing," and, according to others, he left "treatises, one On the Solstice and one On the Equinox."[2] It is widely accepted that Thales concerned himself mostly with nature and astronomy. Thus, Thales, says Hegel, "is universally recognized as the first natural philosopher . . ." (173). Hegel does not find much that is philosophically significant in Thales. Indeed, he thinks that what is attributed to Thales by later commentators could not have belonged to him. Given the nature of his absolute principle, and the specific

---

1. G. W. F. Hegel, *Lectures on the History of Philosophy 1825–6: Greek Philosophy*, ed. Robert F. Brown (Oxford: Clarendon Press, 2006), 15–16.
2. Diogenes Laërtius, *Lives of the Eminent Philosophers*, Vol. 1, trans. Robert Drew Hicks (London: Loeb Classical Library, 1925), 17.

propositions attached to it, "they cannot have had any particular speculative value" (173). Yet, Hegel finds some such speculative value in the principle and propositions of Thales.

By favorably quoting Aristotle, Hegel explains that "'most of the earliest philosophers have placed the principles of everything in something in the form of matter . . .'" Because they perceived the universe essentially as matter, they reasoned that the "'first source'" of everything in existence had to be also of material nature. This "first source" remains eternally present in nature, and "'only changes in its particular qualities.'" They called this source "'the principle of all that exists.'" It follows from this reasoning that "'nothing arises or passes away, because the same nature always remains. For instance, we say that, absolutely speaking, Socrates neither originates if he becomes beautiful or musical, nor does he pass away if he loses these qualities, because the subject, Socrates, remains the same.'" This applies to "'all else,'" in nature. There is thus a permanent principle, or essence, without which "there is no reality or truth" (174–75). All that changes derives from the principle, and is of secondary importance in relation to it.

However, Hegel cautiously asserts that we do not know anything more than Thales's principle, which says that "water is the god overall." The explanation of the "application" of his principle, or "how it is to be proved that water is the universal substance, and in what way particular forms are deduced from it" are lacking. In this sense, too, Hegel shies away from attributing to Thales the Notion that he thought "there is no reality or truth" in change. These thoughts belong to those who came after Thales, as does Aristotle's conjecture that Thales makes "water the absolute essence of everything." This much is not explicitly "acknowledged by Thales" (175). Plutarch also attributes to Thales more than what he could have contemplated. As Hegel quotes him, "'Thales suggests that everything takes its origin from water and resolves itself into the same, because as the germs of all that live have moisture as the principle of life, all else might likewise take its principle from moisture; for all plants draw their nourishment, and thus bear fruit, from water, and if they are without it, fade away; and even the fires of sun, and stars and world are fed through the evaporation of water'" (176). It is in this above sense that water may be considered the essence of everything that exists. Thales' water, according to Plutarch, is thus not simply the permanent and universal ingredient of everything in Nature, but also the source of all life and motion.

"Since Plutarch gives more definite grounds [on behalf of Thales] for holding that water is the simple essence of things," responds

Hegel, "we must see whether things, in so far as they are simple essence, are [really] water." Hegel provides the example of the animal: "The germ of the animal, [which is] of moist nature, is undoubtedly the animal as the simple actual, or as the essence of its actuality, or undeveloped actuality" (ibid.). For Hegel, thus, essence is the Notion, or the Idea, and in this case, the essence of animal is the speculative Notion of the animal. Even though moisture is to be found in the animal, this is not its distinguishing and essential characteristic. In short, "here we have the strife between sensuous universality and universality of the Notion. The real essence of nature has to be defined, that is, nature has to be expressed as the simple essence of thought." The universal, however, has to be completely "devoid of [a determinate] form." But "water as it is, comes into the determination of form, and is thus, in relation to others, a particular existence just like everything that is natural." Yet, water, taken as the principle, has advantages over other elements, such as earth and air. Earth is more evidently formed than the relatively formless water. At the same time, air, which is also relatively formless and simple, has the drawback of being too immaterial. Thus, "if the need of unity impels us to recognize for separate things a universal, water, although it has the drawback of being a particular thing, can easily be utilized as the One, both on account of its neutrality [as opposed to earth], and because it is more material than air" (178).

However, as already indicated, water has its own limitations in this regard. Accordingly, Hegel says, "We certainly grant this universal activity of water, and for that reason call it an element, a physical universal power; but while we find it thus to be the universal of activity, we also find it to be this actual, not everywhere, but in proximity to other elements—earth, air and fire." This indicates that water is just another element with a definite form (a finite), which cannot constitute the essence of all the existents in nature. If it is treated as the universal essence, water has to be speculatively taken to represent the Notion, and not sensuously. "To be speculative universality," Hegel adds, "would necessitate its being Notion and having what is sensuous removed" from it (177). True, speculative universal, then, has to be the Notion, or pure thought.

The main importance of Thales lies in commencing philosophy with the proposition that "water is the Absolute, or as the ancients say, the principle." This is to say, it is the principle as such, and not its sensuous representation (water) that brings consciousness to "essence, truth, that which is alone in and for itself . . ." Thus, the natural world that contains "plenitude of existence," which is manifold and changing, and thus is many, is reduced speculatively "to a simple substance, which, as the ever enduring principle, neither originates nor disappears . . ." It takes "a great robustness of mind" to come up with this in a world in which speculative thought has not been fully cognized. To repeat, the drawback of Thales's universal principle is that it is itself a finite, particular existent, and thus "has no independence, is not true in and for itself, but is only an accidental modification." Nevertheless, there is an "affirmative point of view" involved in his principle in that "all other things proceed from the one [Absolute, universal], that the one remains thereby the substance from which all other things proceed, and it is only through a determination which is accidental and external that the particular existence has its being." It follows also that "all particular existence is transient" (178–79).

Hegel warns here that the universal should not be thought of as something that "stands above, and that down here we have the finite world" (179). This point is immensely important to Hegel, and is often employed by him to controvert various ideas about God, or other expressions of the Absolute. He says, "This idea [of separateness] is often found in the common conception of God—where permanence is attributed to the world and where men often represent two kinds of actuality to themselves, a sensuous and a super-sensuous world of equal standing." Two shortcomings are to be identified with this "common conception." First, because of the equal footing assigned to them, both moments of the totality are erroneously seen as being equally, or in the same way, actual. In contrast, the truly philosophical point of view, says Hegel, "is that the one is alone the truly actual, and here we must take actual in its higher significance, because we call everything actual in common life." To put this somewhat paradoxically, the supersensible One, or the Notion, is more actual than what we ordinarily take to be actuality (180). Second, the particular existents cannot exist without the One. Hegel points out in this regard that "we certainly see this also in living matter, where things happen in another way, for here the Notion comes into existence; thus if, for example, we abstract the heart, the lungs and all else collapse. And in the same way all nature exists only in the unity of all its parts, just as the brain can exist only in unity with the other organs" (182).

Here, Hegel is giving a brief account of the necessary and internal relations of the parts of the whole to each other, and is also highlighting the same relation of the parts to the whole in which they exist. No part can exist apart from the other parts and apart from the whole. However, there is a universal principle which establishes the identity of the parts and the whole, and makes the whole organic and alive. The universal Notion is this principle, according to Hegel. In this sense, the universal is also called the soul.

Diogenes Laërtius says that "'Thales has . . . ascribed a soul to what is lifeless.'" Hegel is skeptical that this thought actually belongs to Thales.[3] Plutarch, on the other hand, says that Thales "'called God the Intelligence of the world.'" Hegel, once again, thinks this thought does not belong to Thales, but was first introduced by Anaxagoras. According to Cicero, "'Thales says that water is the beginning of everything, but God is the Mind which forms all that is, out of water.'" To this Hegel adds, "Thales may certainly have spoken of God, but Cicero has added the statement that he comprehended him as the nous [Mind or intellect] which formed everything out of water." While this attribution by Cicero is historically and factually inaccurate, the more important philosophical point is that in thinking of God as *nous*, or the absolute essence of existence, one must establish its speculative, rational significance. Hegel adds that if Thales did indeed "speak of God [or the soul] as constituting everything out of this same water, that would [still] not give us any further information about this existence; we should have spoken un-philosophically of Thales because we should have used an empty word without inquiring about its speculative significance." The mere assertion of the word of God, or belief in God as the creator, is an empty abstraction. "Similarly the word world-soul is useless, because its being is not thereby expressed" (183–84).

For Hegel, God is not this separate entity which creates the world by manipulating nature from without. God is the essence of all that exists. However, as he explains elsewhere, "When we add that . . . there is a 'highest essence' and that God ought to be designated by that name, two things should be noted:"

> First, . . . the expression "to give" refers to something finite . . . The things that are "given" . . . are such that others are [also] "given" *outside* and *beside* him. But God, as the Infinite itself, is not something that is "given" whilst *outside* and *beside* him there are also other essences. Whatever else is "given" outside of God has not essentiality in its separateness from God; on the contrary, any such thing lacks internal stability and

---

3. Diogenes Laërtius attributes this to Aristotle and Hippias, who "affirm that, arguing from magnate and from amber, [Thales] attributed a soul or life even to the inanimate." Diogenes Laërtius, *Lives of the Eminent Philosophers*, 18.

essence in its isolation, and must be considered as a mere semblance.

And this explanation implies a *second* point too: namely, that all talk of God merely as '*the highest*' essence must be called unsatisfactory. For the category of quantity that is applied here [i.e., the highest] has its place only in the domain of the finite.

In other words, Hegel's main point is that the essence of God cannot be quantified and predicated, since quantification and predication requires equating God to other things, which is inconceivable. For this reason, "God is not merely *an* essence and not merely the *highest* essence either. He is *the* essence."[4]

The general and dialectical point we must get out of these comments is that the totality must not be separated into two externally related independent spheres, one designating the sphere of the absolute essence, and the other that of the particular, finite essences and existents. The latter are internally related to the former and are its immanent manifestations, though, as such, the finite determinations are not the explicit predicates of God. God is neither tall, nor short; neither a tree nor a man. God simply is. As importantly, and to repeat, "Whatever else is 'given' outside of God has not essentiality in its separateness from God; on the contrary, any such thing lacks internal stability and essence in its isolation, and must be considered as a mere semblance." It follows that nothing, or no single thing, can exist or subsist by itself without its essential ties to the Absolute. This rule applies to Nature and cognition.

We have, with Hegel, moved too far afield from Thales. To recapitulate, Hegel summarizes the significance and the limitations of Thales's philosophy as follows: "The philosophy of Thales is comprised in the following simple [moments]: (a) It has constituted an abstraction in order to comprehend nature in a simple sensuous essence. (b) It has brought forth the Notion of ground or principle; that is, it has defined water to be the infinite Notion, the simple essence of thought, without determining it further as the difference of quantity. That is the limited significance of this principle of Thales" (184–85).

As indicated earlier, it is Hegel who defines Thales's water as "the infinite Notion," or as the "simple essence of thought." This Hegelian intervention seems to be necessary for the inclusion of Thales in the annals of proper philosophy for the infinite Notion is a

---

4. Hegel, *The Encyclopaedia Logic*, 177.

necessary prerequisite of such a philosophy. Otherwise, we would have to treat Thales's principle as a dead abstraction, and his philosophy as an immersion into the sensuous nature. This, in turn, would disqualify his principle from being properly philosophical. In a way, in granting this favor to Thales, Hegel has gone against his advice by attributing to him more than he had actually thought and said. Perhaps, his point in doing so was to show the philosophical import of Thales's principle. This is to say, even if his principle is severely limited, the idea behind it—the idea that the One is the *prius* of all truth—is the crux of all philosophical thinking. Perhaps, too, it is because this underpinning idea is so potentially philosophical that his interpreters, including Aristotle, Plutarch, Cicero, and Hegel, were able to attribute to Thales more than he had bargained for.

2.3 Anaximander

It is said that Thales could not convince his friend, Anaximander, that water was the universal principle (185). According to Diogenes Laërtius, Anaximander "laid down as his principle and element that which is unlimited without defining it as air or water or anything else. He held that the parts undergo change, but the whole is unchangeable..."[5] As Hegel interprets Anaximander's principle, first, the undefined "infinite" does not need external material or energy for its "continuous," or spontaneous, "origination." It is a self-generating power. Second, the infinite is the One, and contains within itself all that comes into existence and passes away. In this manner, "Out of the one, Anaximander separates the opposites which are contained in it . . . ; thus everything in this medley [in existence] is certainly there [within the One], but undetermined. That is, everything is really contained therein in possibility [potentiality]," so that, as Aristotle puts it, "'. . . everything arises . . . from incipient being which is not yet in actuality.'" Third, "the infinitude is in size and not in number." With this claim, Anaximander differs from the Atomists, "who maintain the absolute discretion of the infinite, while Anaximander upholds its absolute continuity." In other words, while the Atomists think of the infinite as a medley of discrete, isolated atoms, Anaximander thinks of it as being an undifferentiated One, which then differentiates itself into many parts. As Diogenes Laërtius describes it, "'the parts of the Infinite change, but it itself is unchangeable'" (ibid.). For these three reasons, Hegel considers the

---

6. Diogenes Laërtius, *Lives of the Eminent Philosophers*, 77.

principle of Anaximander a great advance. Given these descriptions of his philosophy, we should add, the resemblance between the principle of Anaximander and the unnamable *Tao* of Lao Tzu is remarkable.

According to Hegel, "the advance made by the determination of the principle as infinite in comprehensiveness rests in the fact that absolute essence no longer is a simple [one-sided, finite] universal, but one which negates the finite." In addition, Anaximander removes from the infinite the individuality, or particularity entailed in Thales's principle (water). In this way, says Hegel, Anaximander's "objective principle does not appear to be material and it may be understood as Thought." However, somewhat confusingly, Hegel adds that "it is clear that he did not mean anything else than matter generally, universal matter." Hegel's point is that the conception of undifferentiated universal matter of this kind can only be expressed as thought, as a mental *conretum*. Whether it is to be taken as pure "Thought" or "universal matter," Anaximander's infinite constitutes an advance in philosophy, and, as such, is not vulnerable to Plutarch's criticism that he did not say whether his infinite is "'air, water or earth.'" For Hegel, and he is stating his own view here, "a definite quality such as one of these [elements] is transient," and should not be conceived as an eternal infinite (187).

As indicated above, potentiality is a key characteristic of Anaximander's principle. This characteristic is also reflected in his theory of causality, which holds that in the process of self-negation of the infinite, "'the like separates itself from the unlike and allies itself to the like; thus what in the whole was gold becomes gold, what was earth, earth, &c., so that properly nothing [new] originates, seeing that it was already there.'" What comes out of the indeterminate infinite as a particular determination, such as gold or earth, is always potentially there, though not in its particular, determinate form. In Eusebius's depiction of Anaximander's thought, we find a similar theory of cosmogony: "'Out of the Infinite [undefined principle], infinite heavenly spheres and infinite worlds have been set apart; but they carry within them their own destruction, because they only are through constant dividing off.'" Hegel interprets this as the determination of finites, "that is, since the Infinite is the principle, separation is the positing of a difference, i.e. of a determination or something finite." Since the seeds of destruction are inherent in the two spheres, they break out into further determinations, such as the earth and the heavenly bodies, according to Anaximander (188).

For Hegel, ultimately these thoughts "are poor [cognitive] determinations, which only show the necessity of the transition from the undetermined to the determined . . ." The reason why Hegel passes this verdict is not clear. Given what follows it, we may surmise that his verdict has something to do with the absence of "real necessity" in Anaximander's cosmogony. Hegel adds in this context that the theory of development has acquired prominence again in more recent times, "but as a mere succession in time." What is lacking here is that "there is no real necessity, no thought, and above all, no Notion contained in it" (ibid.). However, I venture to say, regardless of its perceived shortcomings, among the Ionians the principle of Anaximander resembles that of Hegel the most.

2.4 Anaximenes

Anaximenes's principle is air. Like all philosophical principles, including Hegel's, it assumes that, as Plutarch says, "'Out of it everything comes forth, and into it everything is again resolved.'" Dialectic in its complete movement entails precisely this "coming forth" and returning back to the One. However, because the Ionic principles are natural, and pertain to Nature, the dialectic they produce is not developmental. The return to the One is a return to the original One. Hegel's dialectic of Nature has the same kind of circularity, but not his spiritual dialectic (see Chapter 1). Also, the principle of Anaximenes is a specific element, like Thales's water, instead of the undefinable infinite matter of Anaximander. Anaximenes thought that air has the "advantage of being more devoid of form . . ." than the other elements. The two advantages of air over water are: (a) anything that has a determinate form is necessarily a finite; and (b) air "is less corporeal than water, for we do not see it, but feel it first in movement" (189). In the latter sense, air's advantage is that it is less sensuous.

What we see here is an early attempt to move beyond the fixity of matter and establish the Absolute on the basis of something less sensuous, according to Hegel. The end point of this progression, which would give Hegel more satisfaction, would be achieved when philosophy takes the soul or thought as its principle. In this fashion, it is said by Plutarch that Anaximenes's air is soul-like. "'As our soul, which is air, holds us together, one spirit and air together likewise hold the whole world together; spirit and air are synonymous.'" From this, Hegel concludes that Anaximenes turns the essence into soul, and thus "points out what may be called the transition of natural philosophy into the philosophy of consciousness . . ." Here the "objective [material] form of principle" is left behind (190). The soul (consciousness), says Hegel, "is the universal medium; it is a collection of conceptions which pass away and come forth, while the unity and continuity never cease. It is active as well as passive, from its unity severing asunder the conceptions and sublating them, and it is present to itself in its infinitude, so that negative signification and positive come into unison." There is nothing in this summary of dialectic that cannot be attributed to Hegel also, though he gives credit to "Anaxagoras, the pupil of Anaximenes," for its origination (190).

2.5 Conclusion

According to Hegel, "The principle has to be one, and hence must have inherent unity with itself; if it shows a manifold nature as does the earth [and other elements], it is not one with itself, but [explicitly] manifold." Despite recognizing this important qualification of the universal principle, the principles of the early Ionians remained abstract. Their importance, says Hegel, lies "(a) in the comprehension of a universal substance in everything, and (b) in the fact that it is formless, and not encumbered by sensuous ideas" (191–92). What makes any principle the universal essence is that it is the "substance of everything." What makes the principles of the early Ionians poor abstractions, despite their correct intentions, is that they are still "encumbered" by sensuous ideas since they are derived from sensuous, and thus necessarily finite, *things*. Such things cannot account for the development of everything in the universe. As Hegel puts it, "because the principle of these philosophers is material only, they do not manifest the incorporeal side, nor is the object shown to be the Notion. Matter is indeed itself immaterial as this reflection into consciousness; but such philosophers do not know that what they express is an existence of consciousness. Thus, the first great defect here rests in the fact that the universal is expressed in a particular form" (192). It also becomes clearer here that it is Hegel who translates the material principles of the Ionics into universal thought reflections, and not these Ionic philosophers themselves.

Furthermore, material things cannot accommodate the kind of dialectic the Ionics sought to accomplish. The processes of determination the universal principle undergoes require it to be the "'first cause'" of all that proceeds out of itself, or of all becoming and change. For instance, "'wood neither forms a bed nor does brass a statue, but something else is the cause of the change.'" As we will see again when dealing with Aristotle, matter is only a passive potentiality, and, in this sense, it is a passive principle. To explain the dialectic of change requires establishing "'the Principle of Motion'" which is the first, active principle, or cause. Accordingly, Hegel says, "change is not conceivable out of matter as such." Thus, "here, we see, the Absolute is not yet the self-determining, the Notion turned back into itself, but only a dead abstraction" (193). It follows from this that the real necessity of dialectic can only be found in the Notion as pure thought, which not only implicitly contains the forms of external determinations within itself, but also the principle of motion as well. Properly conceived, the Notion is the self-determining substance/subject of all that exists.

3. Pythagoras and the Pythagoreans

Hegel sees the progression from the sensible principle to supersensible essence, which, again, he calls "the Notion," as a necessary requirement for the development of thought. Thus, "It is now requisite that what is viewed as reality should be brought into the Notion . . ." This progression comes with Pythagoras, who represents "the manifestation of the real side as the ideal . . ." Here, thought becomes more "free from what is sensuous, and, therefore, it is a separation between the intelligible and the real." In this separation, the unity of the intelligible and real is properly posited. Thus, neither the moments nor the movement of what is ordinarily viewed as reality, that is the contradictions and negation of the universal, such as "the moments of division [and separation], condensation, and rarefaction, are not in any way antagonistic to the Notion" (194).

Also, in this "transition from realistic to intellectual philosophy . . . , the absolute is not grasped in natural form, but as a thought determination," and the natural forms become the determinations of thought. To state it plainly, the Pythagorean "essence and the substance of things" is number, because every finite determination in nature entails a quantitative and qualitative measure. In other words, measure-size, or magnitude, is a universal determination inherent in all finite things, and can be expressed in terms of numbers (208).

Hegel summarizes the dialectic of the Pythagorean Notion very succinctly as follows: First, the One is taken as "pure Notion," which is the same as saying that it is "the absolute, simple essence." This essence, "divides itself into unity and multiplicity, of which the one [the simple essence] sublates the other, and at the same time it has its existence in the opposition." Next, "the opposition has at the same time subsistence, and in this is found the manifold nature of equivalent things." In other words, the opposition within the manifold is also based on the unity of the many (equivalency based on the simple essence), and it is this that allows the many to subsist as a whole, or prevents it from extreme dispersion. Third, "the return of absolute essence into itself" represents the "negative unity of the individual subject and of the universal or positive" (219).

This final process represents the "pure speculative Idea of absolute existence . . . ." If we do not know what the speculative is, says Hegel, we will fail to recognize that when

> indicating simple Notions such as these, absolute essence is expressed. One, many, like, unlike, more or less, are trivial, empty, dry moments; that there should be contained in them absolute essence, the riches and the organization of the natural, as of the spiritual world, does not seem possible to him who, accustomed to ordinary ideas, has not gone back from sensuous existence into thought. It does not seem to such a one that God is, in a speculative sense, expressed thereby—that what is most sublime can be put in these common words, what is deepest, in what is so well known, self-evident and open, and what is richest, in the poverty of these abstractions (219–20).

The "common reality" is the manifold manifestation of the absolute, simple essence. The latter "has in itself [implicitly] its opposition and the subsistence of the same." The contemplation of the simple essence as containing the manifold reality within itself, that is, its contemplation as abstract "simple Notion," constitutes an "elevation into thought." Importantly, adds Hegel, this elevation "is not flight from what is real, but the expression of the real itself in its essence." This is also to say that the Notion is the essence of what we ordinarily take to be the real, and we may overlook this important advance in thought if we do not think speculatively. The relation of the Notion, or the absolute simple essence, to reality is expressed also in "the Platonic Ideas, which approximate very closely to these numbers, or rather to pure Notions." In this sense, we should not assume that the Pythagoreans separated the Notion from things, and placed them in separate heavens, above and beyond the material world. As Aristotle summarizes it,

"It is characteristic of the Pythagoreans that they did not maintain the finite and the infinite and the One, to be, like fire, earth, &c., different natures or to have another reality than things; for the Infinite and the abstract One are to them the substance of the things of which they are predicated. Hence too, they said, Number is the essence of all things. Thus they do not separate numbers from things, but consider them to be things themselves. Number to them is the principle and [the essential] matter of things, as also their qualities and forces."

Hegel briefly concludes from this summary that the Pythagoreans thought of Number ". . . as substance, or the thing as it is in the reality of thought" (220–21).

Three categories of thought appear in the Pythagorean approach. These categories, which are crucial to understanding Hegel's dialectic also, pertain to "diversity," "opposition," and "relation." Diversity, as such, refers to considering things only as "for itself," by which Hegel here means *by-itself*, in the same way that the arithmetic one exists as a unit apart from two, three, and so on. This means each thing, "such as horse, plant, earth, air, water and fire," can be taken in isolation, and related "only to itself." The relations of these things to one another are cast aside in the rigid conception of diversity, and the self-identity, or the "independence" of particular existents, is posited instead. Thus, horse is treated merely as horse and nothing else. It is identical only with itself and not with a donkey, and is independent in the sense that it has no essential, inner relations with other similarly independent existents. In this way, the opposition between independent things is posited merely as a contrast, as that which a given thing is not. This impoverished conception of opposition applies both to natural things and thought products alike. What is being said here is that diversity is based only on the self-identity of each existent, and opposition (contradiction) strictly on the non-identity of different existents. However, when their relation is taken into account, as it should be, each object becomes "determined in accordance with its relationship to others, such as right and left, over and under, double and half." The relation in this context is internal. For Hegel, without their internal relations, objects, or atomistic units, are not fully comprehensible. Drawing from Sextus Empiricus, Hegel says, "'The difference between relationship and [mere] opposition is that in [mere] opposition the coming into existence of the 'one' is at the expense of the 'other,' and [vice versa]. If, for instance, motion is taken away, rest commences; if motion begins, rest ceases; if health is taken away, sickness begins, and [vice versa]. In a condition of relationship, on the contrary, both take their rise, and both similarly cease together; if the right is removed, so also is the left; the double goes and the half is destroyed.'" Hegel points out in addition that what "is here taken away is taken not only as regards its opposition, but also in its existence." It follows that the existence of parts is not possible without their contraries, or differences. Continuing with Sextus Empiricus's summary,

> "A second difference is that what is in opposition has no middle; for example, between sickness and health, life and death, rest and motion, there is no third. Relativity, on the contrary, has a middle, for between larger and smaller there is the like; and between too large and too small the right size is the medium." Pure opposition passes through nullity to opposition; immediate [and relative] extremes, on the other hand, subsist in a third or middle state, but in such a case no longer as opposed.

Hegel concludes that this "exposition shows a certain regard for universal, logical determinations, which now and always have the greatest possible importance, and are moments in all conceptions and in everything that is. The nature of these opposites is, indeed, not considered here [by the Pythagoreans], but it is of importance that they should be brought to consciousness" (216–17). It should suffice for now to say that (a) Hegel adopts the relational view, and (b) these issues are fundamental to logic, which Hegel takes up and tries to further resolve in *Logic*.[6] We will revisit them repeatedly throughout this book.

Without the relational view, the number theory falls apart. But, strictly speaking, it is not the Pythagorean theory that faces this fate, according to Hegel. He says that "the [thought] determination through number" is "enigmatic." For instance, in arithmetic the number one is often taken as the most basic unit, since the numerical one is elemental to every other number. This kind of thinking is akin to atomism, which thinks of everything as a composite of independent atoms, or independent differences. For Hegel, the strictly numerical one "is a category of being-for-self, and thus of identity with self . . ." As such, "it excludes all else and is indifferent

---

6. See, for instance, G. W. F. Hegel, *The Encyclopaedia Logic*, 182–86; and *Hegel's Science of Logic*, 431–41.

to what is 'other.'" In other words, the others of one, the other numbers as its relations, are not organically contained within it as its internal potentialities. For this reason, "The further determinations of number are only further combinations and repetitions of the one, which all through remains fixed and external; number, thus, is the most utterly dead, notionless continuity possible." Such continuity "is an entirely external and mechanical process, which is without necessity." According to Hegel, the One as pure, speculative Notion, as distinct from the arithmetical one, contains its determinations within itself. The Notion's others, or opposites/contradictions, are its internal, implicit determinations. What is involved in the arithmetical one, on the other hand, is extreme "externality, in quantitative form, and in that of indifferent distinction."

> In order that anything should have the form of Notion, it must immediately in itself, as determined, relate itself to its opposite [its other], just as positive is [internally] related to negative; and in this simple movement of the Notion we find the ideality of differences and negation of independence to be the chief determination. On the other hand, in the number three, for instance, there are always three units, of which each is independent; and this is what constitutes both their defect and their enigmatic character. For since the essence of the Notion is innate, [arithmetical] numbers are the most worthless instruments for expressing Notion-determinations (210).

However, such a "worthless" mode of Notion-determination cannot be attributed to the Pythagoreans, says Hegel. For them, number is a universal, absolute principle, and "not so much immediate numbers in their arithmetic differences, as the principles of number, i.e. their rational differences." So, *one* in the first instance is taken by the Pythagoreans as the abstract, notional "unity generally," in the same way that Anaximander made his principle the "matter in general." The main difference between the arithmetic and the Pythagorean approaches to number, then, ultimately boils down to the difference between one as an isolated unit and the One as "unity generally" (212). It seems that Hegel takes the Pythagorean *one* to represent the universal Notion of Number, or the One as such. As we will see below, the Eleactics adopt the same principle of the One, and call it *being*, which represents "unity generally," instead of one, isolated *being*.

Out of the Pythagorean One comes "duality [multiplicity] or opposition." The One is an infinite potentiality, and is thus the original unity of the many actual determinations, each of which is a finite difference. For Hegel, "It is most important to trace back the infinitely manifold nature of the forms and determinations of finality to their universal thought [which is] the most simple principle of all determination." To clarify, Hegel provides some examples, and an important conclusion: "Empirical objects distinguish themselves by outward form; this piece of paper can be distinguished from another, shades are different in color, men are separated by differences of temperament and individuality. But these determinations are not essential differences; they are certainly essential for the definite particularity of the things, but the whole particularity defined is not an existence which is in and for itself essential, for it is the universal [Notion] alone which is the self-contained and the substantial." "Pythagoras began to seek these first determinations of unity, multiplicity, opposition, &c." In doing so, he posited that "the first simple Notion is unity . . . ; not the discrete, multifarious, arithmetic one, but identity as continuity and positivity, the entirely universal essence." For this reason, all numbers, as Sextus Empiricus summarizes the Pythagorean view, "'come under the Notion of the one; for duality is one duality and triplicity is equally a one . . . This moved Pythagoras to assert unity to be the principle of things, because, through partaking of it, each is called one'" (212–13). However much things can be divided or multiplied, and they can be divided or multiplied infinitively, what is being divided or multiplied is always a unity, and has *oneness*. One, thus, is the essential form of everything simple and complex. This Pythagorean dialectic is not limited to numbers. A table, for instance, has many parts and attributes. Yet, it is one.

However, Hegel asserts that "necessary progression and proof are not to be sought for here; comprehension," which requires "the development of [multiplicity] out of unity" is lacking with the Pythagoreans. In this way, their thought determinations are still "dogmatic," and are hence "destitute of process or dialectic . . ." (212). Dialectic, then, is essentially a process, and thought becomes more dialectical to the extent that it accounts for the necessity of the development of multiplicity out of the simple, universal essence. Hegel finds a similar criticism "justly" leveled against the Pythagoreans by Aristotle: "'the Pythagoreans do not explain how movement arises, and how without movement and change there can be coming into being and passing away, or the conditions and activities of heavenly objects.'" Hegel finds the source of this "defect" in the fact that "arithmetical numbers are dry forms and barren principles in which life and movement are deficient" (237). The principle should not only be in-itself rich but also capable of engendering life, process, and development. This criticism is already familiar to us, and relates to the issue of the Aristotelian "first cause." It also reverses Hegel's initial assessment of the Pythagorean numbers as being philosophically superior to the strictly arithmetic ones.

Related to the above criticism is the second one which declares number incapable of acting as the universal principle. What is of additional interest in this criticism is the point that corporeal determinations cannot emerge out of numbers, or, as Hegel puts it, "number thus cannot pass into what is concrete."

> For instance, a heavenly sphere and a virtue, or a natural manifestation in the earth, are determined as one and the same number. Each of the first numbers may be exhibited in each thing or quality; but in so far as number is made to express a further determination, this quite abstract, quantitative difference becomes altogether formal; it is as if the plant were five because it has five stamens. This is just as superficial as are determination through elements or through particular portions of the globe; it is a method as formal as that by which men now try to apply the categories of electricity, magnetism, galvanism, compression and expansion, of manly and of womanly, to everything. It is a purely empty system of determination where reality [needs to] be dealt with (238).

How Hegel's own universal Notion, or the Idea, would remedy this problem, "where reality" is dealt with, is not always clear. Obviously, thought cannot produce real, material things simply out of itself, unless it is identified with God, and we take God to possess such powers of material production. Hegel often makes this identification of the Idea and God, especially when he deals with the issues of Nature-creation and history (see Chapter 5). Thus, while reading Hegel, we should not be surprised to find him switch back and forth between God, the Notion, Mind, and so on.

Despite saying things that suggest the contrary above, Hegel concludes that "the Pythagorean philosophy has not yet got the speculative form of expression for the Notion." This is because numbers are only "Notion in the form of ordinary idea or sensuous perception," and do not constitute "pure Notion." He adds that "this expression of absolute essence in what is a pure Notion or something thought, and the movement of the Notion or of Thought, is that which we find must come next and this we discover in the Eleatic school" (239).

4. The Eleatic School

4.1 Introduction

With the Eleatic philosophy, thought becomes "free for itself; and in that which the Eleatics express as absolute essence, we see Thought grasp itself in purity, and the movement of Thought in Notions" (239). The Eleatic principle is simply expressed as "pure Being, the One." This principle is very similar to Hegel's abstract *being*, which, he says, is "nothing but pure being in general," taken "quite abstractly" as "being, and nothing else, without any further specification and filling."[7]

Hegel says that when we think speculatively, we recognize that thought "manifests itself immediately in its rigid isolation and self-identity, and everything else as null." However, thought cannot be retained at this "timid" level of abstraction. It proceeds to ascribe "value to the 'other'" by constituting itself therein and "therefrom." In doing so, it "then grasps the other in its simplicity and . . . shows its nullity." This means that the other of thought, that is, the manifold determinations of existence, is null without thought. In this way, thought "manifests the other in the manifold nature of its [own] determinations" (239).

Hegel adds that "we here find the beginning of dialectic . . ." Where and when dialectic begins is not consistently stated by Hegel, and here we must take him to herald the beginning of dialectic as the "pure movement of thought in Notions." Also, the dialectic involved in the Eleatic philosophy is not clearly stated in the previous paragraph, which includes Hegelian interventions. With the Eleatics, Hegel also says, and this time more accurately, "we see the opposition of thought to outward appearance or sensuous Being . . ." This opposition amounts to the contradiction between "that which is implicit" and "the being-for-another of this implicitness." Stated more simply, this contradiction refers to the opposition between thought and sensuous reality, posited by the Eleatics, the result of which is the nullification of the objective reality in their dialectic. In

---

7. Hegel, *Hegel's Science of Logic*, 69–70.

other words, the manifold is exactly the manifestation of thought, or *being*, but, rather, its denial. While Hegel enthusiastically welcomes the contemplation of this contradiction and the nullification of the sensuous as an advance in cognitive dialectic, he later declares it insufficient for the reason that it fails to establish the unity of thought and sensuous reality (239).

4.2 Xenophanes

With Xenophanes, the absolute as thought is identified with God: "'The all is One and God is implanted in all things; He is unchangeable, without beginning, middle or end.'" As noted by Sextus Empiricus, "'[God] sees everywhere, thinks everywhere, and hears everywhere,' to which words Diogenes Laërtius adds: 'Thought and reason are everything and eternal.' By this Xenophanes denied the truth of the conceptions of origination and of passing away, of change, movement, &c., seeing that they merely belong to sensuous perception . . ." (242). Hegel adds that this "dialectic reasoning of the Eleatics . . . rests on the proposition *ex nihilo nihil fit* [nothing comes from nothing]" (244).

In these brief depictions of Xenophanes's thought, we find several complications. First complication is the unexplained transition from God to "thought and reason." The second complication involves what Xenophanes exactly denies, or nullifies, and in what manner this nullification takes place. In Hegel's view, it does not seem to be the case that Xenophanes denies the manifold reality, or change as origination and passing away, altogether. These "merely belong to sensuous perception," and cannot be grasped rationally. The point seems to be that the Eleatics deny the truth of the many in the rational sense, since they assume that the truth cannot be many. Hegel clearly expresses this view in his discussion of Zeno, as we will see later.

As for *ex nihilo nihil fit*, this proposition has a different meaning in the Eleatic context than it does with the Ionians and with some of the Eastern philosophies discussed previously. In the case of the Eleatics, nothing also comes out of *being*, for such a process of origination would make the One determinate, many, and contradictory. Thus, as Hegel explains, we tend to treat the absolute *being* (God) as a particular determination, and place it "in a line" with all other particular determinations. In Xenophanes, on the other hand, *being* "signifies that all else has no reality [truth] and is only a semblance." It follows that "the truth then simply is that God is the One, not in the sense that there is one God (this is another determination), but only that He is identical with Himself; in this there is no other determination . . ." (243). To put Xenophanes's philosophy from the opposite angle, anything that is determined, and determination involves motion, variation, or predication, is not the One. The One is neither productive nor a product. The One thus does not entail motion, but it cannot be said that it is therefore motionless. To make the One *unmoved* is equally limiting since, quoting Aristotle, "'to be unmoved is non-being, for to it [to *being*, or the One] none other comes, nor does it go into another; but to be moved must mean to be several, for one must move into another. Thus the One neither rests nor is it moved, for it is neither non-being nor is it many. In all this God is thus indicated; He is eternal and One, like Himself and spherical, neither unlimited nor limited, neither at rest nor moved'" (245).

Hegel adds that "we here see a dialectic which may be called metaphysical reasoning, in which the principle of identity is fundamental. The nothing is like nothing and does not pass into Being or conversely; thus nothing can originate from like," since any origination would render the determination unlike the origination (245). Thus, the Eleatics hold that "change does not exist at all." If there is no change, then there is no determination. If *being* is the Absolute One, then ascribing change to it "is contradictory and inconceivable." Change is the determination of "the negative, of the manifold," and must be "withdrawn" from *being*. In this way, the Eleatics, consistently with their speculative idea, "say that only the One exists and that the negative does not exist at all." Even if this conclusion surprises us, says Hegel, it is still to be treated as "a great abstraction" (246). This great abstraction is pure consciousness, and is thus "the pure dialectic, which is negatively related to all that is determined and which annuls [all that is determined]" (248). Here, the word annul is appropriate, since the Eleatics do not have the Hegelian understanding of negation as sublation.

In Xenophanes, the opposition between *being* and the determinate world (*non-being*) is not all that clearly stated. Parmenides, though "unconsciously," sharpens this opposition between *being* and *non-being* implicitly posited by Xenophanes (250), and it is with his philosophy that we must now continue the elaboration of the above outlined Eleatic thoughts.

4.3 Parmenides

As Plotinus, via Hegel, says, "'Parmenides . . . did not place Being in sensuous things; identifying Being with Thought, he maintained it to be unchangeable.'" Thus, in Parmenides's philosophy, "Thought is . . . identical with Being, for there is nothing besides Being." This simply means that *non-being* cannot be thought, and what cannot be thought also cannot be (253–54). The path of *non-being*, says Parmenides, "'is a path quite devoid of reason, for thou canst neither know, or attain to, or express, non-being.'" In confirming this proposition, Hegel adds that "the nothing, in fact, [always] turns into something, since it is thought or is said: we say something, think something, if we wish to think and say the nothing" (252).

In *Logic*, Hegel employs this Eleatic thought himself. By declaring *being* the equivalent of *nothing*, he shows the impossibility of this equivalency, and transitions *being* into the category of *becoming*.[8] However, Parmenides is here speaking of *non-being*, and not *nothing* per se. This distinction is not made by Hegel in the above context. For Hegel, to think of one thing is to think of a finite determination, of a particular something. The *nothing* he formulates at the beginning of *Logic* is not the negation of a particular something. The negative of a particular something, says Hegel, is "non-being instead of nothing." Since the abstract *being* is unmediated and thus undetermined, the contradiction within it is simply an implicit potentiality, or, as Hegel has it, it is "abstract, immediate, negation: nothing, purely on its own account, negation devoid of any relations—what could also be expressed . . . merely by 'not.'"[9] With this distinction in mind, Parmenides's *non-being* is not Hegel's *nothing*, expressed in *Logic*.

Parmenides also denies the possibility of becoming, since motion for him falls under the category of *non-being*. So do the categories of "negation, limitation, the finite, [and] restriction" for the same reason. In this context, Hegel equates this thought of Parmenides with Spinoza's "*determinatio est negatio*" [determination is negation] (252). This is an interesting interjection, though it can cause interpretative complications. We cannot here explore what Spinoza meant by this famous expression. In the Hegelian context, negation often means to sublate, or determine in a more concrete, richer form. What is determined thus becomes "richer by the negation or opposite of" its predecessor, in the sense that it "contains" it, and is therefore "something more" by virtue of being the "unity of itself and its

---

8. Ibid., 83.
9. Ibid.

opposite." [10] However, in its application to Parmenides, the expression *determinatio est negatio* simply means that any determination leads to negation as *non-being*. Indeed, as Hegel points out, "Parmenides says . . . negation . . . does not exist at all" (252). Thus, and more precisely speaking, for him determination as negation is not a process of annihilating or reconstituting reality, but one that does not exist at all.

We conclude this section with the following important remark by Hegel: "Since in this an advance into the region of the ideal is observable, Parmenides began Philosophy proper . . . This beginning is certainly still dim and indefinite, and we cannot say much of what it involves; but to take up this position certainly is to develop Philosophy proper, which has not hitherto existed. The dialectic that the transient has no truth is implied in it, for if these [transient] determinations are taken as they are usually understood, contradictions ensue" (254). With this comment, Hegel tells us that in "dialectic . . . the transient has no truth," which sounds odd, given that many of his interpreters identify his dialectic strictly with the transient. Of course, this Eleatic dialectic is limited for it denies contradictions, or transiency, altogether. In Hegel's dialectic, transiency has truth only insofar as it is grounded by the universal.

4.4 Melissus

Like Parmenides, Melissus held the view that *being* is *not* generated, destructible, divisible, or subject to change and motion. In addition, he held the view that *being* is infinite and spreads in all directions. Since *being* is infinite, ungenerated, indestructible, indivisible, and motionless, it must be One. As Hegel puts it, for Melissus too, "change does not exist" since *being* must be non-contradictory and since change implies contradiction (257).

Hegel says that the reasoning of Melissus is "a dialectic more developed in form, more real reflection," then the one found in Xenophanes and Parmenides (258). Even though the being it contemplates has no motion, Melissus attempts to prove the One with the motion of thought. It is the latter that makes his philosophy dialectical. The first proposition of Melissus is that "'if anything is [being], it is eternal.'" What is meant by "eternal," says Hegel, is not "an infinite length of time . . . but the self-identical, supersensuous, unchangeable, pure present, which is without any time-conception."

---

10. Ibid., 54.

To peg the "eternal" to time is to set it in motion and thus to limit it by giving the eternal the attribute of origination and change. In the "eternal" of Melissus, however, "origination and change are shut out." The reasoning is that if we say being originates at some point in time, we must either assume that before its commencement there was nothing, or that there was something out of which it came. In other words, the concept of origination is necessarily limited to two possibilities: "if it commences, it does so out of nothing or out of Being." As for the first possibility,

> "It is impossible that anything should arise from the nothing. If everything could have arisen, or could it merely not have been everything eternally, it would equally have arisen out of nothing. For, if everything had arisen, nothing would once have existed. If some were alone the existent out of which the rest sprang, the one would be more and greater. But the more and greater would thus have arisen out of the nothing of itself, for in the less there is not its more, nor in the smaller its greater" (258–59).

As for the second possibility, "'No more can anything arise out of the existent [*being*], for the existent already is, and thus does not first arise from the existent.'" It follows from the rejection of both possibilities that, "'As eternal, the existent also is unlimited, since it has no beginning from which it came, nor an end in which it ceases'" (259). This proposition states that what does not begin also does not cease. Likewise, whatever has a beginning must also end. Since the One did not commence, it will not cease to exist. Therefore, the One is eternal, and unmoved.

Clearly, this reasoning rejects the Ionic view that particular things come out of an original *being* (water, air, or general matter). The Eleatic response, found in Melissus, is that if different things were to come out of the One, then the Notion of the One would become self-contradictory in the sense that it could no longer be considered as eternal. It follows that "'the infinite all is one, for, if there were two or more, they would limit one another,' and thus have a beginning and end." Therefore, the One must be "like itself," for if it were not like itself, or gave way to its unlike (its negative), it would cease to be the One which was originally posited, and become many, or different than itself. In short, "'the one, therefore, is in this way devoid of pain or suffering, not changing in position or form, or mingling with what is different. For all these determinations involve the origination of non-being and passing away of Being, which is impossible.'" Hegel concludes that the above propositions firmly establish that when we speak of "origination and passing away," we necessarily speak of "contradiction" (259).

Since Hegel, unlike the Eleatics, takes movement or process as a universal principle, he also accepts the necessary existence, in thought and nature, of contradiction. In *The Encyclopaedia Logic*, he makes this famously clear: "There is *nothing at all* anywhere, in which contradiction—i.e., opposed determinations—cannot and should not be exhibited." In this work, Hegel credits the Eleatics, especially Zeno, for demonstrating that all "movement contradicts itself, and that it therefore *is* not." However, "this dialectic" is faulted for not going "beyond the negative side of the result," and thus not abstracting from "what is effectively given at the same time."[11] We will see the obvious presence of this latter fault, as Hegel conceived of it, when we examine Zeno's dialectic below.

4.5 Zeno

Zeno is known for his paradoxes. It is said that he had produced more than forty of them. Hegel discusses the four well-known paradoxes ("arguments" or "proofs") Aristotle summarizes in *Physics*. The reasoning behind each argument is very similar, and each argument receives a similar Hegelian intervention. There is some confusion as to what Zeno was trying to prove with these paradoxical arguments. The conclusions he arrives at can be interpreted as his own, or his demonstration of what would emerge from *our* presuppositions if we tried to prove *being* on the grounds of the many (*non-being*). Aristotle in *Physics* treats Zeno's conclusions as the products of the latter's absurd reasoning. Hegel, at times, follows Aristotle's interpretation. However, Hegel also recognizes the second, more plausible, possibility, which is elucidated in Plato's dialogue, *Parmenides*.

Plato in this dialogue makes Socrates say: "'Zeno in his writings asserts fundamentally the same as does Parmenides, that All is One, but he would feign delude us into believing that he was telling something new. Parmenides thus shows in his poems that All is One; Zeno, on the contrary, shows that the Many cannot be.'" Indeed, Plato's Socrates here captures Zeno's dialectic accurately. What Zeno intends to show is precisely that "many cannot be." As Zeno

---

11. G. W. F. Hegel, *The Encyclopaedia Logic*, 145–46.

confirms, his arguments are posited "'against those who try to make Parmenides' position ridiculous, for they try to show what absurdities and self-contradictions can be derived from his statements.'" Instead of trying to directly reaffirm Parmenides's principle that *being* is One, Zeno turns the heat on the critics of Parmenides "'who deduce Being from the many . . .'" His purpose, he says, is to show "'that far more absurdities arise from this [derivation] than from the statements of Parmenides.'" This exchange is important for two reasons. On the one hand, it suggests that what Zeno intends to prove with his paradoxes, to repeat, is that "absurdities arise from" the derivation of *being* from the many. On the other hand, Zeno's "dialectic is very well described" in this exchange, says Hegel (264).

I will have more to say on Hegel's assessment of Zeno's dialectic in the next section. This section focuses on Hegel's treatment of the four paradoxes. These paradoxes are not sequential, and my calling them first, second, and so on, below is based on their order of presentation in Hegel's treatment. I will change Hegel's ordering of these paradoxes in my presentation of them below, and begin with the third paradox.

Zeno's third argument ("the Arrow") is this: "'The flying arrow rests, and for the reason that what is in motion is always in the self-same Now, and in the self-same Here, in the indistinguishable'; it is here and here and here." Thus, "it can be said of the arrow that it is always the same, for it is always in the same space and same time; it does not get beyond its space, does not take in another, that is, a greater or smaller space," since each space in which it is found at a given increment of time is the same as the like spaces in magnitude (274). Thus, a flying arrow is motionless (contradiction!) since there is no variation in the space and time it is found in each instance of its flight. While Zeno treats each instant of time as an indivisible moment, he treats the whole time involved in the flight of the arrow as divisible. Thus, the series of indivisible nows constitute the division of the whole. As Hegel rightly says, the argument is based on the "interruption of continuity." At any rate, as Aristotle says, and Hegel takes note of this, Zeno's arrow-proof takes for granted that "'time [only] consists of the Now; for if this is not conceded, [Zeno's] conclusions will not follow'" (275). We can add to this that Zeno's paradox also takes for granted that space consists only of *this* space, here, and here and here. Again, it is possible to think that Zeno might have been making the same point as Aristotle, though from the opposite angle. This is to say, if we take time and space to merely consist of many nows and heres, the absurd conclusion that the *flying* arrow is *not moving* would follow. It is also possible to think, especially if we ignore his exchange with Socrates, that Zeno is trying to prove that time and space are one and indivisible.

"The fourth proof," as Hegel quotes from Aristotle again, "is derived from similar bodies which move in opposite directions in the space beside a similar body, and with equal velocity, one from one end of the space, the other from the middle. It necessarily results from this that half the time is equal to the double of it. The fallacy rests in this, that Zeno supposes that what is beside the moving body, and what is beside the body at rest, move through an equal distance in equal time with equal velocity, which, however, is untrue" (275–76). These bodies are supposed to be in a stadium, and hence this paradox is often called the "stadium paradox."

There are many different interpretations of both Aristotle's cryptic explanation[12] of this proof and what Zeno actually might have had in mind when he proposed it. Actually, the paradox is very simple, and need not be encumbered by the confusing positioning of the three bodies described above. We can express the paradox more simply and in more modern terms as follows: Imagine three trains standing in three parallel railway tracks side by side. Let us call them trains A, B, and C; A being stationary, and B and C moving in opposite directions at the same velocity. Two Zenonian conclusions follow from this example. First, as Aristotle presents it, "half the time is equal to its double,"[13] and, second, half the space (distance) is equal to its double. This is because it is observed by looking at these trains that, as stated above, while "what is beside the moving body, and what is beside the body at rest, move through an equal distance in equal time with equal velocity," the result obtained is the opposite. The fallacy in this conclusion is obvious enough. Two different standards are used to determine the contradiction, one with respect to the stationary A and its relation to one of the trains, and the other with respect to the relationship of two non-stationary trains, B and C. In reality, B has only travelled one mile per hour, and moved only one mile with respect to its original position where A is stationary. With respect to C, it has also travelled at the same speed. The fact that the distance between B and C has become two miles after an hour is not due to B's own velocity alone. It is rather the combination

---

12. It is interesting that Hegel found this fourth proof "too lengthy and difficult" to treat in his 1825–1826 lectures, perhaps due to the cryptic nature of Aristotle's presentation of it. Hegel, *Lectures on the History of Philosophy 1825–6*, 69. For this reason, this argument is missing in this version edited by Brown et al.
13. Aristotle, *Physics*, in *Aristotle: Selections*, trans. Terence Irwin and Gail Fine (Indianapolis: Hackett Publishing, Inc., 1995), 135 (239b-35).

of two trains moving in opposite directions. As Hegel further explains it, "Here the distance travelled by one body is the sum of the distance travelled by both, just as when I go two feet east, and from the same point another goes two feet west, we are four feet removed from one another; in the distance moved both are positive, and hence have to be added together" (277).

Some scholars think that Zeno was too intelligent to make such an obvious mistake in his reasoning.[14] I tend to think that it was not Zeno who made this mistake. To think that Zeno intended to prove the point that "half the time [or velocity] is equal to its double" is to think that he was trying to prove the hypothesis that *being* is many. It is possible to say in this regard that Zeno did not make the mistake of assuming two different standards of measurement to produce the paradox, but demonstrated the absurdity that followed from treating velocity, which is relationship of time and space, as many.

The second paradox, Hegel calls "Achilles, the Swift," and "Achilles and the Tortoise" in contemporary discussions. Hegel, using Aristotle's commentary again, summarizes it as follows:

> Of two bodies moving in one direction, one of which is in front [the tortoise] and the other following at a fixed distance and moving quicker than the first [Achilles], we know that the second will overtake the first. But Zeno says, "The slower [tortoise] can never be overtaken by the quicker [Achilles]." And he proves it thus: "The second one [Achilles] requires a certain space of time to reach the place from which the one pursued [that is, the tortoise] started at the beginning of the given period." Thus during the time in which [Achilles] reached the point where the [tortoise] was, the latter went over a new space which [Achilles] has again to pass through in a part of this period; and in this way it goes into infinity [without Achilles ever overtaking the tortoise] (272).

Zeno's trick in generating this paradox consists in adding the space covered by the tortoise to the increment of space covered by Achilles in each increment of time. Thus, the contestants run in two separate

---

14. For a survey of different and interesting interpretations, see John Immerwahr, "An Interpretation of Zeno's Stadium Paradox," *Phronesis: A Journal of Ancient Philosophy* 23, no. 1 (1978): 22–26; and Kevin Davey, "Aristotle, Zeno, and the Stadium Paradox," *History of Philosophy Quarterly* 24, no. 2 (2007): 127–46.

times and spaces, instead of one. Again, we must remember that Zeno is generating a paradox here between the sensuous reality of Achilles taking over the slower tortoise, and the logical impossibility of this when time and space are taken to be many.

Hegel's response in a nutshell is that "in motion two periods, as well as two points in space, are indeed one." For this reason, "movement means to be in this place [temporarily] and not to be [fixed] in it, and thus to be in both alike; this is the continuity of space and time which . . . makes motion possible." "In our ordinary ideas we find the same determinations as those on which the dialectic of Zeno rests; we arrive at saying, though unwillingly, that in one period two distances of space are traversed [by two contestants], but we do not say that the quicker comprehends two moments of time in one; for that we fix a definite space. But in order that the slower may lose its precedence, it must be said that it loses its advantage of a moment of time, and indirectly the moment of space." In his proof, Zeno only uses "the moment of discretion in space and time," that is, limit and division. Thus, Zeno's abstraction brings the moments of time and space "into forcible opposition." For Hegel, the moments of discretion and continuity "are really united" in motion (273–74). If continuity is ignored, the contradiction involved in the conception of motion naturally follows. Indeed, if his exchange with Socrates, quoted earlier in text, can be of any guidance here, Zeno seems to be making the same point as Hegel, not by directly demonstrating their unity, but, rather, by demonstrating the absurdity that follows from treating them as many. What distinguishes Zeno's approach from that of Hegel ultimately is that the former fails to synthesize the One with the many. He simply reduces all his paradoxes to the contradictions of the many, and considers the viewpoint of discretion alone.

The first argument ("dichotomy") is very similar to the other arguments, especially the one just presented. It goes as follows: "'Movement has no truth, because what is in motion must first reach the middle of the space before arriving at the end.'" The contradiction highlighted here is between the indivisibility (One) and the divisibility (Many) of space. What moves through space must ultimately "reach a certain end," and this space in question constitutes "a whole." However, the body in motion must at some point reach the middle of the initial space. While at this middle point, it can be said that the body has travelled one-half of the initial space. However, in its own right, this first half of space is also a whole space. If it is a whole, it can also be divided into two halves *ad infinitum*. With this argument, Zeno "arrives at the infinite divisibility of space." Thus, as Hegel puts it, "Movement would be the act of passing through these infinite moments, and would therefore never end; thus what is in motion cannot reach its end" (267) for every finite whole is infinitively divisible and the moving body has to go through all of them individually. It follows that the main contradiction highlighted here is that between what is finite and infinite.

We must clarify here that Zeno does not say the body in motion never reaches the end point. If he were to say this, then he would have to also assume that there is no contradiction involved in motion. Instead, he says that when the given finite space is presupposed to be infinitely many, the conclusion that it will never reach its end would naturally follow. The fact that a body in motion, such as an arrow, reaches its end contradicts the presupposition. However, the problem is that he does not say motion is continuous, that is, he does not directly try to prove its oneness, and thus leaves the door open for criticism that he denies motion all together. Consequently, as Hegel points out, "It is known how Diogenes of Sinope, the Cynic, quite simply refuted these arguments against movement; without speaking he rose and walked about, contradicting them by action" (ibid.). Hegel plausibly argues that "the anecdote about Diogenes does not serve at all to refute [Zeno's] dialectic." The intended meaning of Zeno's dialectic "is not that there is no motion at all, for the fact of motion, that this phenomenon exists, is not the point in question, and it never occurred to Zeno to deny motion in this sense."[15]

With this clarification we come across a dilemma. Aristotle says that, and this is a standard interpretation, "Zeno denied movement because it contains an inner contradiction." However, all of Zeno's paradoxes involve motion. This dilemma requires an explanation. Hegel offers one: What is denied by Zeno is the *rational truth* of movement. Zeno only held movement "to be untrue, because the conception of it involves a contradiction; by that meant to say that no true Being can be predicated of it" (266).

A problem with Zeno's point regarding movement, according to Hegel, is that the conception of the infinite it entails is "spurious" (268). Even though I am not sure that Zeno thought of the infinite in this sense, this understanding of the infinite concerns Hegel in his other works, especially in *Logic*. He finds the spurious infinite in atomism, natural philosophy (especially of Galileo and Newton), and the practical philosophy of Kant and Fichte.[16] The simplest way to express the spurious infinite is that it consists of an infinite number of finite determinations which do not share a common essence

---

15. Hegel, *Lectures on the History of Philosophy 1825–6*, 66.
16. Hegel, *The Encyclopaedia Logic*, 105–8.

(common identity), and thus are merely externally related to one another.[17] (This is a similar argument to the one Hegel offered against the merely arithmetical theory of numbers above.) In this way, the continuity of motion and space is denied, whereas in the *genuine* infinite the finite parts are seen as internally related moments that are both continuous and distinct. This formulation also applies to Hegel's account of the transition from quantity to quality, as we will see later. The merit of Zeno's dialectic in this regard consists in treating movement as "pure phenomenon" and thus in its true *being*, that is, "in its distinction of pure self-identity and pure negativity, the point as distinguished from continuity." However, this distinguishing is only discretion in which the moments of the whole are treated as discontinuous parts, as mere differences and not relations. For instance, the line is shown to be an infinite number of points which contradict the continuity of the line. The same applies to space and time; the former is treated as here, here, and here, and the latter as a series of nows. For Hegel,

> When we speak of motion as such, we say a body is in place, that it moves further along and then it is in turn in another place. Where is it while it is moving? While it moves, it is no longer in the first place. If it were [merely] in the first, it would be at rest; and if it were [merely] in the second, it would also be at rest. If we say it is in between these two places, that is empty talk . . . for in between the two it is also in a place . . . [Thus] "to move" is to be in one place and not to be in one place. The latter is the continuity of time and space, and this is what makes motion possible"[18]

Hegel adds, "To us there is no contradiction in the idea that the here of space and the now of time are considered as a continuity and length" and that "their Notion is [also] self-contradictory" (268).

Hegel also points out that the contradiction between continuity and the point (negativity) is actually a strictly subjective contradiction. This Hegelian conclusion is derived from the Aristotelian conception of potentiality, and says that continuity is only *potentially* divisible. As such, divisibility is a "universal" in the sense that it posits "continuity as well as negativity, or the point . . . in it." Thus, what is divisible is necessarily an internal relationship of continuity and point. The whole

---

17. Ibid., 148–52.
18. Hegel, *Lectures on the History of Philosophy 1825–6*, 68.

is both the sum total of its parts (points) and something in which the parts disappear. An hour is an hour as it is also sixty minutes, 3,600 seconds, and so on. However, the point, or a part, in actuality can only be "posited as moment, and not as existent in and for itself." In dividing the whole infinitely, "I do not really divide it into infinitude." In such a mentally divided infinite, no single moment has actual reality apart from the whole in which it exists. A second cannot exist without a minute, and a minute without an hour, and an hour without a day, month, etc., until we reach the conception of time as the infinite. Thus, the finite necessarily implies the infinite, as much as divisibility implies continuity, and *vice-versa*. It follows from this logic that the division in question is nothing but a mental abstraction of the divisible parts from the infinite whole. Likewise, taking the infinite as an absolute, indivisible whole constitutes an abstraction whereby the fact of its divisibility is overlooked. Thus, it "never does happen that, in itself, one or other—absolute limitation or absolute continuity—actually comes into existence in such a way that the other moment disappears." In speculative thought, and in actuality, both moments are each other's internal relations (269–70).

We can say the same thing about space and time more specifically. "The partition of space as divided, is not absolute discontinuity, nor is pure continuity the undivided and indivisible; likewise time is not pure negativity or discontinuity, but also continuity." Their unity is "manifested in motion." Motion, on the other hand, "is just this actual unity in the opposition, and the sequence of both moments in this unity." It follows that the concrete Notion of motion must assume the "unity of negativity and continuity," and to express the Notion of motion is to express its supersensible "essence." If negativity and continuity "are manifested indifferently," that is, as isolated, externally related moments, "their Notion is no longer posited, but their [merely sensuous] existence. In them as existents, negativity is a limited size, and they exist as limited space and time; actual motion is progression through a limited space—and a limited time and not through infinite space and infinite time" (270–71). Said differently, what we have here is the contradiction of sensuous existence in that, apart from its essence, existence appears as indifferently lined up parts to our senses.

The above discussion basically summarizes the relationship of the whole and its parts in the Hegelian dialectic, which also coincides with the dialectic of Heraclitus to some extent. Zeno's dialectic falls short in comparison. Zeno's perceived shortcomings do not deter Hegel from concluding that "this is the dialectic of Zeno; he had a knowledge of the determinations which our ideas of space and time contain, and showed in them their contradiction." The advance made my Zeno in this regard parallels the achievements of "Kant's antinomies," which "do no more than Zeno did here." The comparison of the Eleatic dialectic, with Zeno at its helm, to Kant is usefully further explained as follows:

> The general result of the Eleatic dialectic has thus become, "the truth is the one, all else is untrue," just as the Kantian philosophy resulted in "we know appearances only." On the whole the principle is the same; "the content of knowledge is only an appearance and not truth," but there is also a great difference present. That is to say, Zeno and the Eleatics in their proposition signified "that the sensuous world, with its multitudinous forms, is in itself appearance only, and has no [philosophical] truth." But Kant does not mean this, for he asserts: "Because we apply the activity of our thought to the outer world, we constitute it [as] appearance; what is without [our thought], first becomes an untruth by the fact that we put therein a mass of determinations. Only our knowledge, the spiritual, is thus appearance; the world is in itself absolute truth; it is our [mental] action alone that ruins it, our work is good for nothing."

According to Hegel, this Kantian "excessive humility of mind," which believes that "knowledge has no [absolute] value," is one of the most important shortcomings of Kant. What is targeted here is the Kantian assertion that the thing-in-itself cannot be known. In this context, Hegel equates this humility in modern, Kantian dialectic with the reduction of human beings to the status of animals ("sparrows"). For this reason, "Zeno's dialectic has greater objectivity than this modern dialectic" because it grants our consciousness the possibility of absolute knowing (277).

4.6 Zeno's Dialectic and Beyond

Hegel begins the section on Zeno with a declaration that dialectic "characterizes" Zeno's philosophy, and, "properly speaking, begins with him" (261). Since Hegel has already spoken of some kind(s) of dialectic involved in the philosophies of Zeno's predecessors, and repeats this claim later, we cannot assume that dialectic begins with

Zeno. What begins with him is the *proper* dialectic. Understanding what Hegel means by this claim requires investigating what he means by dialectic "properly speaking." In this sense, Hegel's history of dialectic differs slightly from Aristotle. The latter called Zeno the inventor of dialectic. For Hegel, Zeno is the originator of "the true objective dialectic," and this is the beginning of dialectic "properly speaking" (263). To anticipate what is to come below, Hegel also calls Zeno's dialectic "subjective." This creates some confusion since objective and subjective seem to be contradictory terms. However, the confusion stems from the multiple meanings Hegel, and we, attribute to these two terms. I will try to explain what Hegel means by both objective and subjective dialectic within the contexts in which he uses these terms.

What objective dialectic means can be partially explained in contrast to the subjective dialectic of Xenophanes, Parmenides, and Melissus. It helps to clarify what Hegel means here in pointing out that he refers to the subjective individualism of the Sophists, and some of the Socratics, in a similar manner. In this sense of the subjective, what is meant is the absence of universal, objective thought, which holds true in all circumstances. With subjectivity in this sense, what we have is the relativity of the truth claims, your truth versus mine. Thus, Hegel says the three Eleatics mentioned above "start with the proposition: 'Nothing is nothing; the nothing does not exist at all, or the like is real existence,' that is, they make one of the opposed predicates to be existence." In other words, the real existence is likeness, and any unlike determination (difference of any sort, quantitative and qualitative) is nothing because it indicates opposition. For instance, briefly and generally speaking, to say that *being* is nothing, or *non-being*, is contradictory since the subject and predicate oppose each other. "Now when they encounter the opposite in a determination, they demolish this determination . . ." by definitional fiat. What makes their method subjective is that the demolition of a contradictory determination is the result of an equally determinate assertion, of "my assertion, through the distinction that I form . . ." In this way, they have "proceeded from a definite proposition," or a hypothesis, in which "the nullity of the opposite does not appear in itself," but rather in the assertion itself. What is not shown is that the content of the proposition inherently self-negates, or that "it contains a contradiction in itself," a contradiction that could be affirmed by all rational cognition. To clarify further, Hegel says, "For instance, I assert of something that it is the null; then I show this nullity by another hypothesis regarding motion, and it follows that [motion] is the null." In a sense, I prove my point axiomatically, or ex vi termini. However, another thinking subject ("another consciousness") may not accept my hypothesis since it has not been proven objectively (universally), and may, with equal validity, or lack thereof, assert a hypothesis that directly declares motion to be true by definition.

> Similarly what seems to be the case when one philosophic system contradicts another is that the first is [axiomatically] pre-established, and that men starting from this point of view, combat the other. The matter is thus easily settled by saying: "The other has no truth, because it does not agree with me," and the other has the right to say the same. It does not help if I prove my system or my proposition and then conclude that thus the opposite is false; to this other proposition the first always seems to be foreign and external. Falsity must not be demonstrated through another, and as untrue because the opposite is true, but in itself.

Hegel adds that "we find this rational perception," or objectivity, in Zeno. The "special aim of objective dialectic" is to "see the battle fought with new vigor within the enemy's camp." In this battle, "we no longer maintain simple thought for itself," but, rather, negate the negation. For this reason, "Dialectic has in Zeno this negative side." In this sense, we must conclude that Zeno's dialectic is only negatively objective, and thus lacks the positive proof of the One. Hegel adds that dialectic "has also to be considered from its positive side," as the positive, affirmative proof of the truth (263–64). As we are about to see, it is precisely the lack of positive proof that makes Zeno's dialectic subjective, though in a different sense of subjective than the one described above.

Hegel goes on to offer an important discussion in which he distinguishes different forms of dialectic, subjective and objective, though he also calls them external and immanent dialectic, respectively. He begins this passage by saying, "According to the ordinary ideas of science, where propositions result from proof, proof is the movement of intelligence, a connection brought about by mediation." We may say for the purposes of illustration that Zeno's propositions follow from his proofs, whereas the subjective dialectic of the other Eleatics reverses this order. After this statement, Hegel proceeds to divide dialectic into two camps: "Dialectic is either (a) external dialectic, in which this movement is different from the comprehension of the movement, or (b) not a movement of our intelligence only, but what proceeds from the nature of the thing itself, i.e. from the pure Notion of the content." His description of the first form of dialectic is rather cryptic. His comment that this form of dialectic is to be found with the Sophists suggests that it is a form of relativistic subjectivism (264). This association of the external dialectic with Sophism implies, on the one hand, that this form of dialectic individualizes truth, and, on the other, attempts to destroy every absolute truth claim. Because the "power of thought treats everything dialectically," nothing remains secure, and everything can be proved or disproved (369). We will, with Hegel, have more to say on the Sophists in Chapter 6.

The second form of dialectic "is the immanent contemplation of the object; it is taken for itself, without previous hypothesis, idea or obligation, not under any outward conditions, laws or causes; we have to put ourselves right into the thing, to consider the object in itself, and to take it in the determinations which it has" (265). Notice that this form of dialectic coincides with Hegel's method, described in Chapter 1. Here, objective dialectic acquires an additional meaning. Instead of being the antithesis of the subjective dialectic discussed above, it now means (also) the speculative contemplation of the object, that is, the comprehension of it in itself. Clearly, Hegel favors this form of immanent dialectic, and defends it in detail in *The Phenomenology of Mind*.[19]

More importantly for our purposes here, the identifying characteristic of dialectic begins to emerge here amidst different forms of dialectic. The immanent dialectic "shows from itself that it contains opposed determinations, and thus breaks up." The subjective dialectic does the same thing, though "from external grounds" and moderately, "for it grants that: 'In the right there is what is not right, and in the false the true'" (265). Thus, the subjective dialectic too brings out contradictions, and this is a common element of all forms of dialectic. Even though Hegel only says this of the second form of dialectic, it is safe to assume that both forms of dialectic are destructive, the second being more thoroughly and radically so: "True [immanent] dialectic leaves nothing whatever to its object, as if the latter were deficient on one side only; for it disintegrates itself in the entirety of its nature. This true dialectic may be associated with the work of the Eleatics [above, Hegel associates it with Zeno alone]." From his criticism of True dialectic, which "got no further than the fact that through contradiction the object is a nothing," we sense the presence of a third form of dialectic. In short,

---

19. Hegel, *The Phenomenology of Mind*, 34.

"The result of [Zeno's] dialectic is null, the negative; the affirmative in it does not yet appear" (265). Hegel's dialectic is essentially affirmative, even if affirmation must go through a process of the immanent negation of the Notion, and this is its distinguishing characteristic. Hegel says with regard to Zeno that "the reason that dialectic first fell on [the] movement [of consciousness] is that the dialectic is itself this movement, or movement itself the dialectic of all that is. The thing, as self-moving, has its dialectic in itself, and movement is the becoming another" (266). Dialectic is thus essentially developmental movement.

In contrast, Zeno's dialectic is pure negation. Because it is immanent, the "dialectic of Zeno thus lays hold of the determinations which rest in the content [of thought] itself . . ." For this reason, it may "also be called subjective dialectic, inasmuch as it rests in the contemplative subject . . ." What this means is that dialectic as movement exists only in the head of the thinking subject (Zeno). This meaning of subjective is different than the one employed earlier. Here, it means one-sided idealism in which thought fails to synthesize itself with the material, objective reality. What is lacking in this latter form of subjective dialectic is precisely the outward objectification of the absolute *being*, namely, the concretion of thought (278).

"The next step from the existence of the dialectic as movement in the subject, is that it must necessarily itself become objective." This next step is taken by Heraclitus, who "at least understands the absolute as just this process of the dialectic." This step taken by Heraclitus makes dialectic "three-fold." Thus, we have:

> (a) the external dialectic, a reasoning which goes over and over again without ever reaching the soul of the thing [subjective dialectic in the first sense]; (b) immanent dialectic of the object, but falling within the contemplation of the subject [Zeno's subjective dialectic in the second sense]; (c) the objectivity of Heraclitus which takes the dialectic itself as principle. The advance . . . made by Heraclitus is the progression from Being as the first immediate thought, to the category of Becoming as the second. This is the first concrete, the Absolute, as in it the unity of opposites. Thus with Heraclitus the philosophic Idea is to be met with in its speculative form; the reasoning of Parmenides and Zeno is abstract understanding. Heraclitus was thus universally esteemed a deep philosopher and even was decried as such. Here we see land; there is no

proposition of Heraclitus which I have not adopted in my Logic (278–79).

In other words,

> . . . Zeno expressed the infinite, but on its negative side only, in reference to its contradiction as being the untrue. In Heraclitus we see the perfection of knowledge so far as it has gone, a perfecting of the Idea into a totality, which is the beginning of Philosophy, since it expresses the essence of the Idea, the Notion of the infinite, the potentially and actively existent, as that which it is, i.e. as the unity of opposites. From Heraclitus dates the ever-remaining Idea which is the same in all philosophers to the present day, as it was the Idea of Plato and of Aristotle (282).

Hegel has already given us different versions of when true philosophy and dialectic begins. Now, he says both true dialectic and true philosophy begins with Heraclitus. Overlooking this inconsistency, we find in the above passage what Hegel deems to be the most properly philosophical comprehension of the Idea with Heraclitus.

However, as we will find out in due course, Hegel's conclusion above is premature. For instance, the Sophists and Atomists do not subscribe to the same Idea. Indeed, Hegel's claim depends, in part, on the assumption that Heraclitus came after the Eleatic philosophers. This is not true. Parmenides was born in 540 or 515, Melissus in 500, and Zeno in 490 BCE. Heraclitus, who was born in 535 BCE, was possibly even older than Parmenides, though it is safe to say they were contemporaries. The main problem here is not that Hegel gets his chronological facts wrong. It is, rather, that he manipulates them at times to suit his general claim regarding the progression of the Idea in the history of philosophy. Another problem with Hegel's assessment above is that it gives Heraclitus too much credit. He retreats from this assessment in the next section.

CHAPTER 4

First Greek Period, First Division -
Part II: Heraclitus, the Atomists, and Empedocles

1. Introduction

This chapter examines Hegel's lectures on Heraclitus, the Atomists (Leucippus and Democritus), and Empedocles. What ties these otherwise diverse philosophers together is the acceptance of process, which the philosophical schools discussed in the previous chapter either deny or overlook. At the same time, these philosophers also introduce new innovations with regard to the Notion. Thus, "Heraclitus declares the Absolute to be this very process," and makes the transition from *being* to becoming possible. Instead of the Absolute, "Empedocles, Leucippus, and Democritus . . . go to the opposite extreme, to the simple, material, stationary principle, to the [atomic] substratum, which underlies the process." Their contribution mainly consists in reaffirming Nature as *being* that stands on its own grounds (170).

2. Heraclitus

As we have seen in the previous chapter, the Eleatics propose the "abstract understanding that Being is alone the truth," *Non-being*, on the other hand, is transitory, in motion, a manifold of finites, contradictory, and is thus untrue. Hegel says that Heraclitus was the first to propose the "universal principle" that "'Being and non-being are the same; everything is and yet is not'" (282). Hegel quotes this passage from Aristotle, who actually attributes this "universal principle" to the Atomists. What Aristotle says of their principle more precisely is that they think of the universe to consist of two kinds of "elements," which are "the full [atomic substances] and the empty [space]." For them, "the full and solid is what *is*, and the empty is what is not. That is why they also say that what *is* is no more of a being than what is not, because body is no more of a being than the empty is."[1] In other words, because the empty *is*, it is as much of a

---

1. Aristotle, *Metaphysics*, in *Aristotle: Selections*, trans. Terence Irwin and Gail Fine (Indianapolis: Hackett Publishing, Inc., 1995), 232 (985b.5–10).

being as the solid body. It is possible that Hegel confused this passage with another one where Aristotle says that "for Heraclitus 'all things are and are not' and all things are true and all are false."[2]

Obviously, what Hegel, via Aristotle, attributes to Heraclitus above signifies something other than the principle of the Atomists. "'Being and non-being are the same; everything is and yet is not'" highlights the identity of opposites. The identity of opposites is consistent with Heraclitus's philosophy. The Atomist principle, on the other hand, simply grants that the empty, that is, what we perceive to be *not*, has as much existence as the body. In this proposition, nothing is said of the identity of the empty and the full body. Moreover, the Atomists do not, strictly speaking, acknowledge *non-being* as such for the empty also *is*. In contrast, for Heraclitus, as Hegel correctly ascertains, the truth consist in "the unity of distinct opposites and, indeed, of the pure opposition of being and non-being." For Heraclitus, the truth of *being* entails its *non-being*. To wit, *up* entails *down* and cannot be conceived without it. Hegel says this unity of opposites is the expression of the "Absolute" that he also adopts in his own philosophy (282).

As we will see below, this Heraclitean approach depends on the principle of *becoming*, which is a category that indicates precisely the unity of *being* and *non-being*, or the negativity entailed in the unfolding processes of *being*. In this unity, something is said to *be* and *not be* at the same time. The flowing river is the same and not the same river simultaneously, much like the flying arrow which is here and not here. To speak anachronistically, the Atomists do not subscribe to this kind of Hegelian logic one finds in Heraclitus. At the same time, this logic opposes the reasoning of Zeno, who deems such contradictory states of being irrational and untrue.

Heraclitus's proposition, "Being is and yet is not," may not by itself make much sense, says Hegel. Its meaning has to be supplemented by another one of his propositions. Heraclitus also says that "'everything is in a state of flux; nothing subsists nor does it ever remain the same.'" However, by including this passage to illustrate the identity of the opposites in Heraclitus, Hegel undermines his own purpose. If everything is always in a "state of flux," if nothing ever remains the same, then we cannot speak of the identity of opposites, or of the permanency of *being*. Hegel thus overlooks the fact that his evidence reduces *being* to pure change. A similar complication arises when Hegel quotes the famous river argument Plato attributes to

---

2. I borrow this clarification from the editors of Hegel, *Lectures on the History of Philosophy 1825–6*, 73n192.

Heraclitus in *Cratylus*: "'[Heraclitus] compares things to the current of a river: no one can go twice into the same stream'" (283).

Some scholars think that Plato and Aristotle wrongly reduce Heraclitus's principle to pure flux.[3] Aristotle does nothing of this sort. As Hegel quotes him, he says of the river paradox that "Heraclitus' successors even said 'it could not once be entered,' for it changed directly." This comment by Aristotle, as Hegel acknowledges, does not demolish the identity of the river, for it also remains the same river. In this passage, which comes from *Metaphysics* (IV, 5), Aristotle is clearly referring to Heraclitus's "successors," especially Cratylus, who criticized Heraclitus for not going far enough with the principle of flux. As it turns out, Plato's version of Heraclitus in *Cratylus* comes from Cratylus himself. Thus, Plato confuses Cratylus's criticism of Heraclitus with the latter's own views. As for Hegel, he swings back and forth between the Plato and Aristotle interpretations of Heraclitus.

In the second volume of *Lectures*, Hegel revisits this theme and says that "the Becoming of Heraclitus is a true and real determination . . ." However, he confusingly adds that, with Heraclitus, "change yet lacks the determination of identity with itself." By this latter point, he means to point out the absence of "the constancy of the universal" in Heraclitus's dialectic. In illustrating this absence, Hegel posits his own version of the river analogy: "The stream is ever changing, yet it is nevertheless ever the same, and is really a universal existence." But, as we are about to see, in a different rendition of the river example, Heraclitus also makes the same claim. To complicate things further, Hegel also says Aristotle "is controverting the opinions of Heraclitus and others when he says that Being and non-being are not the same, and in connection with this lays down the celebrated maxim of [non]contradiction, that a man is not at the same time a ship" (II,140). We will have to deal with this maxim in due course, which has much to do with Aristotle's formal logic. The point is that in order for Aristotle to controvert Heraclitus

---

3. "Aristotle accepted the Platonic flux-interpretation and carried it still further," reads one interpretation. However, the authors of this line go on to say that Aristotle, in carrying the flux-interpretation further, criticized Heraclitus for holding that "opposites are 'the same.'" G. S. Kirk, J. E. Raven, and M. Schofield, *The Presocratic Philosophers: A Critical History with a Selection of Texts*, second edition (Cambridge, UK: Cambridge University Press, 1983), 186. However, Aristotle's criticism is not an extension of the Platonic pure flux-interpretation, but, rather, its denial.

in this manner, the latter would have to think that the opposites are in unity of some sort.

Indeed, this latter view is precisely what emerges from different renditions of Heraclitus's celebrated saying. For instance, he is also quoted as saying, "in the same rivers ever different waters flow." This statement implies that the motion (change) of rivers is predicated upon the same-ness of the flowing rivers. This is to say, the permanency of the changing rivers is presupposed. In another rendition of the saying, Heraclitus says "we step and do not step into the same rivers, we are and we are not." Heraclitus also says, according to Plutarch, "the same thing, there are present living and dead, the awake and the sleeping, young and old; for the latter change and are the former, and again the former change and are the latter." These statements obviously indicate the unity of opposites. After all, Heraclitus himself declares that, "it is wise to agree that all things are one,"[4] and the One is the universal *Logos*. In short, Heraclitus holds that there is universal truth, the One, which permeates all things in existence. Hegel adopts this alternative interpretation of Heraclitus when, quoting Aristotle again, he says that Heraclitus "declares that 'there is only one that remains, and from out of this all else is formed; all except this one is not enduring'" (283). This proposition cannot be reduced to the pure-flux theory.

The last point requires us to think of existence as the unity of *being* and *non-being*. Hegel says, "If we do not take the conception of existence as complete, the pure Being of simple thought . . ." that is, *being* taken in isolation merely as thought, becomes perceived as "the absolute negative." This amounts to the notion of *being* which denies "everything definite," and keeps us at the level of Zeno, who "remained at the proposition, 'From nothing [non-being], comes nothing.'" Only by recognizing the identity of *being* and *non-being*, or that "the moment of negativity is immanent in *being*," can we understand that *non-being* comes out of *being* and forces it into becoming. What is being emphasized here is that "when we look closer, we find that Heraclitus also conceived of the opposites and their unification in a more definite [concrete] manner." Further evidence for this conclusion is found in what Sextus Empiricus attributes to Heraclitus, which Hegel quotes in this context: "'The opposites are combined in the self-same one, just as honey is both sweet and bitter'" (283–84).

---

4. Jonathan Barnes, ed., *Early Greek Philosophy* (London: Penguin Books, 2001), 70, 63, 50.

However, Hegel proceeds to confuse us once again when he quotes Sextus Empiricus's conclusion to this last remark: "'Heraclitus, like the Skeptics, proceeds from ordinary ideas; no one will deny that healthy men call honey sweet, while those who are sick will say it is bitter.'" The Skeptical argument, as Hegel points out, is that "if it is only sweet, it cannot alter its nature in another individual; it would in all places and even to the jaundiced patient be sweet" (284). It follows from this Skeptical argument that since the nature of sweet is altered in the "jaundiced patient," the universality of sweetness cannot be established. But, this is not Heraclitus's intended meaning. In other words, turning Heraclitus into a Skeptic would imply precisely that he has no notion of unity. In turn, this implication would contradict what Hegel is attempting to show on Heraclitus's behalf, namely, that "opposites are combined in the self-same one, just as honey is both sweet and bitter."

Further evidence to prove the unity-of-opposites interpretation of Heraclitus's philosophy is found in Aristotle's following quotation of Heraclitus: "'Join together the complete whole and the incomplete . . . what coincides and what conflicts, what is harmonious and what is discordant, and from out of them all comes [O]ne, and from [O]ne, all.'" For Hegel, this means "whole makes itself the part, and the meaning of the part is to become the whole." The One with Heraclitus is "not an abstraction, but the activity of [the One] dividing itself into opposites" (284). This is the essential formulation of the Hegelian dialectic also, which he states elsewhere as follows: "The moving principle of the concept, which not only dissolves the particularizations of the universal but also produces them is what I call *dialectic*."[5]

Moreover, Heraclitus "determined the real process in its abstract moments by separating two sides in it." For instance, "the way upwards and the way downwards" is such a separation, which designates ". . . the existence of opposites . . ." This expression also captures "the unification of these existent opposites" because it is stated that the up and down are in some sense identical (288). Here, Hegel has in mind the necessary internal relations of the opposite determinations. As Hegel puts it in his own terms, "each particular only is, in so far as its opposite is implicitly contained in its Notion" (285). In order for this unity and opposition to hold true simultaneously, the opposing moments must be in a circular process. This is where the category of *becoming* becomes so essential.

---

5. Hegel, *Elements of the Philosophy of Right*, 60.

After considering similar examples that indicate the unity of opposites found in Heraclitus, Hegel concludes that "everything is three-fold and thereby real unity; nature is the never-resting, and the all is the transition out of the one into the other, from division into unity, and from unity into division" (288). The whole "Nature is thus a circle. With this in view, we find Heraclitus . . . saying: 'The universe was made neither by God nor man, but it ever was and is, and will be, a living fire, that which, in accordance with its Laws, kindles and goes out'" (289). This circular and triadic dialectic is also raised to prominence in Hegel's *Logic*[6] and *Elements of the Philosophy of Right*.[7] The circular process of becoming captures the entire movement of dialectic. However, as we are about to find out, Hegel demotes Heraclitus's dialectic from "three-fold" to two-fold, to the transition from *being* to *becoming* in which everything vanishes.

Hegel says in *Lectures* that "the truth of Being [is] Becoming." This principle emerges directly out of the principle of contradiction, that is, out of the unity and opposition of *being* and *non-being*. Because *non-being* constantly emerges out of *being*, the principle of *becoming* naturally follows. For this reason, as Hegel puts it, both "origination" and "passing away" belong to *being*. Origination and passing away, furthermore, are not merely separate processes. They are also "identical." What comes to be is simultaneously a process of vanishing and is in this sense also *non-being*. Living and dying are identical both in cognitive and natural terms (283).

In Hegel's assessment,

> It is a great advance in thought to pass from Being to Becoming, even if, as the first unity of opposite determinations, [becoming] is still abstract. Because in this relationship both [*being* and *non-being*] must be unrestful and therefore contain within themselves the principle of life, . . . [Thus] motion, which Aristotle has demonstrated [to be lacking] in the earlier philosophies is supplied, and . . . even made to be the principle [by Heraclitus]. This philosophy is thus not one past and gone; its principle is essential, and is to be found in the beginning of my Logic, immediately after [the categories of] Being and Nothing.

---

6. Hegel, *Hegel's Science of Logic*, 71.
7. Hegel, *Elements of the Philosophy of Right*, 26.

Thus, the essential philosophical advance made by Heraclitus consists in the recognition "that Being and non-being [if isolated from one another] are abstractions devoid of truth, that the first truth is to be found in Becoming . . ." Such an abstraction as isolation belongs to "the understanding," which "comprehends both [*being* and *non-being*] as having truth and value in isolation; [Speculative, philosophical] reason, on the other hand, recognizes the one in the other, and sees that in the one its 'other' is contained" (ibid.).

What is somewhat unclear from the above discussions is whether or not Hegel thinks Heraclitus's dialectic is complete. Elsewhere, Hegel tells us that if the Eleatic school stops at the abstractly universal being ("being-itself-at-home-with-itself," which is thinking's "immediacy"), Heraclitus stops at "becoming."[8] Likewise, he says Heraclitus's *being* is just "process." With him, "Becoming existed only as the transition of Being into nothing where each is negated" (302). Similarly, according to Hegel,

> Heraclitus, indeed, says that everything flows on, that nothing is existent and only the one remains; but that is the [abstract] Notion of the unity which only exists in opposition and not of that [of Notion] reflected within itself. This one [of Heraclitus], in its unity with the movement of the individuals, is the genus, or in its infinitude the simple Notion as thought; as such, the Idea has still to be determined, and we shall thus find it again as the νοῦς [nous] of Anaxagoras. The universal is the immediate simple unity in opposition which goes back into itself as a process of differences; but this is also found in Heraclitus . . . He calls this "the ethereal body, the seed of the Becoming of everything;" that to him is the Idea, the universal as reality, as process at rest (292–93).

Hegel, to my knowledge, never successfully clarifies what Heraclitus precisely leaves out in his dialectic. The difficulty in trying to determine what is left out has much to do with the difficulties involved in Hegel's own philosophy. While this is not the place to explain such difficulties in detail, it is worth pointing out that there is a well-known dilemma in Hegel, which can be highlighted by the following question: Does the Absolute Idea represent the true reconciliation of contradictions and thus signify the truth of *being* at a

---

8. Hegel, *The Encyclopaedia Logic*, 37.

higher level than becoming? In my view, because Hegel is not consistent on the issue of what happens to contradictions within the realm of the Absolute Idea, it is not possible to definitively decide whether or not the end result, the Hegelian Absolute Idea, contains the dialectic of negation and becoming. While Hegel at times suggests that the Absolute would not be absolute if it did not contain contradictions, he also depicts the final stage as a stage of "reconciliation" of the Idea "with" and "within" itself. For instance, much like his criticism of Heraclitus, he criticizes the Indians for holding that "the third [and final stage of dialectic] is still change and negation" (136).

Some of Hegel's able interpreters try to explain this dilemma away. As John McTaggart sees it, even though "contradictions are the cause of dialectic process . . . , truth consists, not of contradictions, but of moments which, if separated, would be contradictions."[9] In some sense, McTaggart's conclusion resonates well with Hegel's philosophy. Hegel says after all that anything short of the Absolute Idea, "is error, confusion, opinion, endeavor, caprice and transitoriness; the absolute Idea alone is *being*, imperishable life, *self-knowing truth*, and is *all truth*."[10] However, Hegel also says in *The Encyclopaedia Logic* that "it is the contradiction that moves the world";[11] and in *Science of Logic* that the "law of contradiction" is that "*everything is inherently contradictory*";[12] and this "law" "expresses . . . the truth and the essential nature of things."[13] These statements suggest that the "transitoriness" driven by contradictions is the incontrovertible absolute truth.

J. N. Findlay takes a shot at this dilemma also, but, inevitably, ends up making confusing statements. On the one hand, he says "dialectic . . . for Hegel . . . is only a 'moment,' and aspect in philosophical thinking," which is "overcome in the higher thought of reason . . ." by "uniting or reconciling" contradictions. On the other hand, "Speculative Thought" also contains "the dialectical element, together with its contradictions: these too will persist and be preserved in the results of Reason."[14]

Given these difficulties, Hans-Georg Gadamer suggests that Hegel himself may have thought that the task of full comprehension "cannot be completed." The "insoluble problem" in this respect is

---

9. McTaggart, *Studies in the Hegelian Dialectic*, 10.
10. Hegel, *Hegel's Science of Logic*, 824.
11. Hegel, *The Encyclopaedia Logic*, 187.
12. Hegel, *Hegel's Science of Logic*, 439–40.
13. Ibid., 439.
14. Findlay, *Hegel: A Re-examination*, 63–64.

the tension between "the inherent disquietude of the dialectical process," and the superseding of all disquietude by the "Absolute knowing as thinking of totality."[15] To my knowledge, there is no direct evidence that would allow us to attribute this claim to Hegel himself.

A less charitable interpretation of Hegel's Absolute Idea and its relationship to dialectic is given by Frederick Engels:

> [H]owever much Hegel, especially in his *Logic*, emphasized that this eternal truth is nothing but the logical, or, the historical, process itself, he nevertheless finds himself compelled to supply this process with an end . . . In his *Logic*, he can make this end a beginning again, since here the point of the conclusion, the absolute idea—which is only absolute insofar as he has absolutely nothing to say about it—"alienates", that is, transforms, itself into nature and comes to itself again later in the mind, that is, in thought and in history. But at the end of the whole philosophy, a similar return to the beginning is possible only in one way. Namely, by conceiving of the end of history as follows: mankind arrives at the cognition of the self-same absolute idea, and declares that this cognition of the absolute idea is reached in Hegelian philosophy. In this way, however, the whole dogmatic content of the Hegelian system is declared to be absolute truth, in contradiction to his dialectical method, which dissolves all dogmatism.[16]

Engels correctly states that Hegel "was compelled to make a system and, in accordance with traditional requirements, a system of philosophy must conclude with some sort of absolute truth." As Engels also indicates above, the absolute is also used as the beginning of the system. Such an absolute, according to Engels, is contrary to the spirit of dialectic. In dialectic, he says, "nothing is final, absolute, sacred. It reveals the transitory character of everything and in

---

15. Hans-Georg Gadamer, *Hegel's Dialectic: Five Hermeneutical Studies* (New Haven: Yale University Press, 1976), 82, 84.
16. Frederick Engels, "Ludwig Feuerbach and the End of Classical German Philosophy," in *Karl Marx and Frederick Engels Collected Works*, Vol. 26 (New York: International Publishers, 1990), 360–61.

everything; nothing can endure against it except the uninterrupted process of becoming and passing away."[17]

Engel's version of dialectic thus coincides with the pure-flux interpretation of Heraclitus, and may be the main reason why many Marxists, even the Hegelian ones, think of dialectic strictly in these terms. However, how Engels interpreted Heraclitus's dialectic cannot be conclusively ascertained. He says, for instance, that in Heraclitus dialectic, "everything is and is not, for everything is fluid, is constantly changing, constantly coming into being and passing away." The context in which Engels discusses Heraclitus suggests the pure-flux theory.[18] However, the information he provides is too brief to warrant conclusive results in this regard.

By claiming that Heraclitus's philosophy does not go beyond the category of becoming, Hegel, in a way, reaffirms the pure flux interpretation of Heraclitus's dialectic. However, for the reasons indicated above, Hegel himself is inconsistent, if not self-contradictory, on the possibility of bringing dialectic to a halt beyond becoming. For this reason, the precise nature of his criticism of Heraclitus remains unclear.

A further question arises in Hegel's treatment of Heraclitus's philosophy: Is thought, or the Notion, the universal principle of Heraclitus? Hegel goes on to say that Heraclitus did not simply express himself "in Notions." He also gave his Notion, "a real and more natural form . . ." Some claim that he made fire his principle; others say it was air, vapor, or time. Because of these natural principles attributed to him, "he is still reckoned as belonging to the Ionic school of natural philosophers." The misguided conclusion, according to Hegel, that he was strictly a natural philosopher may be due to the obscure ways in which Heraclitus expressed himself (285). However, when his conceptions are examined more closely, "Heraclitus could no longer, like Thales, express water, air or anything similar as an absolute principle—he could no longer do so in the form of a primeval element from which the rest proceeds." This is "because he thought of Being as identical with non-being, or the infinite Notion; thus the existent, absolute principle cannot with him come forth as a definite and actual thing such as water, but must be water in alteration, or as process only" (286).

---

17. Ibid., 360.
18. Frederick Engels, "Socialism: Utopian and Scientific," in *Karl Marx and Frederick Engels Collected Works*, Vol. 24 (New York: International Publishers, 1989), 299.

In other words, "his philosophy has, on the whole, a bent towards a philosophy of nature, for the principle, although logical, is apprehended as the universal nature-process." This principle, of course, is different than the principles that are derived from natural things, such as water. The universal here is not the elements of nature, but the super-sensuous process that sets these elements in motion. However, "From his principle that everything that is, at the same time is not," which also amounts to saying everything is in a state of process, "it immediately follows that he holds that sensuous certainty has no [absolute] truth; for it is the certainty for which something exists as actual, which is not so in fact. Not this [sensuous] immediate Being, but absolute mediation, Being as thought of, Thought itself, is the true Being." This is none other than reason "'as the judge of truth.'" The "only wisdom is," thus, "to know the reason that reigns overall." All knowing without this universal One is "arbitrary" (293–94). In short,

> However much Heraclitus may maintain that there is no [absolute] truth in sensuous knowledge because all that exists is in a state of flux, and that the existence of sensuous certainty is not while it is, he maintains the objective method in knowledge [the knowledge of the universal] to be none the less necessary. The rational, the true, that which I know, is indeed a withdrawal from the objective as from what is sensuous, individual, definite and existent; but what reason knows within itself is necessity or the universal of being; it is the principle of thought, as it is the principle of the world. It is this contemplation of truth that Spinoza in his *Ethics* calls "a contemplation of things in the guise of eternity" (296–97).

With these comments, Hegel pushes Heraclitus's principle toward the universal Notion, which, he tells us later, is first properly posited by Anaxagoras. Besides the necessary presence of the Notion as the principle, which Hegel somewhat imposes upon Heraclitus, what Heraclitus permanently contributes to the system of philosophy is the category of becoming, which is necessarily related to the theory of the unity of opposites. This theory derives from the principle that contradictory categories, such as *being* and *non-being*, are also identical. Another *possible* contribution Heraclitus makes is contained in his thought that *non-being* emerges out of the One. This claim lends itself to the theory of potentiality, which is essential to Hegel's dialectic. However, Heraclitus is not usually associated with this theory.

3. Leucippus, Democritus, and Empedocles

3.1 Introduction

Whether or not these three philosophers belong to the same school of philosophy is questionable. Hegel treats Empedocles together with Leucippus and Democritus because, he says, their thought manifests the "ideality of the sensuous." This means that they manifest the manifold sensuous reality as "universal determinateness." In this, they "transition to the universal" from the sensuous determinations. In Hegel's estimation, the emergent universal can only be expressed as the ideal *being*. However, this transition to the universal may be less true of Empedocles, who had the Ionic "tendencies" of natural philosophy. Thus, in Empedocles "we see the commencement of the determination and separation of principles. The becoming conscious of difference [between the ideational and the sensuous] is an essential moment, but the principles here have in part the character of physical Being, and though partaking also of ideal Being, this form is not yet thought-form." Leucippus and Democritus, on the other hand, inherited the tendencies of the Eleatic school. For this reason, these two "philosophers belong to the same philosophic system ... [and] must be taken together as regards their philosophic thought." In their thought, we find "the more ideal principles, the atom and the Nothing," and the "deeper immersion of thought-determination" in the sensuous, objective existence. This is the "beginning of a metaphysics of body," which means that "the significance of the material" is expressed in terms of "pure Notions," even though their thought is "on the whole, immature ..." (298). Hegel's outline above, as becomes clear in the following section, is not altogether applicable to these three philosophers. Consequently, he ends up wavering on their idealism.

3.2 Leucippus and Democritus

Very little is known of Leucippus's writings. Indeed, besides certain interpretations of him, there seems to be only one surviving sentence that can be directly attributed to him: "Nothing happens in vain, but all things for a reason and by necessity."[19] What is known as Leucippus's philosophy, we may add, has reached us through the works of his student-friend Democritus. These two philosophers are treated as identical by Hegel and others.

Hegel says we are "greatly indebted" to Leucippus because he "is the originator of the famous atomic system . . ." and, by extension, "our ordinary physics" (300). In understanding this system, it would be helpful to include here a fragment from Aristotle's lost work, *On Democritus*, which is not considered by Hegel:

> Democritus thinks that the nature of eternal things consists in small substances, limitless in quantity, and for them he posits a place, distinct from them and infinite in extent. He calls place by the names "empty [void]", "nothing" and "limitless"; and each of the substances he calls "thing", "solid" and "existent". He thinks that the substances are so small that they escape our senses, and that they possess all sorts of forms and all sorts of shapes and differences in size. From them, as from elements, he produces and compounds the visible and perceptible bodies. The atoms struggle and are carried about in the empty [void] because of their dissimilarities and the other differences mentioned, and as they are carried about they collide and intertwine in a way which makes them touch and be near one another but which does not produce any truly single nature whatever from them; for it is utterly foolish to think that two or more things might ever become one. He explains that the substances remain together for a certain time because the bodies entangle with and grasp hold of one another; for some of them are scalene, some hooked, some concave, some convex, and others have innumerable other differences. So he thinks that they hold on to one another and remain together up to the time when some

---

19. Quoted in Barnes, *Early Greek Philosophy*, 202.

stronger necessity reaches them from their surroundings and shakes them and scatters them apart.

Simplicius concludes from this fragment that Democritus "speaks of generation and of its contrary, dissociation, not only of animals but also of plants and worlds—and in general of all perceptible bodies. So if generation is an association of atoms, and destruction their dissociation, then according to Democritus too, generation will be an alteration."[20] Generation, then, is not the coming into being of perceptible bodies out of nothing. It is instead association of variously shaped and always present atoms, that is, their coalescing together. Their passing away is simply a process of separation, and not their destruction.

The fragment above and Similicus's commentary put us in a better position to make sense of Diogenes Laertius's commentary, which Hegel quotes in describing the philosophy of the Atomists.

> "Atoms, divergent in form, propel themselves through their separation from the infinite, into the great vacuum." (Democritus adds to this, "by means of their mutual resistance and a tremulous, swinging motion." [Hegel's note]) "Here gathered, they form one vortex where, by dashing together and revolving round in all sorts of ways, the like are separated off with the like. But since they are of equal weight, when they cannot, on account of their number, move in any way, the finer go into outer vacuum, being so to speak forced out; and the others remain together and, being entangled, run one against another, and form the first round system. But this stands apart like a husk that holds within it all sorts of bodies; since these, in pressing towards the middle, make a vortex movement, this encircling skin becomes thin, because from the action of the vortex, they are continually running together. The earth arises in this way, because these bodies, collected in the middle, remain together. That which encircles and which is like a husk, again becomes increased by means of the adherence of external bodies, and since it also moves within the vortex, it draws everything with which it comes in contact to itself. The union of some of these bodies again forms a system, first the moist and slimy, and then the dry, and that which circles in the vortex of

---

20. Ibid., 206–7.

the whole; after that, being ignited, they constitute the substance of the stars. The outer circle is the sun, the inner the moon," &c.

Hegel finds little value in these ". . . confused ideas of circle-motion," which in later times is called "attraction and repulsion." What is valuable in them is merely "the fact that the different kinds of motion are looked at as the principle of matter" (309–10). However, what comes about as a consequence of motion is "merely a combination," and both the process and the form sensuous objects take are "altogether external and accidental." Thus, "unity is quite disregarded, and . . . no rational word is uttered in regard to the transition of phenomena, but only what is tautological" (307). Here, Hegel is repeating Aristotle's complaint that "these men" have an inadequate sense of motion, because they "blithely" ignore the question of "whence and how the existing things acquire" their motion.[21] In other words, motion is not shown to inhere in the bodies that move about, nor is there any explanation of whence it originates—if not from within the bodies themselves. As we have seen in Chapter 2, the Indian Atomists argue that action inheres in the substances (atoms), and is a category of nature in this sense. This idea, or something akin to it, is not found in these Greek Atomists.

As for the unity found in existence, the system of Atomists, says Hegel, is based on the separation of "the universal and the sensuous, or the primary and the secondary, or the essential and the non-essential qualities of body." With this comment, Hegel intervenes here to make the atomism of Leucippus and Democritus a speculative philosophy. In speculative reasoning the universal qualities of the sensuous, "corporeal" body are treated as Notions, and seen as the primary, or essential, qualities, "such as form, impenetrability and weight . . ." Speculatively speaking, "essential existence" is the manifold determinations of the universals. The latter exist in themselves. Such an existence refers to the "abstract content," or essence, of "the reality of existence" the corporeal bodies take. Thus, "To body as such, there is nothing left for the determination of reality but pure singularity; but it is the unity of opposites [of singularity and universality], and the unity of these predicates constitutes" the concrete reality of bodies in existence (300–301).

Existence as the unity and opposition of singularity and universality undergoes another division in atomism, the division between the body and the empty. Hegel, quoting Aristotle, says,

---

21. Barnes, *Early Greek Philosophy*, 207.

"'Leucippus and his friend Democritus maintain that the full and the empty are the elements, and they call the one the existent, and the other the non-existent; that is, the full and solid are the existent, the empty and rare, the non-existent.'" The wording in this sentence is misleading since it may suggest that the empty does not exist at all. This is not Hegel's intention. As Hegel points out, the Atomists "also say that Being is no more than non-being because the empty is as well as the bodily; and these form the material sources [causes] of everything" (301). This clarification is derived from the passage from Aristotle, which I have quoted in the section on Heraclitus.

Hegel proceeds to say that "the determination of being-for-self belongs to Leucippus." This, adds Hegel, is a "great principle," which we have not seen in the previous philosophers. For instance, "Parmenides establishes Being" only as "the abstract universal," that is, merely as *in-itself*. In this, he "says that the nothing [or non-being] does not exist at all." In contrast, Leucippus's non-being is a material precondition of existence. Heraclitus's *being*, on the other hand, is just "process." With him, "Becoming existed only as the transition of Being into nothing where each is negated." In further contrast to this view, "the view that each is simply at home with itself, the positive as the self-existent one and the negative as empty, is what came to consciousness in Leucippus, and became the absolute determination." Thus, from Leucippus's point of view, the positive self-existent *(for-itself)* bodies, as atoms, do not pass away. They must "always exist" (302).

Not incidentally, the transition from Parmenides to Heraclitus and then to Leucippus, says Hegel, parallels the transition from the abstract *being (being-in-itself)* to becoming, and then to the *being-for-itself* in Hegel's *Logic*. In this regard, Hegel enthusiastically declares on behalf of the Atomists that "the full [body] has the atom as its principle, the Absolute, what exists in and for itself, is thus the atom and the empty" (301). Hegel's enthusiasm here is not well-grounded for the Atomists do not see the body and the empty, the positive and the negative, existing in relational unity. For this reason, Hegel's following conclusion is also too enthusiastic: This principle of unity, says Hegel, is the "principle of one" because "it is wholly ideal." This is to say, the principle "pertains wholly to thought, even though the assertion that the atom also exists was intended." Hegel's assumption here is that when the principle of unity is thought, it is necessarily thought, speculative, as the One, since thought, as the principle, is always in unity within itself, and that "thought is the true essence of things." For this reason, adds Hegel, "the philosophy of Leucippus is no empirical philosophy and the atom is nothing empirical."[22]

Before the Atomists, the ideality of the One appeared merely "in the sense of being in thought" alone (Eleatics). This meant that the Nature, "this world," did not have its own internal principle or foundation. According to Hegel,

> The Atomists are . . . , generally speaking, opposed to the idea of the creation and maintenance of this world by means of a foreign principle . . . For if nature is represented as created and held together by another, it is conceived of as not existent in itself, and thus as having its Notion outside itself, i.e. its principle or origin is foreign to it and it has no principle as such, only being conceivable from the will of another; as it is, it is contingent, devoid of necessity and Notion in itself.

"It is in the theory of atoms that science first feels released from the sense of having no foundation for the world." The Atomist foundation as atom and the void, Hegel repeats, cannot be reduced to rigid empiricism. In the atomism of Leucippus and Democritus, "we have the conception of the inherency of nature, that is to say, thought finds itself in it, or its principle is in itself something thought, and the Notion finds its satisfaction in conceiving and establishing it as Notion." Thus, "In abstract existence, nature has its ground in itself and is simply for itself; the atom and the vacuum are just such simple Notions." However, "we cannot here," in these Atomists, "see or find more than the formal fact that quite general and simple principles . . . are represented" (306). The last point suggests that Hegel has been all-along attributing to the Atomists more than what their "simple principles" represent.

For Hegel, "The atom may be taken materially, but it is supersensuous, purely intellectual." In this sense, the atom is the Notion, and this Notion necessarily entails the One. Hegel's reasoning behind this interpretation is simple enough: "The atoms of Leucippus are . . . not molecules, the small particles of [modern] Physics. In Leucippus, according to Aristotle, there is to be found the idea that 'atoms are invisible because of the smallness of their body,' which is much like the way in which molecules are nowadays spoken of: but this is merely a way of speaking of them." The atom "can neither be seen nor shown with magnifying glasses or measures, because it is an

---

22. Hegel, *Lectures on the History of Philosophy 1825–6*, 91.

abstraction of thought; what is shown is always matter that is put together." What Hegel means here is that the matter that is put together originates from the soul-like, supersensible Notion of atom. For this reason, Leucippus inevitably conceived of the atom as the inner-most soul, or essence, of the existing bodies: "Leucippus understood it so, and his philosophy is consequently not at all empirical" (303).

There is no evidence that Leucippus actually "understood it so." It is one thing to say we must understand the Notion of the atom this way, quite another to say that Leucippus also thought this way. Hegel conflates these two forms of reasoning here. He seeks to find further evidence for his interpretation in the claim, attributed to Democritus by Sextus Empiricus, that "it is not the senses through which we become conscious of the truth, and thereby he has established an idealism in the higher sense and not one which is merely subjective" (303). This point, however, does not furnish evidence against the said empiricism of the Atomists. It does not say that the atom is essentially ideational, soul-like Notion, nor does it explicitly deny the priority of sense-perception in knowledge. More importantly, this point pertains to epistemology, and not to the ontology of the atoms and the empty, entertained by the Atomists. Said differently, it is possible to argue, as the Indian Atomists had done, that the invisible atoms, which are material, coalesce into compound objects and produce sensation, though it is reason that discriminates between different kinds of sensation and produces the knowledge of them. This argument does not put reason before, or within, the substance or the sensation. It is Hegel who does this on behalf of the Greek Atomists. The merit of Hegel's intervention for us thus reduces itself to a useful insight into Hegel's own philosophy. In Hegel's own words, this insight may be summarized as follows: "It is just as futile when, as in modern times, men try by the microscope to investigate the inmost part of the organism, the soul, and think they can discover it by means of sight and feeling. Thus the principle of the One is altogether ideal, but not in the sense of being in thought or in the head alone, but in such a way that thought is made the true essence of things" (303–4). The implications of the last sentence are far-reaching. It indicates that the Notion, or *nous*, also resides in things (Nature) as their "true essence." This claim will be further articulated in the chapter on Anaxagoras.

3.3 Empedocles

In yet another confusing restatement Hegel says the "speculative Idea" of Heraclitus "is process," which combines opposites, "but this [combination] is so without the individual moments in reality being mutually related as Notions" (313). It seems that Hegel simply means by this restatement that Heraclitus did not contemplate the category, or the Notion, of synthesis. Perhaps, this is also what he meant by his earlier claim that Heraclitus did go beyond the category of becoming. If so, Hegel's criticism of Heraclitus resolves into a mere formal technicality. Indeed, Heraclitus's combination of opposites strongly implies the notion of synthesis. Hegel claims that it is Empedocles who first introduces this Notion. However, as we will see, the Notion of synthesis proposed by Empedocles is not really a Hegelian synthesis, but a combination of externally related parts, or mere differences. Hegel ultimately rules that the true universal is missing in Empedocles's synthetic view.

At any rate, Hegel says the "Notion" that governs Empedocles's philosophy is "Combination or Synthesis." Indeed, his "conception of synthesis holds good to the present day . . ." Empedocles is "the originator of the common idea that" everything is a combination of four "fundamental" elements, namely, fire, air, water, and earth (313–14.) For this reason, his philosophy resembles the Ionic philosophy with the major difference that, instead of one, four fundamental material elements constitute his theory of origination. In this way, he is also related to the Atomists who, chronologically, come after him. The generation of the One is a process of the many coming together. The advantage of Empedocles over the Atomists is that he proposes two forms of opposing prime movers, Love (sometimes referred to as Friendship) and Strife (Enmity). These two forces explain the reason and necessity for movement of the many into a combination and separation. Empedocles also accepts the Eleatic principle that "nothing comes out of nothing." The four elements and the two powers are eternally present. However, Empedocles departs from the Eleatics, who deny the truth of both motion and the many.

Empedocles also declares God to be immortal. At times, he presents God as a powerful and wise figure in human affairs.[23] God is also described cosmologically as an encircled stillness, equal only to itself in every dimension, without any beginning or end. This stillness of God is not an existence apart from the movement of the mortal or

---

23. Barnes, *Early Greek Philosophy*, 112.

natural things, which are ceaselessly combined and dissociated within this circle, though leaving God unaltered.[24]

Hegel mostly focuses on the relationship of the four elements and the two powers enumerated above. By quoting Aristotle, he sums up the general ideas of Empedocles as follows:

> "To the three elements, fire, air, and water, each of which was in turn considered as the principle from which everything proceeded, Empedocles added the Earth as the fourth corporeal element." These elements "always remain the same, never becoming, but being united and separated as the more or the less, combining into one and coming out of one" . . . Aristotle further says in reference to the abstract Notion [combination] of their relation to one another that Empedocles did not only require the four elements as principles, but also Friendship and Strife; . . . it is at once evident that these [two principles] are of another kind, because they are, properly speaking, universal. He has the four natural elements as the real, and friendship and strife as the ideal principles . . . (314)

It may be thought that "nothing metaphysical is signified by" these four real-material elements in Empedocles's philosophy. Hegel says this is not true, and proceeds to rescue Empedocles from empiricism by implanting the metaphysical Notion into his philosophy. In this spirit, Hegel says,

> [W]ith Empedocles this undoubtedly is the case: every particular thing arises through some kind of union of the four. These four elements, to our ordinary idea, are not so many sensuous things if we consider them as universal elements; for, looked at sensuously, there are various other sensuous things. All that is organic, for example, is of another kind; and, further, earth as one, as simple, pure earth, does not exist, for it is in manifold determinateness. In the idea of four elements we have the elevation of sensuous ideas into thought (314).

---

24. Ibid., 125.

Hegel's intervention is logical enough in its own right. But we must reserve the right to question whether or not Empedocles actually thought in these "metaphysical" terms. The fact that Hegel himself criticizes Empedocles's views on the following grounds justifies our reservation.

Though, perhaps, on somewhat different grounds than the ones given above, Hegel now proceeds to take the universal, metaphysical Notion away from Empedocles:

> Empedocles ... represented ... [the unity of elements] as a combination. In this synthetic union, which is a superficial relation devoid of Notion, being partly related and partly unrelated, the contradiction necessarily results that at one time the unity of elements is established and at another, their separation: the unity is not the universal unity in which they are moments, being even in their diversity one, and in their unity different, for these two moments, unity and diversity, fall asunder, and union and separation are quite indeterminate relationships (315).

In contrast, for Hegel, things never "fall asunder" in their diversity or separation because they are internally related. The moments of the whole do not appear in diversity at one moment in time and place, and then come back together again. Nor are they merely combined, as in a mechanical synthesis, which seems to be the case with Empedocles's theory of combination. Treating combination and separation in this mechanical manner is the result of overlooking the "universal unity" of the elements. This unity is made possible with the universal Notion. Thus, this problem pertaining to the unity of elements stems from the absence of the simple, universal essence in Empedocles's philosophy. As quoted by Sturz, Empedocles says "'There is no such thing as a Nature, only a combination and separation of what is combined; it is merely called Nature by men.'" It is clear from the context of Hegel's discussion here that by "Nature" is meant *essence*, and not the world out there. Hegel thus interprets Empedocles as saying,

> that which constitutes anything, as being its elements or parts, is not as yet called its nature [essence], but only its determinate unity. For example, the nature [essence] of an animal is its constant and real determinateness, its kind, its universality, which is simple. But Empedocles

does away with nature [essence] in this sense, for everything, according to him, is the combination of simple elements, and thus not in itself the universal, simple and true: this is not what is signified by us when we speak of nature [essence] (ibid.).

When Hegel speaks of essence elsewhere, he says "there is something that abides in things, and this is, in the first instance, their essence."[25] "Because that which is implicit [the simple universal, essence] comes into existence, it certainly passes into change, yet it remains one and the same, for the whole process is dominated by it" (22).

Hegel proceeds to tell us that essence "moves in accordance with its own end . . ." What it becomes is thus implicitly present within it. Since Empedocles treats the four elements as mere existents, he finds "no process established in them." Their motion is merely an external movement, and not the unfolding and becoming of what is implicit in them. There is no necessity in, say, water to become a particular combination, or determination. Moreover, because the "simple and true" (essence) is not considered, the elements involved in the process become "only vanishing moments, and not [also] existent in themselves." Without the implicit and permanent essence, the elements cannot "constitute themselves into a unity; for in the one their subsistence, or their implicit existence would be destroyed." Hegel, somewhat confusingly adds to this that "because Empedocles says that things subsist from these elements, he immediately establishes their unity" (315–16). To be consistent with the preceding, "immediately" here seems to mean *hastily*. Better yet, it means the absence of mediation the essence undergoes in becoming a unity of the manifold.

Hegel concludes the section on Empedocles with five points of criticism. These critical points are taken from Aristotle, and are reconsidered through Hegel's own views. First, Aristotle finds in Empedocles's principles of Love and Strife the bases of the universal principles governing all that is good and bad, or evil. With this, "Aristotle shows the trace of universality present here." The universal Aristotle is looking for is necessarily "the Notion, or the thought which is present in and for itself." Hegel says such a principle is found in Anaxagoras for the first time, and thus is missing in Empedocles. The principle of the good, properly understood, explains the "why" of the process. This is because the good is an "end in and for itself," meaning that its telos is implicit within itself,

---

25. Hegel, *The Encyclopaedia Logic*, 176.

and that the process takes place "on its own account," and that "all else *is*" (italics added) in and through it. In this way, "the end has the determination of activity, the bringing forth of itself, so that it, as end to itself, is the Idea, the Notion that makes itself objective and, in its objectivity, is identical with itself." This Notion as an end in and for itself, and, consequently, process as the objective activity of the Idea is not found either in Empedocles or in Heraclitus, says Hegel (316–17).

Second, Aristotle also finds fault with the way Empedocles utilizes the "'two universal principles of Friendship and Strife, as of union and separation.'" With him, "'friendship [also] frequently divides and strife unites.'" This is the opposite of the intended power of these principles for the former is also meant to unite and the latter to divide. When the parts of the whole ("'all'") fall "'asunder through strife . . . ,'" all four elements are also united into one. This is to say, the separation process brings each one of the elements back into unity with itself, whereas in combination they were in unity as an admixture of four elements. Likewise, "'. . . when everything through friendship goes back into one, it is necessary that the parts of each element undergo separation again.'" In other words, in combining the four elements into One, which makes the One a "manifold" of four elements, what we have, adds Hegel, is "a diverse relation of the four diversities, and thus the going together is likewise a separation." Empedocles does not recognize this contradiction. For Hegel, this is actually "the case generally with all determinateness, that it must in itself be the opposite, and must manifest itself as such. The remark that, speaking generally, there is no union without separation, no separation without union, is a profound one; identity and non-identity are thought-determinations of this kind which cannot be separated." Hegel does not make it very clear as to who makes this "profound" remark, though it seems that he has Aristotle in mind. All the same, Hegel makes this remark his own. I think Empedocles's problem boils down to this: "'he did not assert that the principle of motion is one, but that it is different and opposed . . .'" (317). In other words, he asserted two principles of motion, combination and separation. We can say in certain terms that in Hegel's dialectic the motion is one, and it simultaneously contains within itself the contradiction of combination and separation. Motion separates and unites at the same time, and this contradiction is a cardinal rule in Hegel's dialectic.

Third, Empedocles does not seem to speak of the four elements as "equivalents in juxtaposition," but as two, since fire is put by itself, apart from the other three (water, earth, air). This point does not go very far in his hands, except that Hegel says, "What would be most interesting is the determination of their relationship." The fourth point of criticism is also very brief: "In what deals with the relationship of the two ideal moments, friendship and strife, and of the four real [material] elements, there is . . . nothing rational, for Empedocles . . . did not properly separate, but coordinated" the ideal with the material. Thus, "we often see them in proximity and counted as having equal value; but it is self-evident that Empedocles also separated these two sides, the real and the ideal, and expressed thought as their relation." This point is also suggested in Hegel's argument above that there is "nothing rational" in the separation and combination proposed by Empedocles. Rational thought (Reason) for Hegel is concrete, and thus finds itself as the ideal within the real (318). As he puts it elsewhere, "Reason . . . is *consciously* aware of itself as its own world, and of the world as itself . . ." This makes Reason the ". . . essence that is *in* and *for itself*, and which at the same time actual as consciousness and aware of itself . . ."[26] It is this rational essence and its awareness of itself that seems to be missing in Empedocles.

Fifth, "Aristotle says with justice that 'Empedocles contradicts both himself and appearances.'" This is because he maintains, on the one hand, that "'none of the elements springs out of the other.'" Instead, "all else comes from" the combination of four elements. On the other hand, "'he makes them into a whole through friendship, and again destroys this unity through strife. Thus through particular differences and qualities, the combined object becomes,'" through separation, once again "'water, . . . fire, &c. Now if the particular differences are taken away (and they can be taken away since they have arisen), it is evident that water arises from earth, and the reverse. The All was not yet fire, earth, water, and air, when these were still one, so that it is not clear whether he made the one or the many to be, properly speaking, real existence.'" It follows that, as Hegel contemplates, "Because the elements become one, their special character, that through which water is water, is nothing in itself, that is, they are passing into something different; but this, contradicts the statement that they are the absolute elements, or that they are implicit. He considers actual things as an intermingling of elements, but in regard to their first origin, he thinks that everything springs from one through friendship and strife." On the basis of this last point, Hegel issues a general complaint: "This customary absence of thought is in the nature of synthetic conceptions; it now upholds unity, then multiplicity, and does not bring both thoughts together as sublated,

---

26. Hegel, *The Phenomenology of Mind*, 251 (§ 438).

one is also not one" (318–19). Multiplicity, in other words, is the sublated One, and this is precisely what is meant by the Hegelian notion of the unity of opposites.

The problem is that Empedocles never held such a notion of the One out of which all else proceeds in the first place. Indeed, properly speaking, he did not have a theory of the One at all. Consequently, he does not assert that each of the elements emerge out of one another, or out of the One, in which they are implicitly present. His view was akin to the Atomist view of generation, or combination, which simply assumes that parts coalesce and separate, and nothing more.

CHAPTER 5

First Greek Period, First Division - Part III: Anaxagoras

1. Introduction

According to Michelet, who was present at Hegel's lectures, the latter "always connected the Atomists with the Eleatics and Heraclitus, and took Empedocles ... as the forerunner of Anaxagoras" (319n1). While Empedocles was possibly of the same age as Leucippus and was older than Democritus, all three were born after Anaxagoras. Thus, Empedocles is seen by Hegel as the forerunner of Anaxagoras in the philosophical and not chronological sense. Hegel thought Anaxagoras presented the most advanced philosophical principle yet. For this reason, he placed Anaxagoras at the end of the first leg of the tripartite first Greek period in his lectures.

Anaxagoras's principle is *nous*. Hegel refers to Anaxagoras's *nous* as "Mind," "Thought," "Reason," and "Understanding." He says that before Anaxagoras, "we have had Being, Becoming, the One, as principles." Even though these categories "are universal thoughts," their "content" is still "... taken from what is sensuous, and they are thoughts in some sort of a determination." With Anaxagoras, on the other hand, "it is the Universal, Thought itself, in and for itself, without opposition, all embracing, which is the substance or the principle." Anaxagoras thus opens up a "quite new ground" in the development of philosophy. On the basis of this new ground, the first period of philosophy "concludes" and "a fresh one begins" (319–20).

While this summary highlights the importance of Anaxagoras in the history of philosophy, as Hegel saw it, it also offers some complications. Basically, Hegel's interpretation of Anaxagoras's *nous* is confusing. Hegel says here that the *nous* of Anaxagoras is "in and for itself." This suggests a developed form of the principle which one finds only in Hegel. Relatedly, Anaxagoras's *nous* is also said to be "the substance or the principle" of the universe. Equating *nous* with the substance of the universe suggests that the essential origin of the universe is *nous*, and that *nous* is also the essence of the universe. This is not exactly the case in Anaxagoras's own thinking. A similar complication emerges from Aristotle's remarks, which Hegel quotes in this context. Anaxagoras's *nous*, says the former, "'lives in nature,'" or "'is the origin of the world and of all order'" (320). Living in nature, and causing it to move, is not necessarily the same as being the "origin" of nature. The "origin" view suggests that everything originates out of *nous*, which further suggests that *nous* is the simple essence of the world it creates. Again, this is not the case with Anaxagoras's own thinking. Because of this complication, Hegel at times misleadingly suggests that nature is the inherent *end* of *nous* for Anaxagoras.

2. The Cosmogony of Anaxagoras

Confusing statements regarding Anaxagoras's principle are not entirely due to Hegel's misinterpretation of him. In what is known as Fragment 11, Anaxagoras says that "in everything there is a portion of everything except thought," and adds, rather confusingly, that "in some things thought too is present." In Fragment 12, he says, "other things share a portion of everything, but thought is something limitless and independent, and it has been mixed with no thing."[1] It is clear that he holds *nous* to be pure and unmixed. However, it is unclear whether or not *nous* penetrates some things in Nature. Consequently, his philosophy appears to be dualistic. What also emerges from these fragments is that *nous*, due to its purity, does not entail Nature within itself as its teleological end.

According to Anaxagoras, *nous* rules the universe. The principal role of *nous* in ruling the universe is, like Empedocles's two principles (Love and Strife), one of mixing and dissociating the "existing things," that is, the existing elemental units in Nature (Fragment 17). These elements are present in "seeds." The term *seed* is suggestive of potentiality, since seeds are said to contain everything. However, these seeds, in which everything is supposed to be contained, are devoid of inherent activity. For this reason, they merely constitute the material cause of the universe as Nature. Their potentiality is a passive one, and requires the intervention of *nous* from without.

Unlike Empedocles, who has two forces, Love and Strife, which set the elements in motion, Anaxagoras contemplates only one such force, which is *nous*. The functions of this force are clearly indicated in Fragments 13 and 14. In the former he says: ". . . when thought began to move things, things were separating off from everything which was being moved, and everything which thought moved was

---

1. All of the fragments from Anaxagoras, quoted or cited below, come from Barnes, *Early Greek Philosophy*, 185–98.

dissociated"; and, in the latter, "Thought had power over whatever exists and now is where all the other things also are—in the surrounding mass and in what has come together and in what has separated off." It follows that *nous* actually resides in the universe which it rules, though in proximity to the mass of compound things. This basically describes Anaxagoras's cosmogony.

As Aristotle, via Hegel, further explains it,

> "Anaxagoras sets forth" (in respect of the material) "infinitely many principles, for he maintained that, like water and fire in Empedocles' system, nearly all that is formed of like parts only arises from union and passes away through separation . . ." That is, the existent, the individual matter such as bones, metal, flesh, &c., in itself consists of parts like itself—flesh of small particles of flesh, gold of small gold particles, &c. Thus he said at the beginning of his work, "All has been alike." (i.e. unseparated as in a chaos), "and has rested for an infinitude of time; then came the *nous*, and it brought in movement, separated and brought order into the separated creation, in that it united the like" (334–35).

In the view of the Atomists and Empedocles, matter is "the absolute . . . objective existence." This existence, first "separate only in form," is further "determined" in such a way that simple elements-atoms become "existing things" in "their syntheses and combinations." In contrast, as Aristotle adds, "'Anaxagoras maintains what are of like parts such as flesh, bones, or the like to be simple materials; such things as water and fire, on the contrary, are a mixture of the original elements. For any one of these four consists of the infinite admixture of all invisible existing things of like parts, which hence come forth from these [four]." Anaxagoras thus adopts the Eleatic principle that "'the like only comes out of the like; there is no transition into the opposite, no union of opposites possible,'" whereas with Empedocles it is precisely the unity of (four) opposite, unlike elements, each of which Anaxagoras treats as an "infinite admixture," which makes the existing things possible (335). It follows that, to Anaxagoras, concludes Hegel, "all change is . . . only a separation and union of the like." Hence, Anaxagoras's process of formation involves the combination of homogenous substances. Such a process is called *homoeomeries*. For this reason, the dialectic of formation in Anaxagoras does not reflect "true change," since "change as true change would be a Becoming out of the negative of itself" (336).

The process of Nature-formation, as described by Anaxagoras, is caused by *nous*. In this sense, *nous* acts like a cosmic force. However, *nous* also comes into play as human cognition. According to Anaxagoras, the seeds are too tiny to be sensed. Their sense perception becomes possible after they are forced into becoming existent things through separation and association of the parts that are alike. But he tells us in Fragment 21 that the truth cannot be ascertained through sense-perception. Only reason (*nous*) is capable of grasping the truth. The details of how this cognitive process comes about are not given. For this reason, whether or not thought is prior to sensation is unclear, as is the relationship of human thought to the cosmic *nous*. This ambiguity is also present in Hegel's treatment of Anaxagoras. As we will see later, Hegel switches back and forth between three different, albeit related, meanings of *nous*, including the *nous* in Nature (laws of Nature), *nous* as human thought, and *nous* as a God-like cosmic force.

Moreover, Anaxagoras distinguishes the animate existents from the inanimate ones. The former are fitted with a soul, and (some) humans are distinguished from other living beings in that they also have reason (Fragment 4). In this sense, *nous* is also treated as an eternal soul, residing in the body of animate beings. While the material body is transient, the soul lives on, undying. But, as Aristotle notes, what Anaxagoras says about the relationship of *nous* and the soul is "obscure." "Anaxagoras . . . declares the moving cause of things to be soul." In "many places he tells us that the cause of beauty and order is mind, elsewhere that it is soul; it is found, he says, in all animals, great and small, high and low, but mind (in the sense of intelligence) appears not to belong alike to all animals, and indeed not even to all human beings."[2] While the relationship of *nous* to *soul* is unclear, Anaxagoras seems to accept that *nous* as rationality resides only in some human beings. This view is also found in Plato and Aristotle. The latter, after all, argued that some individuals are intended by nature to function as slaves, as "animate tools."[3]

The more relevant point for our purposes is that *nous* as human intelligence is distinct from the *nous* as cosmic force. In Anaxagoras,

---

2. Aristotle, *Politics*, trans. C. D. C. Reeve (Indianapolis: Hackett, 1998), 6 (1253b.25–30).
3. "De Anima," Aristotle, I, 2. The Internet Classics Archive, MIT, accessed January 22, 2013, http://classics.mit.edu/Aristotle/soul.1.i.html. See also Hegel (329–30).

the two senses of *nous* are possibly related, though their relationship remains unclear. Indeed, whether or not the cosmic *nous* is intelligence is not indicated at all. As we will see later, Hegel insists, perhaps rightly, that Anaxagoras's (cosmic) *nous* is not conscious, intelligent thought. From the Hegelian point of view, what is clearly missing in Anaxagoras is *nous* within Nature. For this reason, Hegel thinks Anaxagoras, and ancient Greeks in general, overlook the fact that there is reason, albeit an unconscious one, within Nature.

Even though the complications mentioned above are present in Anaxagoras's writings, he does not seem to suggest anything like what Hegel attributes to him in the following sentence: "the logical principle of Anaxagoras was that he recognized the *nous* as the simple, absolute essence of the world." According to Hegel, "The simplicity of the *nous* is not a [determinate] Being but a universality which is distinguished from itself, though in such a way that the distinction is immediately sublated and the identity is set forth for itself. This universal for itself, sundered, exists in purity only as thought; it exists also in nature as objective existence, but in that case no longer purely for itself, but as having particularity as an immediate in it . . ." In a nutshell, what Hegel describes here is the dialectic of the "pure," abstract Notion, the simple essence, which realizes "itself into a system, organized as a universe." In this sense, *nous* transitions from *in-itself* to *in-and-for-itself*. However, by the end of the paragraph, Hegel suggests that this simple essence, as the Notion in-itself, which becomes objective and *for-itself*, is "certainly not found with the ancients" (329). Thus, Hegel's above assertion that Anaxagoras "recognized the *nous* as the simple, absolute essence of the world" falls apart. Hegel gradually moves away from this assertion and treats Anaxagoras's *nous* differently.

In "Thales and Heraclitus," for instance, everything emerges out of the One, which is both the "possibility" and "actuality" of all that exists. In contrast, Anaxagoras argues that "concrete things arise through the severance of [the] infinitely many principles . . . ," which is also a sorting process of the like from the unlike. Thus, the formation of the concrete things is the coming together of the likes "since like finds like." For this reason, "The activity of the *nous*, as the sundering of the like out of the chaos and the putting together of the like, as also the setting at liberty again of this like, is certainly simple and relative to itself, but purely formal and thus for itself content-less" (336–37). Because of the reduction of *nous* to mere content-less formality, and its activity to mere "sundering," "in objective existence, or in matter, universality and thought abandon Anaxagoras . . ." What Hegel means by this statement is simply that Anaxagoras fails to see *nous* in objective, material existence, and, by extension, his *nous* is not truly universal. His *nous*, then, "is only what binds and separates, what divides and arranges" (338–39). As we will see later, this function of *nous* is similar to the religious saying that *Providence rules the world*. For this reason, Anaxagoras's *nous*, defined as "the soul of the world and the organic system of the whole," remains "a mere word" because *nous* is taken to be a content-less external force that rules the world from without (339–40).

As Hegel further explains, "Thought moves on account of something: the end is the first simple which makes itself result; this principle with the ancients grasped as good and evil, i.e. end as positive and negative. This determination is a very important one, but with Anaxagoras it was not fully worked out." Because the principles of the ancients are "material," they cannot fully account for causality. Agreeably quoting Aristotle, Hegel notes that such material principles "'are not sufficient to beget the nature [essence] of things.'" Thus, the ancients "'abandon such matters [of causality] to hazard and to chance'" (329–31). Consequently, in Anaxagoras's thought, too, "we find nothing further than the activity determining from out of itself, which sets up a limit or measure; further than the determination of measure, development does not go. Anaxagoras gives us no more concrete definition of the *nous* . . . ; we thus have nothing more than the abstract determination of the concrete in itself [*by-itself*]" (333).

In short, Anaxagoras presents an inadequate view of the "going forth of the *nous* into further determinations." Instead, "this universal [nous] is confronted by Being." The latter is taken to mean mere "matter," or "the manifold generally." Consequently, Anaxagoras treats *being* (Nature) as material "potentiality," and *nous* "as actuality." However, says Hegel, "the universal [*nous*], as the self-moving, may rather be called the actual in itself . . . ," if "the Good or the end is also determined as [the] potentiality" of *nous*. In other words, *nous* should be viewed as the active potentiality, or implicit actuality, and the material, manifold world as the particularization and determination of what is implicitly entailed in *nous* as its end (333–34). Anaxagoras does not go this far.

3. The Good and Causality

"Aristotle says of Anaxagoras . . . that he appeared as a sober man among the drunken."[4] This statement from *The Philosophy of History* is repeated almost verbatim in *Lectures* (319). What is meant by it is that, for the first time, philosophy becomes aware of the rationality in nature. Its motion and existence is no longer treated as accidental, or without rational purpose. Hegel adds that "Socrates adopted [this] doctrine from Anaxagoras, and it forthwith became the ruling idea in Philosophy—except in the school of Epicurus, who ascribed all events to chance."[5] This comment further implies that, in Hegel's words, in Anaxagoras's *nous* "we have the end or the Good" (332).

In describing Hegel's interpretation of them, Michelet points out that Empedocles "swayed to and fro between the One . . . and the Many . . . , without . . . adhering to either of these one-sided determinations . . ." In this ambiguity, Empedocles "opened a way for the Anaxagorean conception of end." As mentioned in the previous chapter, the *end* and the Good are related. The idea behind this relation is that the "manifold of phenomena" in nature is implicit in the One, and thus constitutes its end, or teleological purpose. Said reversely, the One, as *nous*, is seen as the "immanent source" of the many (n319). However, Michelet's Hegel inspired point here is inaccurate. More importantly, Hegel himself wavers on this issue and makes it difficult for us to follow his treatment of Anaxagoras. Ultimately, Hegel accepts the view that the idea of the end is absent in Anaxagoras. For this reason, he treats the nous in Anaxagoras's philosophy merely as a formal, separate force that rules the world from without.

Unlike what Hegel suggests above, Socrates did not exactly "adopt" the doctrine of end or Good from Anaxagoras. Indeed, he thought that Anaxagoras failed altogether to grasp the end, or the Good, implied in the proposition that reason rules the world. Socrates's dismay with Anaxagoras's failure is exhibited in Plato's *Phaedo*, where Plato makes Socrates say, and Hegel himself quotes,

> "I was delighted with the sentiment and hoped I had found a teacher who would show me Nature in harmony with Reason, who would demonstrate in each particular phenomenon its specific aim, and in the

---

4. Hegel, *The Philosophy of History*, 12.
5. Ibid.

whole, the grand object of the Universe. I would not have surrendered this hope for a great deal. But how very much was I disappointed, when, having zealously applied myself to the writings of Anaxagoras, I found that he adduces only external causes . . ."

The "defect" Socrates finds in "Anaxagoras's doctrine does not concern the principle itself," says Hegel. That is, both Socrates and Anaxagoras accept the principle that reason rules the world. Hegel adds that when reason rules the world, "each particular phenomenon" in the world is given "its specific aim," which must be the Good.[6] However, Socrates's point is not that Anaxagoras misapplied the principle of the Good, as Hegel seems to assume here. Rather, it is that he did not consider it at all. Aristotle, too, states that Anaxagoras makes *nous deus ex machine* "for the production of universe."[7] This is consistent with Socrates's saying, as quoted above, that Anaxagoras "adduces only external causes."

In the same work, that is, Plato's *Phaedo*, Socrates gives additional explanation regarding Anaxagoras's shortcomings:

> It seemed to me that [Anaxagoras] was just about as inconsistent as if some were to say, "The cause of everything that Socrates does is mind"—and then, in trying to account for my several actions, said first that "the reason why I am lying here now [in prison awaiting his execution] is that my body is composed of bones and sinews, and that the bones are rigid and separated at the joints, but the sinews are capable of contraction and relaxation, and form an envelope for the bones with the help of the flesh and skin, the latter holding all together, and since the bones move freely in their joints the sinews by relaxing and contracting enable me somehow to bend my limbs, and that is the cause of my sitting here in a bent position." Or again, if he tried to account in the same way for my conversing with you, adducing causes such as sound and air and hearing and a thousand others, and never troubled to mention the real reasons, which are that since Athens has thought it better to condemn me, therefore I for my part have thought it better to sit here, and more right to stay and

---

6. Ibid.
7. Aristotle, *Metaphysics*, 231 (985b.18–25).

submit to whatever penalty she orders. Because, by dog, I fancy that these sinews and bones would have been in the neighborhood of Megara or Boeotia long ago—impelled by a conviction of what is best!—if I did not think that it was more right and honorable to submit to whatever penalty my country orders rather than take to my heels and run away.

In the above passage, Socrates distinguishes between different kinds of causality. These different types of causality are expressed more succinctly as follows: First, "If it were said that without such bones and sinews and all the rest of them I should not be able to do what I think is right, it would be true." However, and second, "But to say that it is [solely] because of them that I do what I am doing, and not through choice of what is best—although my actions are controlled by mind—would be a very lax and inaccurate form of expression." Thus, we should "distinguish between the cause of a thing and the condition without which it could not be a cause!"[8] As Hegel puts it, Socrates, "here correctly places the two kinds of reason and cause in opposition to one another—the cause proceeding from ends, and the inferior, subject, and merely external causes of chemistry, mechanism, &c.—in order to show the discrepancy between them, as here exemplified in the case of a man [i.e., Socrates] with consciousness." This statement also affirms that Hegel himself subscribes to these two kinds of causality, one of which ("cause proceeding from ends") is of superior nature. Hegel now says, Anaxagoras attempts to define an end within *nous*, "but he immediately lets this go again and proceeds to quite external causes" (341–42).

What is of special interest here is Hegel's statement that there are "two kinds of reason and cause." What Hegel means to say is that, in his view, there is also reason in nature, which both Anaxagoras and Socrates fail to see. He says of the latter that his criticism of Anaxagoras, even though "a good example for showing that we miss the end in such modes of explanation," is also shortsighted. This is "because [the end] is taken from the kingdom of the self-conscious will" alone. It is true that "Anaxagoras made no application of his *nous* to reality." However, "the positive element in the conclusion of Socrates seems to [also] desire causes for nature which do not appear to be in it, but which fall outside of it in consciousness." This is to

---

8. Plato, "Phaedo," in *Plato: The Collected Dialogues, Including the Letters*, eds. Edith Hamilton and Huntington Cairns (Princeton: Princeton University Press, 1961), 79–81 (97c-99d).

say, the end, "or purposive action, is mainly an act of consciousness and not of nature. But in so far as ends become posited in nature, the end, as end, on the other hand, falls outside of it in our judgment only; as such it is not in nature itself, for in it there are only what we call natural causes." Accordingly, "we distinguish, for instance, in Socrates the end and ground of his action as consciousness, and the causes of his actual action: and the latter we would undoubtedly seek in his bones, muscles, nerves, &c. Since we banish the consideration of nature in relation to ends—as present in our thought and not existent in nature" (343).

Hegel's criticism above is applicable to Anaxagoras more than Socrates. Anaxagoras did not grasp the "immanent" causes in nature, nor did he adequately explain how reason rules the world from without. By "immanent" causes, as we will see below, Hegel has in mind the inherent laws of nature, which he identifies with *nous*.

4. How Mind Rules the World

Hegel agrees in principle that *nous* rules the world. The cosmic *nous*, which he often calls God, Reason, and Spirit/Mind, splits itself into two distinctive realms of activity. In this way, *nous* comes to rule the spiritual and natural worlds in distinctive, yet related, ways. Because for Hegel *nous* by its nature is always one, its bifurcated showings are not to be treated as two externally related forms of *nous*. Indeed, even in the history of philosophy, which falls under the spiritual world, the cosmic *nous* manifests itself in a diversified way, as many finite minds possessed by as many philosophers. However, as we have seen in Chapter 1, these finite minds, or spirits, are one with the cosmic Mind. They are both its particular manifestations and bearers. Likewise, the *nous* in Nature is a moment of the cosmic *nous* as much as Nature is a bearer of the latter.

According to Hegel, "the nature is not formed from without as men make a table . . . *Nous* is thus not [merely] a thinking existence from without, which regulates the world." *Nous* is also within nature, ruling it from within by establishing its laws of motion. "The laws of nature are themselves nature's immanent essence," and these laws correspond to *nous* because they entail rationality. Thinking of *nous* as "an individual," that is, as merely "a unit from without," is to adopt the view of "ordinary conception," and leads to the "dualism" of thought and Nature, or Mind and *being* (331–32). Thus, the main "shortcoming" of Anaxagoras lies in the fact that he does not deduce Nature "from that principle" of *nous*. Each side, Nature and *nous*, "remains in fact a mere abstraction," an isolated realm onto itself. Nature thus is not treated as the "development" of *nous*, or as "an organization produced" by its internal needs.[9]

As Hegel tells us in *Philosophy of Mind*, "From our point of view mind has for its presupposition Nature, of which it is the truth, and for that reason its *absolute prius*." To this, he adds, "External nature . . . , like mind, is rational, divine, a representation of the Idea." Here, we see three forms of *nous* being related to each other. The human mind and external nature are both rational, and are representations of the Idea. Thus,

> philosophical thinking knows that Nature is idealized not merely by us . . . , but that the eternal Idea immanent in Nature or, what is the same thing, the essence of mind itself at work within Nature brings about the idealization, the triumph over the asunderness [of Nature] . . . The procession of mind or spirit from Nature must not be understood as if Nature were the absolutely immediate and the *prius*, and the original positing agent, mind, on the contrary, were only something posited by Nature; rather is it Nature which is posited by mind, and the latter is the absolute *prius* [of nature] . . . The transition from Nature to mind is not a transition to an out-and-out Other, but is only a coming-to-itself of mind out of its self-externality in Nature.[10]

Consequently, adds Hegel, Mind

> knows that it posits being itself, that it is itself the creator of its Other, of Nature and finite mind, so that this Other loses all semblance of independence in the face of [cosmic] mind, ceases altogether to be a limitation for mind and appears only as a means whereby mind attains to absolute being-for-itself, to the absolute unity of what it is in itself and what it is for itself, of its Notion and its actuality. The highest definition of the Absolute is that it is not merely mind in general but that it is mind which is absolutely manifest

---

9. Hegel, *The Philosophy of History*, 12.
10. Hegel, *Hegel's Philosophy of Mind: Part*, 8–15, § 381, and *zusatze*.

to itself, self-conscious, infinitely creative [and creating] mind.[11]

In the above passage, Hegel first distinguishes the cosmic mind, which he also calls "God," from the *nous* in Nature and from the finite mind of the individual. In the latter part, he subsumes the human mind under the absolute Mind. The latter unity is possible when human consciousness recognizes the Absolute Mind within itself, and thus becomes infinite Mind, *in-and-for-itself*.

What is somewhat confusing is Hegel's claim that Mind "is the creator of its Other," that is "of Nature and finite mind." By "the creator," Hegel clearly means God. This meaning becomes all the more clear when Hegel adds that, in modern times, it was Spinoza who grasped God as the substance, or "absolute foundation of everything." In this, the unity of thought and *being* resurfaces in philosophy. But, the "defect of Spinozism consists . . . just in this, that in it substance does not progress to its immanent development, the manifold [in Nature simply] is added to substance in an external manner." Retuning to Anaxagoras, "the same unity of thought and being is contained in the *nous* of Anaxagoras; but this *nous* fails even more than Spinoza's substance to achieve its development."[12]

In his *Lectures on the Philosophy of Religion*, Hegel explains this triadic dialectic of creation in some detail. The first logical stage is "the absolute, eternal Idea," which is "in its essential existence, in and for itself, God in His eternity before the creation of the world, and outside of the world." The second logical stage is the creation of the world. What is "created" is "this otherness or other-Being." By this expression, Hegel means that the world is the "other" of the Absolute Idea, which, in turn, means that the world is not a totally separate entity, which is indifferent to the Absolute Idea, or God. This "other" further "divides within itself into two sides, physical Nature and finite Spirit." The third stage consist of the reconciliation process whereby the world, which appears separated and alienated from God, is brought back by the Absolute Spirit "into harmony with itself." The "three forms indicated here are: [1] eternal Being in and with itself, the form of Universality; [2] the form of manifestation or appearance, that of Particularization, Being for another; [3] the form

---

11. Ibid., 19, or § 384, and *zusatze*.
12. Ibid., 31, or § 389, and *zusatze*

of the return from appearance [and particularization] into itself, [which is] absolute Singleness or individuality."[13]

The point I wish to emphasize here is that the world is split into "two sides," each of which entails the Idea, and that the Idea entailed in these two sides emanates from the cosmic Idea, or God. Thus, we have three forms of the Idea, though they are ultimately in harmony, of one piece, and reemerge at the end of the dialectical process of differentiation and particularization in the form of "absolute Singleness." On the one hand, this process of reemerging is both historical (in the world of finite spirit), and natural (in Nature.) On the other hand, it is also an intellectual process of Spirit becoming conscious of itself and its deeds in these two worlds. What is lacking in Anaxagoras, and even such modern thinkers as Schelling to some extent, says Hegel, is this explicit conscious thought. Consequently, Anaxagoras's *nous* is this "unconscious active rationality," or "the ruling of the world" by *nous* unconsciously.[14] Repeating the same claim in *Lectures on the History of Philosophy*, Hegel says, in Anaxagoras, "Thought as pure, free process in itself, is the self-determining universal, and is not distinguished from conscious thought" (320). This distinction is important in the sense that conscious thought as *nous*, according to Hegel, knows itself, "as the truly actual." Thus, the comprehending "mind" is not merely given by the sensuous world, nor is it fully separated from it. Instead, such a mind "is for itself" and "grasps itself" in the sensuous object it thinks. In other words, thought does not think something completely external to itself when it thinks of an object, or the laws of Nature. Rather, it confronts "the 'other' of itself as a negation [sublation] of consciousness" (327). The ancient Greeks, including Anaxagoras, were not cognizant of this dialectic.

The dialectic described here, which requires consciousness to find itself in the operations of the world, also dictates the cognition that *nous* is the simple essence, that is, the substance of the world. Hegel also calls this substance the "ideality" of nature. Epicurus fails to grasp this, says Hegel. What he critically says of Epicurus's philosophy in this regard is also applicable to Anaxagoras: God, or *nous*, is "not beside the things, in the process, like the God of Epicurus, but actually in the things." Hegel's point seems to agree

---

13. G. W. F. Hegel, *Lectures on the Philosophy of Religion,* Vol. 3, trans. Rev. E. B. Spiers and J. Burdon Sanderson (New York: The Humanities Press Inc., 1962), 1–2.
14. G. W. F. Hegel, *Lectures on the Philosophy of Religion,* Vol. 2, trans. Rev. E. B. Spiers and J. Burdon Sanderson (New York: The Humanities Press Inc., 1962), 1–2, 55.

with Pantheism. However, unlike Pantheism, Hegel holds that the things in Nature are not truly (independently) real. Their reality depends on their ideality. God is thus "the absolutely One Substance," the universality that permeates everything and posits its ideality therein in doing so. This dialectic is different than the Pantheistic notion that God is the combination of all things in the universe, "as allness or totality." In this Pantheistic view, God is seen as a mere combination of dispersed, independent things, just as much as the Atomists and Empedocles saw *being* as a combination of atoms and elements, as did Anaxagoras in his own way. The principle that God is the "absolutely One Substance," as suggested earlier, was first introduced by Spinoza. However, we now find out, Spinoza fails to realize that this substance is also the dialectical "subject," which actively and consciously posits itself in its other. It appears that this consciousness becomes possible with the spiritual development of "man," with the development in which the human individual acquires "personality." With this development, says Hegel, the finite "spirit enters into God."[15]

The above synopsis of Hegel's view describes how reason rules the world implicitly, and, once it becomes conscious thought, explicitly as well. Elsewhere, Hegel says that there are generally "two phases and points of view that concern the generally diffused conviction that Reason has ruled, and is still ruling in the world, and consequently in the world's history." The "Greek Anaxagoras was the first to enunciate the doctrine that *nous*, Understanding generally, or Reason, governs the world." However, his *nous* ". . . is not intelligence as self-conscious Reason—not a Spirit as such that is meant; and we must clearly distinguish these from each other." Spirit as such, we must note, has a self-actualizing, penetrative, and reflective power. It realizes and recognizes itself in and through Nature. To give an example to illustrate, "The movement of the solar system takes place according to unchangeable laws. These laws are Reason, implicit in the phenomena in question. But neither the sun nor the planets, which revolve around it according to these laws, can be said to have any consciousness of them."[16] The law of motion of planets is their inherent "reason," but it is only the self-conscious reason, or "Spirit as such," which is conscious of this law.

The question, then, becomes: What makes human reason able to understand the hidden *nous* in nature? Hegel's answer to this question is clear enough: "To him who looks upon the world rationally, the

---

15. Ibid., 55–56.
16. Hegel, *The Philosophy of History*, 11.

world in turn presents a rational aspect. The relation is mutual." Reason thus resides in the world and rules it through natural law(s). Reason is also in the mind of the thinking subject. We come to understand the natural world because (a) we are capable of reason, and (b) the world we seek to understand is itself rational. True, or philosophical, science is only possible when the mutuality of (a) and (b) is explicitly understood. This, Hegel calls "reflection," as in (an intelligent) light targeting its intelligible object, illuminating it, and returning to its source where the object is reflected as an image. Thus, the thinking subject also finds the object and its laws of motion within itself, and becomes aware of itself as a thinking, knowing subject. It is "indispensable," says Hegel, "that Reason should not sleep—that reflection should be in full play."[17]

The maxim "that Reason directs the World . . ." also applies to the science of "Universal History," which deals with "political affairs," and to "the *religious truth*." In religious truth, for instance, the principle demonstrates "that the world is not abandoned to chance and external contingent causes, but that a *Providence* controls it." Hegel says in this connection that "the truth," namely, that "a Providence (that of God) presides over the events of the World, consorts with the proposition in question; for *Divine* Providence is Wisdom, endowed with an infinite Power, which realizes its aim, viz., the absolute rational design of the World." "Reason," says Hegel, "is Thought conditioning itself with perfect freedom." But, stated merely as such, the maxim that reason, or Providence, rules the world is no more than a *belief*, and thus not the concrete truth. Therefore, "a contradiction" inevitably arises "between this belief and our principle," that is, Hegel's principle, "just as was the case in reference to the demand made by Socrates in the case of Anaxagoras's dictum [that reason rules the world]."[18]

The reason for this contradiction is that the religious belief stated above, as is also the case with Anaxagoras's dictum, is "indefinite." In other words, the principle that reason rules the world is "not followed out into definite application, or displayed in its bearing on the grand total," which is the "entire course of human history." In the case of Socrates, this demonstration is still limited and revolves around the consciousness and actions of the individual, finite spirits. In the case of Anaxagoras, we find neither the application of *nous* to individual action, nor to the origination and processes of nature, not to mention

---

17. Ibid.
18. Ibid.

the complete ignorance of the demonstration of the maxim in history.[19]

"In the conception that God [eternal *nous*], as wisdom, rules the world in accordance with an end, . . . the Good in the end gives content to itself, so that while it is active with this content, and after it has entered into externality, no other content comes forth than what was already present." What emerges as the product is precisely what went into it. Thus, the product is nothing but the concrete manifestation of the original *being* (332–33). This is demonstrated, according to Hegel, only at the end of history. The history of religion, societies, and philosophy demonstrates precisely this fact. At the end, what is cognized is this:

> Everything that from eternity has happened in heaven and earth . . . ; the life of God and all the deeds of time simply are the struggles for Mind to know itself, to make itself objective to itself, to find itself, be for itself, and finally unite itself to itself; it is alienated and divided, but only so as to be able thus to find itself and return to itself. Only in this manner does Mind attain its freedom, for that is free which is not connected with or dependent on another (22–23).

For Hegel, explaining how reason rules history and Nature concretely requires *demonstrating* the "'plan' of Providence" in what only appears to be contingent human or natural affairs. Yet, in various religious doctrines, "this very plan . . . is supposed to be concealed from our view: . . . It is deemed presumption, even to wish to recognize [this plan]." Hegel's target of criticism here is not simply various religious doctrines but also Kant, who declared the truth in the phenomenal world beyond the human understanding. As for Anaxagoras, his "ignorance . . . as to how intelligence reveals itself in actual existence, was [still] ingenuous" for his times. His ignorance consists in the fact that "he had not attained the power to apply his general principle to the concrete, so as to deduce the latter from the former." To his credit, however, Anaxagoras "did not take up a *hostile* position toward such an application. The common belief in Providence [on the other hand] *does*; at least it opposes the use of the principle on the large scale, and denies the possibility of discerning the plan of Providence."[20] Once again, Hegel claims that "discerning

---

19. Ibid.
20. Ibid., 13.

the plan of Providence" is possible only at the end of the realization of this cosmic plan. The history of philosophy, in its own but fundamental ways, is precisely the demonstration of this plan.

Hegel concludes his treatment of Anaxagoras in *Lectures* with a generous evaluation of the latter's philosophy. With Anaxagoras, and for the first time in the history of philosophy,

> we have the beginning of a more distinct development of the relationship of consciousness to Being, the development of the nature of knowledge as a knowledge of the true. The mind has gone forth to express real existence as Thought; and thus real existence as existent, is in consciousness as such . . . The mind has no longer to seek existence in something foreign, since it is in itself (349).

It is not necessary to reexamine to what extent we can actually attribute to Anaxagoras what Hegel attributes to him in this passage. The more important point is that Hegel thinks Anaxagoras, either directly or indirectly, has played a significant role in raising *nous* to its proper significance in the history of philosophy. The period coming after Anaxagoras makes *nous* as such the centerpiece of its philosophy.

CHAPTER 6

First Greek Period, Second Division - Part I: The Sophists

1. Introduction

In the second division of the first Greek period, we find the Sophists, Socrates, and the Socratics. "Here the self-determining thought is conceived of as present and concrete in me," that is, in the thinking individual. Hegel calls this "the principle of subjectivity," though in this period this principle also assumes the form of "infinite subjectivity, for thought first shows itself here only partly as abstract principle and partly as contingent subjectivity" (165). The grasping of *nous* subjectively means that the end, or the Good, in thought is determined by me. Grasping *nous* as "infinite subjectivity," or as "contingent subjectivity," means abolishing any sense of the universal in *nous*. It is only later, in the third division of the first Greek period, that Plato and Aristotle represent *nous* as "what is on the whole an objective way, as genus or Idea," even though Socrates already initiates this development in the second period. From this mode of thinking in the second period "arises an age of subjective reflection; i.e. there begins in this period . . . the principle of modern times," which is based on the thinking "I," or I as the active subject. Thus, thought also becomes "posited as subject" in this period. (350).

In this chapter, we examine Hegel's interpretation of the Sophists—Protagoras and Gorgias. Sophism has been associated with the pursuit of self-interest. The fact that they were known to charge fees helped galvanize this suggestion. Relatedly, in various dialogues of Plato, the relationship between Sophism and true philosophy is questioned, since Sophism is assumed to deny the possibility of any rational or moral absolute principle, which proper philosophy depends upon. This denial suggests that the Sophists were also the progenitors of skepticism. Hegel tries to cast aside this interpretation of the Sophists, and looks for the universal, philosophical basis of their teachings.

In introducing their thought, Hegel says that "the Notion [of the Sophists] . . . is the simple negative into which all determination, all that is existent and individual [particular] sinks." Thus, "Before the Notion nothing can exist, for it is simply the predicateless absolute to which everything is clearly a moment only; for it there is thus nothing

[else] . . . permanently fixed and sealed." This fluidity of all else in their relation to the Notion comes across also in Heraclitus's philosophy: "the constant change . . . , the movement, the causticity, which nothing can resist" is the Notion of Heraclitus. "Thus the Notion which finds itself, finds itself as the absolute power before which everything vanishes; and thereby all things, all existence, everything held to be secure, is now made fleeting" (352).

The Sophists thus do not have anything like the universal Notion of the previous philosophers. Their Notion is an open-ended negation, what Hegel calls the "simple negative," of all that is positively asserted. For this reason, the Sophists are "decried" from two different, but related angles: by "the healthy human understanding" and "morality." The former denounces the Sophists "on account of their theoretic teaching," which is assumed to be based on the meaningless saying that "nothing is." This theoretical teaching, it is said, translates into their amoral practice, in which they presumably "subvert all principles and laws." By "the healthy understanding," Hegel has in mind a kind of *unhealthy* reasoning. Briefly stated, this mode of understanding "possesses the modes of thought, maxims, and judgments of its time, the thought-determinations of which dominate it without its being conscious thereof." The "healthy" understanding thus takes what is given at any particular time, both in terms of moral maxims and scientific discoveries, as being eternally fixed. If this reasoning were to be transplanted before the discoveries of Copernicus, it would have denied, as the healthy understanding back then did, the fact that the earth revolves around the sun. Likewise, it would have found the presence of another continent, America, implausible before Columbus's voyage. For the same reason, "a republic" in India or China is nowadays considered to be "contrary to healthy reason" (379).

Hegel's criticism of the "healthy" understanding is actually a criticism of phenomenology, which finds the universal in what is necessarily fluid and transient, in sensuous, particular determinations (appearances). There is, then, a kind of unconscious hypocrisy involved in the criticism of the Sophists by "the healthy understanding" for it takes what is changing and vanishing to be universal, while accusing Sophism of doing away with the universal.

It is with the influence of Socrates and Plato that sophistry has, even today, become "a word of ill-repute." Consequently, "the word usually now signifies that, by false reasoning, some truth is either refuted and made dubious, or something false is proved and made plausible." Hegel says we should forget this "evil significance" attributed to the Sophists, and "consider further from the positive and properly speaking scientific side, what was the position of the Sophists in Greece." The "scientific side" of the Sophists emerges from their application of the "simple [negative] Notion as thought . . . to worldly objects generally." It also emerges from the penetration of "all human relations" by such thought. This Sophistical subjective thought, because it "is conscious of itself as the absolute and single reality, and, jealous of all else, exercises its power and rule in" this world, on worldly objects and human relations. The Sophist thought is thus "identical with itself," and "directs its negative powers towards the manifold determination of the theoretical and the practical, the truths of natural consciousness and the immediately recognized laws and principles." In this way, what seems to the ordinary conception as fixed and given "dissolves itself" in the Sophist thought. What remains "first and fixed" is the "particular subjectivity," which relates "everything to itself" (353–55). The particular subjectivity, then, becomes with Sophism the *nous* that rules the world, not by organizing it into a coherent whole, as it is with Anaxagoras, but by making it vanish. In short, "It appears that the Sophists were conscious of this reasoning . . . that everything could be proved." Consequently, the Sophists "knew that . . . nothing was secure because the power of thought treated everything dialectically" (369).

The dialectic of the Sophists, according to Hegel, remained merely negative for two fundamental reasons: "Because, on the one hand, the need of subjective freedom existed merely to give effect to that which man himself perceives and finds present in his reason (thus laws, religious ideas, only in so far as I recognize them through my thought), on the other hand, no fixed principle had so far been found in thought; thought was rather reasoning, and what remained indeterminate could thus only be fulfilled through self-will." In modern Europe, by contrast, culture has reached the heights of "presupposing a knowledge of the eternal nature of Spirit and of the absolute end, of the end of man, to be in a spiritual way actual and to posit himself in unity with the absolute spirit. Thus here there is a groundwork of a fixed spiritual principle which thus satisfies the needs of the subjective mind; and from this absolute principle all further relationships, duties, laws, &c., are established" (365–66).

In terms of cognizing the Absolute thought as Spirit, Socrates and Plato may be placed somewhere in between the Sophists and the modern times. The content of Socrates's thought was "the beautiful, good, true, and right, as the end and aim of the individual, while with the Sophists the content was not present as an ultimate end, so that all this was left to the individual will." While Socrates's philosophy too remains subjective, it is also objective subjectivity, since the content-end contained in it is universal. The Sophists lacked this universality, "and this is certainly their defect." Consequently, "in distinction to Plato" and Socrates, the Sophist reasoning makes "duty" rely on "external reasons through which right and wrong, utility and harmfulness, are distinguished." Thus, "that which has to be done [duty]," does not arise from "the Notion of the thing as determined in and for itself . . ." that is, from the Absolute Notion. In other words, the Sophists do not consider the universal essence of the conditions in determining the course of action, since they do not accept that the universal Notion is present in the conditions and the things in existence. In contrast, "Socrates and Plato wished to bring forward this Notion as opposed to the consideration of things from points of view and reasonings which are always merely particular and individual, and thus opposed to the [universal] Notion itself. The distinction in the two points of view is thus that cultured reasoning only belongs, in a general way, to the Sophists, while Socrates and Plato determined thought through a universal determination (the Platonic Idea), or something fixed, which mind finds eternally [within] itself" (366–67).

By "cultured reasoning," Hegel means "that what free thought is to attain must come out of itself and be personal conviction; it is then no longer [dogmatically] believed but investigated—in short, it is the so-called enlightenment of modern times." The truth, then, must be accepted by the rational individual on rational grounds, on the grounds that the individual discovers for himself-herself through free thought. This non-dogmatic dialectic is the positive contribution of the Sophists to philosophy, even if its "cultured reasoning" lacks the cognition of the Idea in its reasoning. With Sophism, thus,

> Thought seeks general principles [rules] by which it criticizes everything which is by us esteemed, and nothing has value to us which is not in conformity with these principles. Thus, thought undertakes to compare the positive content with itself, to dissolve the former concrete of belief; on one side to split the content up, and, on the other, to isolate these individualities, these particular points of view and aspects, and to secure them on their own account. These aspects, which are properly not independent, but only moments of a whole, when detached from it, relate themselves to themselves, and in this way assume the form of universality. Any one of them can thus be elevated to a reason, *i.e.* to a

universal determination, which is again applied to particular aspects.

For example, "A judge knows the various laws, i.e. the various legal points of view under which a thing is to be considered; these are already for him universal aspects through which he has a universal consciousness, and considers the matter in a universal way." Likewise, "A man of culture thus knows how to say something of everything, to find points of view in all," and relate all to the universal standpoint. In this way, thought, as such, comes to exercise authority. It is this ascendance of thought to prominence that makes Sophism a "culture in philosophy as much as in eloquence" (356–57). However, we must not rush to the conclusion that the universal standpoint in Sophism and in the mind of "a man of culture" is the Hegelian universal. There is some sarcasm involved in Hegel's usage of "culture" in this context, which assume that "a man of culture" may discuss things endlessly without leading anywhere.

2. Protagoras

Protagoras is mostly known for two of his surviving statements, which are quoted by Hegel. The first statement says: "'As to the gods, I am not able to say whether they are or not; for there is much which prevents this knowledge, both in the obscurity of the matter, and in the life of man which is so short.'" Notice that Protagoras does not explicitly deny the existence of gods. He simply presents an agnostic point of view. The second statement posits, perhaps more famously, that "'man is the measure of all things.'" According to Hegel, this second statement constitutes the "main point" of Protagoras's system (373).

In these statements, Hegel detects in Protagoras "a philosopher who reflected on fundamental determinations of an altogether universal kind." What this means, continues Hegel, is that Protagoras first grasps "thought as determined and as having content," and then finds "the determining and content-giving." The content-giving is the "universal determination," which "then becomes the standard by which everything is judged." Presumably, this universal determination is "man," as indicated in Protagoras's proposition that "man is the measure of all things" (ibid.). Hegel's attempt to demonstrate the presence of such a standard in Protagoras eventually fails.

According to Hegel, Protagoras's "assertion is in its real meaning a great truth, but at the same time it has a certain ambiguity." We will discover later that the "real meaning" of this assertion belongs to Socrates and Plato, and not Protagoras, even in Hegel's own account. The "ambiguity" Hegel detects in the assertion is this: The assertion may mean that "as man is the undetermined and many-sided, either he may in his individual particularity, as this contingent man, be the measure," or that "self-conscious reason in man, man in his rational nature and his universal substantiality, is the absolute measure." If, says Hegel, "the statement is taken in the former sense, all is self-seeking, all self-interest, the subject with his interests forms the central point; and if man has a rational side," in the second sense, "reason is still something subjective, it is 'he,'" the individual person who reasons subjectively. Hegel says that both possibilities are "just the wrong and perverted way of looking at things." It is on the basis of such misguided interpretations that the Sophists are reproached, namely, that "they put forward man in his contingent aims as determining; thus with them the interest of the subject in its particularity, and the interest of the same in its substantial reason are not distinguished" (373–74).

The evidence to controvert the above reproach, says Hegel, is to be found in Protagoras's other statements. However, as it turns out, the so-called evidence fast turns against Hegel's own interpretation. For instance, he quotes Protagoras as saying, "'Truth is a manifestation for consciousness. Nothing is in and for itself one, but everything has a relative truth only,' i.e. it is what it is but for another, which is man." Hegel admits that what is presented in this statement is the "relativity" of truth. Indeed, continues Hegel, the "insignificant examples" which he adduces to prove his point "show that in Protagoras' understanding what is determined is not grasped as the universal and identical with self." For example, Protagoras says, "'in a wind it may be that one person is cold and another is not; hence of this wind we cannot tell whether in itself it is cold or hot.'" It follows from Protagoras's statement that, as Hegel puts it, "Frost and heat are thus not anything which exist, but only are in their relation to a subject; were the wind cold in itself, it would always be so to the subject." Or again, Protagoras argues, "'if we have here six dice, and place by them four others, we should say of the former that there are more of them. But, again, if we put twelve by them we say that these first six are the fewer.'" It follows that, Hegel adds, "the more and the less," which others may take as universals, "is merely a relative determination; thus what is the object, is so in the idea present to consciousness only." It follows that, for Protagoras, the truth of the thing is relative. Clearly, Protagoras here rejects the Pythagorean view that one and the many, or more or less, have the same essence, or universal measure. Hegel admits as much when he finds in Plato this Pythagorean view in contrast to Protagoras: "Plato, on the contrary, considered one and many, not like the Sophists in their distinction, but as being one and the same." It follows that, for the Sophists, "what is said in defining anything never concerns the thing as in itself, but clearly only as being related to something else. Nothing is thus constituted in and for itself as it appears, but the truth is just this phenomenon to which our activity contributes." Hegel now says that Protagoras's approach is based on "double relativity," since he says "'Matter is a pure flux, it is not anything fixed and determined in itself, for it can be everything, and it is different to different ages and to the various conditions of waking and sleep, &c.'" (376–77). The double relativity referred to here is that both the thinking subject and the phenomenal object are relative. Hegel, in short, fails to find the universal Notion in Protagoras for the simple reason that the latter simply rejects it altogether.

For the purpose of understanding the history of philosophy, the links Hegel establishes between various philosophers and Protagoras prove more interesting. For instance, in contrast to Protagoras's double relativity, Kant has single relativity: "Kant separates himself from this standpoint only in that he places the relativity in the 'I,' and not in objective existence." In objective existence, there is "an unknown x," the unknowable universal. It is through our subjectivity that the objective world is perceived to be a diversity of contradictory determinations.

More simply put, according to Kant, basically, one cannot know anything without experience through the senses. However, knowledge we acquire through the senses is ultimately made sense of through the categories that are innate in our minds. It follows that we can only know things as they appear to us, and not as they are in existence. There is a gap between what appears to us and reality, and this gap indicates the dualism of consciousness and the real world. In Kant's view, adds Hegel,

> Even if there were an objective ground for our calling one thing cold and another warm, we could indeed say that they must have diversity in themselves; but warmth and cold first become what they are in our feeling [and not objectively]. Similarly it can only be in our conception that things are outside of us, etc. But if the experience is quite correctly called a "phenomenon," i.e. something relative, because it does not come to pass without the determinations of the activity of our senses,

nor without categories of thought, yet that one, all-pervading, universal, which permeates all experience, which to Heraclitus was necessity, has to be brought into consciousness [though as an unknown x] (377).

As it turns out, the universal, absolute Notion is nowhere to be found in Protagoras's own understanding of the proposition that "man is the measure of all things." Hegel finds this Notion in the modified way in which the proposition was used by Socrates and Plato. In their usage, the statement means "man, in that he is thinking and gives himself a universal content, is the measure." According to Hegel, with their usage,

> the great proposition is enunciated on which from this time forward, everything turns, since the further progress of Philosophy only explains [the proposition] further: it signifies that reason is the end of all things. This proposition further expresses a very remarkable change of position in asserting that all content, everything objective, is only in relation to consciousness; thought is thus in all truth expressed as the essential moment, and thereby the Absolute takes the form of the thinking subjectivity which comes before us principally in Socrates. Since man, as subject, is the measure of everything, the existent is not alone, but is for my knowledge. Consciousness is really the producer of the content in what is objective, and subjective thinking is thus really active. And this view extends even to the most modern philosophy, as when, for instance, Kant says that we only know phenomena, i.e. that what seems to us to be objective reality, is only to be considered in its relation to consciousness, and does not exist without this relation. The fact that the subject as active and determining brings forth the content, is the important matter, but now the question comes as to how the content is further determined—whether it is limited to the particularity of consciousness or is determined as the universal, the existent in and for itself. God, the Platonic Good, is certainly at first a product of thought, but in the second place He is just as really in and for Himself. Since I, as existent, fixed and eternal, only recognize what is in its content universal, this, posited as it is by

me, is likewise the implicitly objective, not posited by me (374–75).

The Protagorean influence, now Hegel admits, also extends to the later Skeptics. Protagoras's "great powers of reflective thought" brought forth to philosophical consciousness the "reflection on consciousness." However, he brought it forth in the "form of manifestation" that served the purposes of later Skeptics. It is argued by the Skeptics that "the phenomenal is not sensuous Being, for because I posit this as phenomenal, I assert its nullity," or "'What is, is only for consciousness,' or 'The truth of all things is the manifestation of them in and for consciousness.'" For Hegel, these statements are contradictory. The contradiction consists in the fact that they assume "first that nothing is in itself as it appears, and then that it is true as it appears." In other words, the Skeptical view holds that "objective significance must not be given to the positive, to what is true." This amounts to saying as if "this were white in itself because it appears so; for it is only this manifestation of the white that is true, the manifestation being just this movement of the self-abrogating sensuous Being, which, taken in the universal, stands above consciousness as truly as above Being. The world is consequently not only phenomenal in that it is for consciousness, and thus that its Being is only one relative to consciousness, for it is likewise in itself phenomenal" (377–78).

In short, the skeptical "element of consciousness which Protagoras has demonstrated, and owing to which the developed universal has in it the moment of the negative Being-for-another, has thus indeed to be asserted as a necessary moment; but taken for itself, alone and isolated, it is one-sided, since the moment of implicit Being is likewise essential" (ibid.).

3. Gorgias

The skepticism found in Protagoras "reached a much deeper point in Gorgias of Leontium." Skepticism, since it is a practice of negation, is essentially dialectical. For this reason, the word *dialectic* assumes a significant presence in Hegel's treatment of Gorgias. Even though Gorgias is assumed to be Empedocles's disciple, his "dialectic partakes of the manner and method" of the Eleatics. In some sense his thought also manifests the Sophist "eloquence" of reasoned argumentation, which is a "requisite" of the cognitive dialectic method. However, "his pre-eminence lies in his pure dialectic [with respect to] the quite universal categories of Being and non-being, which indeed is not like that of the [other] Sophists." It is the practice of this "pure dialectic" that brings Gorgias closer to the Eleatics, especially Zeno (378). However, Gorgias also departs from the Eleatics in a significant way, since he calls into question the Eleatic principle that only *being*, as the *One*, exists. His dialectic is similar to Zeno's only in the sense that he too disputes the claim that that sensuous existence *is*.

In this, his dialectic is similar to that of Protagoras, except that the "dialectic of Gorgias moves more purely in Notion than that found in Protagoras." As Hegel explains, "Since Protagoras asserted the relativity, or the non-implicit nature of all that is, this only exists in relation to another which really is essential to it; and this last, indeed, is consciousness. Gorgias' demonstration of the non-implicitness of Being is purer, because he takes in itself what passes for real existence without pre-supposing that other [the subjective side], and thus shows its own essential nullity and separates therefrom, the subjective side and Being as it is for the latter" (378–79). A simpler way to say what Hegel is saying here is that Gorgias dealt with purely logical categories.

Moreover, the dialectic of Gorgias differs from the dialectic of later Skeptics, such as Sextus Empiricus. Gorgias presented proofs, "and this is what the Skeptics later "ceased to do." Thus, in Gorgias's dialectic, "very abstract," that is, pure, "thought-determinations regarding the most speculative moments of Being and non-being, of knowledge, and of bringing into existence, of communicating knowledge, are involved." Hegel adds that "this is no idle talk, as was formerly supposed, for Gorgias' dialectic is of a quite objective kind, and is most interesting in content" (379). What Hegel means by the objectivity of Gorgias's dialectic is that his conclusions are meant to be universally acceptable. Said differently, Gorgias's truth is not your truth versus mine. It is no longer the truth "to me" alone, but the truth, if logically considered, *to all* rational consciousness. The irony involved in this objective truth, which all reason must accept, is that it denies the universality of truth itself.

Gorgias's dialectic is found in his treatise, *On Nature or the Non-Existent*. According to Sextus Empiricus, who was instrumental in preserving some key portions of this treatise in his *Against the Schoolmasters*, Gorgias's work has three parts, which Hegel quotes as follows: "'In the first he proves that' (objectively) 'nothing exists, in the second' (subjectively), 'that assuming that Being is, it cannot be known; and in the third place' (both subjectively and objectively), 'that were it to exist and be knowable, no communication of what is known would be possible'" (379–80). We observe here that the dialectic of Gorgias begins with ontological arguments and winds up with epistemological ones. It begins by nihilistically establishing the claim that "nothing exists." For this reason, he even acquired the nickname the Nihilist. At the same time, his epistemological conclusions are more in tune with the agnosticism of the Kantian kind than with nihilism.

Hegel provides a very brief account of Gorgias's first proof, which attempts to show that nothing exists (380). A useful rendition of Sextus's summary of Gorgias's first proof would be this: *If* anything exists, it must exist as *being* (as existent) or as *non-being* (as nonexistent), or both as *being* and *non-being*. What Gorgias attempts to prove is that neither *being* nor *non-being* exists. By extension, *being* and *non-being*, taken together, also does not exist. If *non-being* does not exist, then nonexistence also does not exist. It follows, when the proof is given, that "nothing exists." His proof is as follows: "the nonexistent does not exist; for if the nonexistent exists, it will both exist and not exist at the same time, for insofar as it is understood as nonexistent, it will not exist, but insofar as it is nonexistent it will, on the other hand, exist." His reasoning seems to be this: *non-existence* (or *non-being*) means the absence of existence. To say non-existence exists is to necessarily say *it is* and *it is not*. However, Gorgias reasons that it would "be entirely absurd for something to exist and at the same time not to exist." Since it is "absurd," or contradictory, he reaches the conclusion that "the nonexistent, therefore, does not exist." To add to this, "if the nonexistent exists, the existent will not exist, for these are opposites to each other, and if existence is an attribute of the nonexistent, nonexistence will be an attribute of the existent. But it is not, in fact, true that the existent does not exist. <Accordingly>, neither will the nonexistent exist."[1]

In his second refutation, Gorgias tries to prove that "the existent does not exist either." To say that something exists is to assume that it has either existed eternally, or was generated at a particular point in time. Gorgias finds both possibilities implausible. His intention here, as Hegel notes, is to show that it is impossible for *what is* to be either with or without beginning. In the first place, reasons Gorgias, "if the existent is eternal (one must begin with this point) it does not have any beginning." If it is without a beginning, it must be "without limit [infinite]." If something is without limit, it cannot be said that it has a

---

1. Gorgias of Leontini, "On the Nonexistent," in Sextus Empiricus, *Against the Schoolmasters*, Vol. VII, 65–87, accessed February 5, 2013, http://www.wfu.edu/~zulick/300/gorgias/negative.html

spatial presence. Thus, what is infinite "is nowhere." If we say that it is somewhere, we assume that it is in something other than itself. This assumption poses two related contradictions. First, "if the existent is contained in something it will no longer be without limit." It will thus be a finite. It also follows from this that the space in which it is contained must be "greater than the contained, but nothing is greater than the unlimited, so that the unlimited cannot exist anywhere." Second, if it is contained in something, "it is not contained in itself." If it is contained in it itself, the "container and contained will be the same, and the existent will become two things, place and body (place is the container, body the contained). But this is absurd. Accordingly, existence is not contained in itself." In short, "if the existent is eternal, it is not existent at all."[2]

Gorgias also reasons that existence cannot be either generated or un-generated, or both generated and un-generated. It follows that, if an existent cannot be either or both, it cannot amount to existence. His reasoning runs as follows: If something is generated, it comes into *being*. "If it has come into being, it has come either from the existent or the nonexistent." However, it is absurd to say that it has come from the already existent, "for if it is existent, it has not come to be, but already exists." Thus, existence necessarily assumes eternal existence, which has already been disproven above. It is also not possible for the existent to come out of the non-existent. The reason is that "the nonexistent cannot generate anything, because what is generative of something of necessity ought to partake of positive existence." In conclusion, "it is not true either, therefore, that the existent is generated."[3]

Hegel, by agreeing with Aristotle, adds that Gorgias's reasoning is "the dialectic already brought forward" by "Melissus and Zeno." The basic logic behind it is that "'if Being is, it is contradictory to predicate a quality to it, and if we do this, we express something merely negative about it'" (380). This is because any quality would render *being*, which is supposed to be the infinite One, finite or many. What is meant here can be further clarified with Hegel's similar argument in *The Encyclopaedia Logic*, which I have already quoted in the section on Thales. Hegel says there that when we say God is the "highest essence," we give a finite quality and quantity to what is infinite. "The expression 'to give' refers to something finite . . . The things that are 'given' . . . are such that others are [also] 'given' *outside* and *beside* him." Thus, "the category of quantity that is applied here

---

2. Ibid.
3. Ibid.

[i.e., the highest] has its place only in the domain of the finite."[4] In making these points, Hegel, of course, does not completely agree with Gorgias. He simply agrees that the reasoning Gorgias refutes, which stems from predicating the Absolute, is faulty.

However, Gorgias's reasoning is also faulty, according to Hegel, especially when he attempts to refute the infinite.

> This dialectic of Gorgias regarding the infinite is on the one hand limited, because immediate existence has certainly no beginning and no limit, but asserts a progression into infinitude; the self-existent Thought, the universal Notion, as absolute negativity, has, however, limits in itself. On the other hand, Gorgias is quite right, for the bad, sensuous infinite is nowhere present, and thus does not exist, but is a Beyond of Being; only we may take what Gorgias takes as a diversity of place, as being diversity generally. Thus, instead of placing the infinite, like Gorgias, sometimes in another, sometimes within itself, i.e. sometimes maintaining it to be different, sometimes abrogating the diversity, we may say better and more universally, that this sensuous infinite is a diversity which is always posited as different from the existent, for it is just the being different from itself (381).

Here, Hegel is asserting the unity of the infinite and the finite, which we have explained in the section on Zeno.

As for the question of the generation or origination of the infinite raised by Gorgias, Hegel makes a broader critical point, which comes to inform the difference between his own logic and formal logic. In this instance, Hegel has in mind the logic of the Skeptics, in which "the object to be contemplated hence ever becomes posited under determinations with 'either' 'or.'" If something is said to be one thing, or has *this* predicate, it cannot also be said to be another. This is known in formal logic as the *law of identity*. But, if it is shown to be another, then there arises a contradiction. According to Aristotle, the law of (non)contradiction, the "firmest principle of all," is that "it is impossible for the same thing [predicate] both to belong and not to belong at the same time to the same thing [subject] and in the same respect . . . ."[5] Skepticism, including that of Gorgias, agrees with this

---

4. Hegel, *The Encyclopaedia Logic: Part I*, 177.
5. Aristotle, *Metaphysics*, 251.

law with a fundamental difference. Formal logic does not deny the truth of existence. It simply denies that existence, or truth about existence, can be contradictory. Skepticism, on the other hand, assumes that because everything can be seen as either-or, all affirmations of existence are inevitably contradictory, and hence untrue.

"But," warns Hegel, "that is not the true dialectic, because [with Skepticism] the object resolves itself into those [two] determinations [of either/or] only." Consequently, in this faulty dialectic, "when nothing follows respecting the nature of the object itself, then, as is already proved, the object must be necessarily in one determination, and not in and for itself" (382). For Hegel, on the other hand, contradiction is an essential aspect of the truth of existents: ". . . only the unity of opposites is the truth—that in every statement there is truth and falsehood, if truth is to be taken in the sense of the simple, and falsehood in the sense of the opposed and contradictory; in it the positive, the first unity, and the negative, this last opposition, fall asunder" (458). Hegel's point here is related to the notion of the unity of the opposites, which we have also discussed previously.

Gorgias also says, "Of course, if the existent is the same as the nonexistent, it is not possible for both to exist. For if both exist, they are not the same, and if the same, both do not exist. To which the conclusion follows that nothing exists. For if neither the existent exists nor the nonexistent nor both, and if no additional possibility is conceivable, nothing exists."[6] Hegel grants limited validity to this argument. He says,

> In speaking of Being and non-being, we always say the opposite to what we wish. Being and non-being are the same, just as they are not the same; if they are the same, I speak of the two as different; if different, I express the same predicate of them, [that is. their] diversity. This dialectic is not to be despised by us, as if it dealt with empty abstractions, for these categories are, on the one hand, in their purity the most universal, and if, on the other hand, they are not the ultimate, yet it is always Being or non-being that are in question; they are not, however, definitely fixed and divided off, but are self-negating. Gorgias is conscious that they are vanishing moments, while the ordinary unconscious conception

---

6. Gorgias of Leontini, *On the Nonexistent*,
http://www.wfu.edu/~zulick/300/gorgias/negative.html.

also has present to it this truth, but knows nothing about it (382–83).

Even though Hegel's consideration of Gorgias does not include it, the latter also refutes existence on the grounds of the contradiction of the one and the many. It is here that we see a more direct resemblance of Gorgias's dialectic to Zeno's paradoxes. As Gorgias reasons in this context, if something exists, it must be "either one or many." Neither possibility is plausible. If the existent is one, "it is an existent or a continuum or a magnitude or a body. But whatever of these it is, it is not one, since whatever has extent will be divided, and what is a continuum will be cut." Similarly, magnitude is also divisible, and a body is necessarily "three dimensional." Since it is absurd to say that "the existent is none of these things," we must conclude that "the existent is not one." But, to say that the existent is many is equally absurd. This is because "if it is not one, it is not many either, since the many is a composite of separate entities [and is hence one composite] and thus, when the possibility that it is one was refuted, the possibility that it is many was refuted as well. Now it is clear from this that neither does the existent exist nor does the nonexistent exist."[7]

Indeed, what Gorgias actually proves here is simply that one may be perceived as many, and many as one. However, instead of seeing them as the unity of opposites, as Hegel does, in that each, of necessity, entails the other, he brings the contradiction to impossibility. In order to accept the conclusion he reaches, we have to accept that existence can only be considered as either one or many, and each side of this consideration is illogical for there is no such thing as pure one, or pure many. In this sense, his proof merely succeeds in calling into question the Notion of the Eleatics, who took the One to be such a pure *being*, and the Notion of the Atomists and Empedocles who treated *being* as simply the compound of many.

For Hegel, and Aristotle, the One and the many exist in a dialectical relationship. Repeating Aristotle in a different context, Hegel says,

> As regards merely empirical existence, it may easily be shown that each quality exists on its own account, but in the Notion they only are, through one another, and by virtue of an inward necessity. We certainly see this also in living matter, where things happen in another way,

---

7. Ibid.

for here the Notion comes into existence; thus if, for example, we abstract the heart, the lungs and all else collapse. And in the same way all nature exists only in the unity of all its parts, just as the brain can exist only in unity with the other organs (182).

We now have to consider Gorgias's epistemological arguments, which rest upon his ontological ones presented above. His main point in this context is that "even if anything exists, it is unknowable and incomprehensible to man." On the one hand, "if things considered in the mind are not existent, the existent is not considered." If the existent is not considered, what the mind considers cannot be the knowledge of the existent. On the other hand, "if things considered are existent, all things considered exist, and in whatever way anyone considers them." But, Gorgias reasons, this is also "absurd." With a considerable leap of logic, he argues that "if one considers a man flying or chariots racing in the sea, a man does not straightway fly nor a chariot race in the sea. So that things considered are not existent." Clearly, it should have been said here that what mind considers does not *necessarily* exist in actuality. In other words, his reasoning suffers from a selection bias in which the thinking of the implausible presumably proves that what "mind considers" does not exist. Continuing with this faulty logic from the opposite angle, Gorgias argues,

> In addition, if things considered in the mind are existent, nonexistent things will not be considered. For opposites are attributes of opposites, and the nonexistent is opposed to the existent. For this reason it is quite evident that if "being considered in the mind" is an attribute of the existent, "not being considered in the mind" will be an attribute of the nonexistent. But this is absurd. For Scylla and Chimaera and many other nonexistent things are considered in the mind. Therefore, the existent is not considered in the mind.

In conclusion, it is "absurd" to believe that "chariots race in the sea," just because someone considered it in his/her mind. "Therefore, the existent is not an object of consideration and is not apprehended."[8]

---

8. Ibid.

After quoting a smaller portion of the above arguments of Gorgias, Hegel says the former, "pronounces a just polemic against absolute realism, which, because it represents, thinks to possess the very thing itself, when it only has a relative." But Gorgias ends up falling "into the false idealism of modern times, according to which thought is always subjective only, and thus not the existent, since through thought an existent is transformed into what is [only] thought" (383).

From this reasoning, Gorgias presents another set of arguments to prove that, as Hegel summarizes it, "knowledge cannot be imparted" (ibid.). From the conclusion that the existent cannot be apprehended, Gorgias now wishes to stand on a safer ground: "if it should be apprehended, it would be incapable of being conveyed to another." His reasoning begins with the following question: "For if existent things are visible and audible and generally perceptible, which means that they are external substances, and of these the things which are visible are perceived by the sight, those that are audible by the hearing, and not contrariwise, how can these things be revealed to another person?" This question is posed in response to the claim that things are sensed and known according to their own sense-criterion. Gorgias's argument is that whatever we come to know through sense-perception, if we do know it at all, cannot be imparted to the others. The reason is that we reveal knowledge through "*logos* [discourse, or logic]." However, "*logos* is not substances and existing things." For this reason, *logos* is both different than sense perception, and the organs of sense-perception, and incapable of communicating what is being sensed. It follows from this premise that we cannot "reveal existing things to our neighbors, but *logos*." Therefore, "just as the visible would not become audible, and vice versa, similarly, when external reality is involved, it would not become our *logos*, and not being *logos*, it would not have been revealed to another."[9]

In response to Gorgias's reasoning, Hegel briefly concludes that "in this manner Gorgias' dialectic is the laying hold of this difference [between the subjective and objective] exactly as again occurred in Kant; if I maintain this difference, certainly that which is, cannot be known." The difference that Gorgias and Kant maintain is the one between the subject and object, that is, between that which thinks and "that which is." Gorgias's dialectic is, adds Hegel, "undoubtedly impregnable to those who maintain sensuous Being [alone] to be real." That is, his dialectic holds good against *absolute realism*. For Hegel, "That this existent cannot be imparted, must likewise be held most

---

9. Ibid.

strongly, for this individual [existent] cannot be expressed. The Sophists thus also made dialectic, universal Philosophy, their object, and they were profound thinkers." However, "the truth of [Gorgias'] dialectic is only this movement to posit itself negatively as existent, and the unity is the reflection that the existent, comprehended also as non-existent, becomes, in this comprehension of it, universal." It follows that "Philosophic truth is thus not only expressed as if there were another truth in sensuous consciousness." *Being* is also "present" in the truth, in the philosophical thought (380–84).

Gorgias's *logos* is devoid of this inherence of *being* in thought. This issue closely pertains to presence of the *end* in *nous*, which forcefully emerges for the first time with Socrates. The end, which in Socrates grounds thinking, or gives dialectic content, vanishes with the Sophists in an ironic way. Elsewhere, Hegel points out in this regard that

> the Sophists came on the scene among the Greeks at a time when they were no longer satisfied with mere authority and tradition in the domain of religion and ethics. They felt the need at that time to become conscious of what was to be valid for them as a content mediated by thought. This demand was met by the Sophists because they taught people how to seek out the various points of view from which things can be considered; and these points of view are, in the first instance, simply nothing but grounds . . . However, since a ground does not yet have a content that is determined in and for itself, and grounds can be found for what is unethical and contrary to law no less than for what is ethical and lawful, the decision as to what grounds are to count as valid falls to the subject. The ground of the subject's decision becomes a matter of his individual disposition and aims. In this way the objective basis of what is valid in and for itself, and recognized by all, was undermined . . .

Socrates fought Sophism on two main fronts. First, he tried to show that the individualistic, subjective grounds are untenable, since they always lead to contradiction. Second, he tried to show that only the universal is valid *in-and-for-itself*, and deduced the universal from what is "just and good."[10] It is to this Socratic advance in dialectic that we must now turn our attention.

---

10. Hegel, *The Encyclopaedia Logic*, 191.

CHAPTER 7

First Greek Period, Second Division - Part II: Socrates

1. Introduction

In order to reiterate one of the main points of *Lectures*, Hegel begins his lecture on Socrates with the statement that the latter "did not grow like a mushroom out of the earth, for he stands in continuity with his time . . ." Socrates's continuity with his time is related to both the development of philosophy and political changes in Athens. But this continuity also entails a significant "mental turning-point . . . in the form of philosophic thought." Philosophy becomes thought thinking about the nature of thought. The ancient Ionics, for instance, did not reflect on thought *in-and-for-itself*. In this way, they neither reflected on thought as such nor defined the products of thought as thought-products. The Atomists "made objective existence into thoughts, but these [thoughts] were . . . only abstractions, pure [sensuous] entities." It was Anaxagoras who first "raised thought as such, into a principle," and treated it as "the all-powerful Notion, as the negative power over all that is definite and existent." Anaxagoras, in turn, failed to give thought any positive existence because, with him, *nous* and *being* remained separated and external to each other (384–85).

The Sophist Protagoras, in contrast, expressed thought "as real existence," though only as "the all-resolving consciousness," or as "the unrest of the Notion." The Notion in Sophism, Hegel now says, is at the same time grounded in the secure and restful "I," the subjective consciousness, which has "the moments of movement outside of it." The "I" with the Sophists retains itself by negating "what is different," that is, consciousness posits itself as the negation of *being* and *non-being*. In this way, the "I" remains an "individual, and not yet the universal reflected within itself," which Hegel calls the "negative unity" of the "I" with existence. Hegel says this fixity of the subjective "I," and its relationship to the fluid objective world creates an "ambiguity" between "dialectic and sophistry." The ambiguity is this: "if the objective disappears, the signification of the fixed subjective [becomes] either that of the individual opposed to the objective . . . , or that of the objective and universal ["I"] in itself" (385). In the first instance, "the contingent and lawless will" arises. In the second instance, the opposite of the contingent and lawless, that is, the objective and universal individual will arises.

However, we must note, this ambiguity between "dialectic and sophistry" is not an ambiguity for the Sophists themselves. The latter option cannot be attributed to them since the Sophists do not posit anything like the idea that the "I" is, or has for its content, "the objective and the universal in itself." Indeed, Hegel himself has declared in the previous chapter that Sophism entails "double relativity," the relativity of the subjective and the objective. The "I" of the Sophists is neither the restful, secure "I," nor does it entail objective universality. For the first time in the history of philosophy, Hegel finds this objectivity in Socrates.

The Socratic position, or opposition to the Sophists, is initially described by Hegel as follows: "Socrates expresses real existence as the universal 'I,' as the consciousness which rests in itself." The universal "is the good as such, which is free from existent reality, free from individual sensuous consciousness of feeling and desire, free finally from the theoretically speculative thought about nature." In this way, Socrates posits the Good as the ground of the subjective will, though not as the ground of nature. With Socrates, "as with Protagoras, the self-conscious thought . . . [negates] all that is determined," and is posited as the "real existence." The difference between them is that, with Socrates, while thought negates all that is determined and particular, because of its universal content, it still retains its internal "rest and security." The rest and security of the subjective thought comes from it having an objective, universal substance within itself. "This substance existing in-and-for-itself, the self-retaining," is "determined as end, and further as the true and the good" (386).

Socrates thus takes further Anaxagoras's underdeveloped principle, namely, that "the understanding is the ruling and self-determining universal . . . ," and firmly establishes self-consciousness as the self-determining universal. Socrates, says Hegel, further posits that the Good, which is the "substantial end [telos]" in the "I," "must be known by me." Thus, the pursuit of the Good in every action becomes a conscious endeavor from within the "I." In this way, the "I" becomes the "ruling and self-determining" universal, though, unlike the Sophist "I," it purports to rule itself on objective, universal, moral grounds. This consciousness of the end as the Good, and the determination of the will on its basis, is also the basis of "the freedom of self-consciousness." Thus, according to Hegel, Socrates's principle dictates "that man has to find [within] himself both the end of his actions and the end of the world, and must attain to truth through himself" (386). In this way, *nous* comes to rule the life of the individual, and merely that. The world at large remains external to *nous*. For this reason, the objectivity of the Socratic principle is still subjective.

The validity of Hegel's interpretation of Socrates, briefly outlined above, depends on which, or whose, Socrates we take into account. This is the famous "Socrates problem," which, in my view, cannot be firmly resolved. There are different accounts of Socrates by his critics and followers. Aristophanes's *Clouds* treats Socrates as a teacher of sophistry and of disrespect for the mores of society. Xenophon and Plato, in their different ways, portray Socrates's teachings more or less in the way Hegel does above. However, as we will see in the next chapter, many followers of Socrates, "the Socratics," take his philosophy in the opposite direction than the one taken by Plato, the most famous student of Socrates. With the Socratics, the objectivity of the "I" vanishes once again. Thought takes the form of what Hegel in the previous chapter has labeled the "infinite subjectivity."

Connected to these diversifications of the Socratic thought is the nature of the famous Socratic irony. Did Socrates take himself to be the wisest man, or was he the person who genuinely believed that he himself knew nothing? If he believed that he knew nothing, what was the purpose of his dialectic? Was it to cast doubt on all claims to knowledge, or was it to bring the universal, objectively true, out of himself and out of the muddled beliefs of his opponents? These are the central questions Hegel seeks to answer below.

2. Dialectic Method and Irony in Socrates

Socrates's philosophy is often identified with his method of inquiry, the "Socratic method," which comes in the form of reasoned dialogues. In these dialogues, a given proposition, a concrete determination, is questioned from a variety of angles until it is shown to be inadequate or self-contradictory. The interrogator, which is Socrates, thus casts doubt on the knowledge of the interrogated. This method is also called "dialectic." Just about everybody agrees with this simple interpretation of Socrates. Disagreements come into play when his interpreters consider the ultimate intention of his inquisitiveness. Was he, in the manner of sophistry, merely interested in casting doubt on all truth claims? Or, was he bent upon establishing the universality of truth himself? These questions pertain to the nature of the *irony* in Socrates.

Hegel says that Socrates's method "must in its nature be dialectic." Hegel's understanding of the Socratic dialectic is different than the usual banality attributed to the latter. For instance, Bertrand Russell describes the Socratic dialectic as "the method of seeking knowledge by question and answer . . ."[1] Hegel sees more than this in the Socratic dialectic. For Hegel, Socrates's dialogical reasoning is not arbitrary. His questions, which shape the form of his dialogues, are justified by the internal reason they contain. What this means is very significant to our understanding of Hegel's own dialectic also: "the principle of [Socrates's] philosophy falls in with the method itself, which thus far cannot be called method, since it is a mode which quite coincides with the moralizing [or philosophizing] peculiar to Socrates" (397). Hegel makes a similar claim about his own method, as we have seen in Chapter 1. We must begin with and follow the rhythm of purely logical Notion. This "demands concentrated attention on the notion as such, on simple and ultimate determinations like being-in-itself [pure *being*], being-for-itself, self-identity, and so on, for these are elemental, pure, self-determined functions . . ."[2] As for Socrates, Hegel thinks, the Notion of the Good is precisely this self-determining universal principle, which is internal to the form the Socratic dialectic method takes. The Good is the content of the Socratic thought.

Socrates, moreover, gives this content of a practical expression. In this sense, "the chief content is to know the good as the absolute," and relate this absolute "to actions."

> Thus it can be said that in content his philosophy had an altogether practical aspect, and similarly the Socratic method, which is essential to it, was distinguished by the system of first bringing a person to reflection upon his duty by any occasion that might either happen to be offered spontaneously, or that was brought about by Socrates. By going to the work-places of tailors and shoemakers, and entering into discourse with them, as also with youths and old men, Sophists, statesmen, and citizens of all kinds, he in the first place took their interests as his topic—whether these were household interests, the education of children, or the interests of knowledge or of truth. Then he led them on from a

---

1. Bertrand Russell, *A History of Western Philosophy* (New York: Simon and Schuster Inc., 1945), 92.
2. Hegel, *The Phenomenology of Mind*, 34.

definite [particular] case to think of the universal, and of truths and beauties which had absolute value, since in every case, from the individual's own thoughts, he derived the conviction and consciousness of that which is the definite [truth] (397–98).

Hegel concludes on the basis of this observation that Socrates's method "has two prominent aspects." These are "the development of the universal from the concrete case, and the exhibition of the notion which implicitly exists in every consciousness" (398).

It is in the first aspect that the so-called "ignorance" of Socrates is to be found. As Hegel explains, Socrates began his discourses "by adopting the ordinary conceptions [i.e., the concrete cases] which they considered to be true. But in order to bring others to express these, he represents himself as in ignorance of them, and, with a seeming ingenuousness, puts questions to his audience as if they were to instruct him, while he really wished to draw [the premises of these conceptions] out. This is the celebrated Socratic irony" (ibid.).

Søren Kierkegaard claims that Hegel, as well as Plato, misinterpreted the Socratic irony. According to Kierkegaard, the dialectic of Socrates involves "absolute negativity," since it "only negates"; and it negates everything. In this sense, it is "infinite" negativity, which amounts to total denial of true knowledge. This is ironic because the Delphic oracle states that Socrates is the wisest man, who knows what is best more than anyone else. The Socratic dialectic thus makes the subject negatively free because the subject (Socrates) lets nothing ground him, or hold his consciousness firm and fixed. Consequently, for Socrates, the entire reality lacks a foundational point of validity, or a ground; the universal principle as a standpoint is thus entirely missing. Socrates used this irony to destroy the "Greek culture." In his thinking and conduct, he maintained ignorance, and tried to show the ignorance of others as well. He thus really meant that "he knew nothing." Eventually, the extreme irony of Socrates consumed him.[3]

It should be obvious by now that Hegel does not share Kierkegaard's interpretation of Socrates. Hegel repeats that Socrates's dialectic is only "a subjective form of dialectic" because it carries "on intercourse between one person and another." In contrast to this subjective form of dialectic, "real dialectic deals with the reasons for things" (ibid.). In the latter kind of dialectic, what this or that

---

3. Søren Kierkegaard, *The Concept of Irony: With Constant Reference to Socrates* (New York: Harper & Row, 1965), 278.

individual thinks is not the determining factor. What matters here are the purely logical dictates of reason. Socrates's subjective dialectic thus tries to bring out the principles of other people first, push each one of them into a "definite proposition" next, and then consequently "deduce . . . the direct opposite of what the proposition stated, or else allow the opposite to be deduced from their own inner consciousness without maintaining it directly against their statements." He thus got his opponents to refute themselves. Socrates "also derived the opposite from . . . concrete case[s] . . . , then went on to show that they contradicted themselves." In an inexplicable turn of reasoning, here Hegel seemingly ends up adopting the other version of the Socratic irony. He now says, "Thus Socrates taught those with whom he associated to know that they knew nothing; indeed, what is more, he himself said that he knew nothing, and therefore taught nothing. It may actually be said that Socrates knew nothing, for he did not reach the systematic construction of a philosophy. He was conscious of this, and it was also not at all his aim to establish a science" (399). In short, he was not feigning his "ignorance" after all.

However, as it turns out, Hegel does not ultimately intend to equate the Socratic "ignorance" suggested here with the purely negative dialectic, suggested by Kierkegaard.

> On the one view, this irony seems to be something untrue. But when we deal with objects which have a universal interest, and speak about them to one and to another, it is always the case that one does not understand another's conception of the object. For every individual has certain ultimate words as to which he presupposes a common knowledge. But if we really are to come to an understanding, we find it is these presuppositions which have to be investigated . . . For if I say I know what reason, what belief is, these are only quite abstract ideas; it is necessary, in order to become concrete, that they should be explained, and that it should be understood that what they really are, is unknown. The irony of Socrates has this great quality of showing how to make abstract ideas concrete and effect their development, for on that alone depends the bringing of the Notion into consciousness (399–400).

Said differently, the ignorance of Socrates implies: "'I do not know what the other person's view is on this matter.' This is always the case. People ["the man of culture"] discuss topics of general interest endlessly and express one view or another about them. Usually each individual takes the latest views and terminology to be generally acknowledged as valid. Familiarity with them is presupposed on all sides. But if we are in fact going to achieve some insight, then it is these very presuppositions—what passes as acknowledged—that have to be investigated."[4] What Hegel opposes here is attributing to Socrates the kind of modern irony, which takes "the subjective" as "the arbitrary will, the inward divinity which knows itself to be exalted above all. The divine is said to be the purely negative attitude, the perception of the vanity of everything, in which my vanity alone remains . . . From this irony of our times, the irony of Socrates is far removed." Hegel proceeds to conclude that Socrates's "premeditated irony" has the "natural aim of leading men, through thought, to the true good and to the universal Idea" (401–2). Thus, Socrates's method involves moving from the uncertain, nay contradictory, realm of the particular cases, or thought determinations, to the universal Idea, which alone is objectively true.

This aim of Socrates brings us to the second aspect of his method, which "Socrates has called the art of midwifery—an art which came to him from his mother." This method coincides with dialectic as positive development, and attempts to overcome the pure negativity of the dialectic of the Sophists. "It is the assisting into the world of the thought which is already contained in the consciousness of the individual—the showing from the concrete [particular], unreflected consciousness, the universality of the concrete, or from the universally posited [by others], the opposite which already is within it" (402). In doing these, Socrates does not begin with an axiomatic universal principle and prove things deductively. Instead, he analyzes the "universality immersed" in every consciousness, and separates this implicit universal from the concrete cases in order to then bring it out more explicitly in opposition to the particular determination. Thus, the "art of midwifery" involves bringing out the implicit universal by a process of separation, or abstraction. This second aspect is intimately related to the first aspect of the Socratic method: One can negate the particular, and thus bring the universal out of it, only if the universal is entailed in the particular. According to Hegel, this is "the same method which forms in every man his knowledge of the universal; an education in self-consciousness, which

---

4. Hegel, *Lectures on the History of Philosophy, 1825–6*, 131.

is the development of reason." The development of reason in this manner requires the articulation of the already implicitly present universal Notion by way of abstracting and isolating it from the particular first, and bringing "what is [abstractly universal, the Notion in-itself] before consciousness." Today, we may not appreciate this process of abstraction because we "are taught from youth up in universal principles . . . , the universal of the concrete case is already present . . . as universal, because our reflection is already accustomed to the universal, and we do not require, first of all, to take the trouble of making a separation" (403–4). Socrates's separation of the universal by way of abstraction and negation was original, and necessary for its times.

The Socratic principle, because it finds the Good implicitly present in every individual consciousness, lends itself to the conclusion that "man can learn nothing [new], virtue included." This conclusion is the opposite of the Sophist endeavor to teach reason and virtue. The Socratic position, which Plato also adopts, does not assume that individuals have "no relation to science," or that they cannot be educated at all. What it assumes instead is that "the good [or the universal] does not come from without . . . ; it cannot be taught, but is implied in the nature of mind. That is to say, man cannot passively receive anything that is given from without like the wax that is molded to a form, for everything is latent in the mind of man, and he only *seems* to learn it" (410, italics added).This Socratic/Platonic position coincides with Hegel's own position, namely that consciousness is no tabula rasa. It is also related to the dialectic of midwifery in the sense that what is already "latent in the mind of man" simply needs to be brought out dialectically. This is also Hegel's strategy in *The Phenomenology of Mind*, where he attempts to bring out the universal Notion by showing its necessary presence in all understanding. His *Science of Logic* simply takes the universal for granted, as something already accomplished.

Hegel proceeds at this point to outline his own perspective on this issue:

> Certainly everything begins from without, but this is only the beginning; the truth is that this is only an impulse towards the development of spirit. All that has value to men, the eternal, the self-existent, is contained in man himself, and has to develop from himself. To learn here only means to receive knowledge of what is externally determined. This external comes indeed through experience, but the universal therein belongs to

thought, not to the subjective and bad [finite and particular], but to the objective and true [infinite, or universal]. The universal in the opposition of subjective and objective, is that which is as subjective as it is objective; the subjective is only a particular, the objective is similarly only a particular as regards the subjective, but the universal is the unity of both.

Hegel adds that "nothing has any value to men to which the spirit does not testify. Man in it is free, is at home with himself, and that is the subjectivity of spirit . . . ; that which is held by me as truth and right is spirit of my spirit." What comes from "passions, likings, and arbitrary desires" is the particular subjectivity, which is different in each person. This is the basis of much of the modern materialism. Hegel does not completely deny the validity of sense-perception, or these impulses for they are also "implanted in us by nature." But they lack universality, which is only possible through true thought, or Reason: "high above" senses and natural impulses is "true thought, the Notion, the rational." Socrates "awakened this real conscience, for he not only said that man is the measure of all things, but man as thinking is the measure of all things" (410–11).

Hegel's point that the Good, or virtue, according to Socrates, is implanted in us clearly comes across in Plato's *Meno*. In this dialogue, Socrates asks Meno to tell him what virtue is. "Meno proceeds to make various distinctions: 'Man's virtue is to be skillful in managing state affairs, and thereby to help friends and harm foes; woman's to rule her household; other virtues are those of boys, of young men, of old men,' &c." Here, Meno makes virtue manifold. Socrates, however, pressures him to define the "virtue in general, which comprehends everything in itself. Meno says 'It is to govern and rule over others.'" Socrates, then, points out that "the virtue of boys and slaves does not consist in governing." Meno concedes to this point and declares himself unable to "tell what is common in all virtue." Socrates "replies that it is the same as figure, which is what is common in roundness, squareness, &c." Here, the universal Idea, or *form*, emerges. All round things share in common *roundness*, and it is on the basis of the universal that we come to know the difference between the round and square, etc. From what Socrates is made to say elsewhere, we can attribute to him the position that all kinds of virtue also partake in the same general *Virtue*, which is the Good in each thing or action. At this point, Meno musters enough courage to say, "'Virtue is the power of securing the good desired.'" This definition of virtue sounds similar to Socrates's position, except that Meno grounds it in desires. Socrates points out that when "men know that something is an evil, they do not desire it." Hegel does not go into the significance of this point, which seems to be twofold: First, virtue can also be that which we do not desire. Second, virtue cannot be determined through desires, but through knowledge alone. Perhaps, this is what Hegel also means when he says that in Socrates's view "the good must be acquired in a right way" (405).

Consequently, Socrates achieves the intended goal of his discussion with Meno: the utter frustration and perplexity of the latter. Meno goes on to say,

> "I used to hear of you, before I knew you, that you were yourself in doubt, and also brought others into doubt, and now you cast a spell on me too, so that I am at my wits' end. You seem, if I may venture to jest, to be like the torpedo fish, for it is said of it that it makes torpid those who come near it and touch it. You have done this to me, for I have become torpid in body and soul, and I do not know how to answer you, although I have talked thousands of times about virtue with many persons, and, as it seemed to me, talked very well. But now I do not know at all what to say. Hence you do well not to travel amongst strangers, for you might be put to death as a magician" (405–6).

As Socrates tries to push him into trying again, Meno manages to turn the argument against Socrates. He asks: "'How can you inquire about what you say you do not know? Can you have a desire for what you do not know? And if you find it out by chance, how can you know that it is what you looked for, since you acknowledge that, you do not know it?'" Here, Meno is presenting what is nowadays called "the learner's paradox." Hegel does not elaborate on the significance of Meno's paradox and Socrates's response to it. He simply concludes that "a number of dialogues end in the same manner, both in Xenophon and Plato, leaving us quite unsatisfied as to the result" (406).

In my view, Socrates's response to Meno fails to directly answer Meno's paradoxical questions. Socrates goes on to manipulate Meno's questions to mean: how could Socrates teach knowledge, or virtue, if he does not know what it is in the first place. In this context, Socrates has already admitted to be ignorant of what virtue is. Socrates proposes some positive ideas to address Meno's paradox, such as the immortality of the soul, the theory of knowledge as recollection (*anamnesis*), etc. The premise of his response is that, because of the immortality of the soul, knowledge is eternally present in every consciousness. "The soul has learned everything that *is*." What needs to be done is not teaching knowledge or virtue, as the Sophists want to do, but to recollect this knowledge "for seeking and learning are nothing but recollection." Socrates illustrates this point by getting one of Meno's slaves to illustrate his implicit knowledge of the geometrical shapes, which the slave was initially unaware of. Meno ends up accepting that all knowledge is ultimately recollection. Thus, Socrates here gives the so-called Socratic irony a different twist. He does not know what virtue is. However, given the demonstrated validity of the recollection theory of knowledge, "I am ready," says Socrates to Meno, "with your help, to inquire into the nature of virtue."[5] In short, Socrates maintains that he himself does not know what virtue is in general. By this, he does not mean that it cannot be brought out of him. The knowledge of virtue is buried in his consciousness, as it is in the consciousness of others. They all simply have to recollect it through the force of dialectic (midwifery).

According to Hegel, this process of recollection also surprises us. It brings out the implicit, which consciousness "never looked for" before, though it was present in it all along. "[F]or example, on the universally known idea of Becoming, we find that what becomes is not and yet it is; it is the identity of Being and non-being, and it may surprise us that in this simple conception so great a distinction should exist." Hegel is clearly referring to the categories in his *Logic* here.[6] The main point, however, is that Socrates's dialectic brings people to say "'that what we [thought we] knew has refuted itself.'" It is important to reiterate that refutation is self-refutation, or self-negation of consciousness, and this can only happen if the universal Notion is already implicit within consciousness. Indeed, the conclusions produced through dialogues are generally accepted by Socrates's opponents at the end of the dialectical process. However, the main "drift of the greater part of Socrates' dialogues," says Hegel, is to bring out the "contradictions" in popular thought, and not to resolve these contradictions back into a unity. That Socrates did not sufficiently take this last step is a reason why Hegel considers the Socratic dialectic insufficient. Consequently, the "main tendency" of these dialogues "was to show the bewilderment and confusion which

---

5. Plato. *Meno,* in *Plato: The Collected Dialogues, Including the Letters*, eds. Edith Hamilton and Huntington Cairns (Princeton: Princeton University Press, 1961), 363–64 (80a-82b).
6. See Hegel, *Hegel's Science of Logic*, 83.

exist in [ordinary] knowledge." At the same time, says Hegel, this stirring-up of trouble in ordinary consciousness, this shock-therapy so to speak, is necessary for the attainment of the truth: ". . . everything must be doubted, all presuppositions given up, [in order] to reach the truth as created through the Notion" (404–6).

3. The Good as the End of Thought

As we have seen in the section on Anaxagoras, Socrates, instead of following his bodily impulses to escape his punishment ("Because, by dog, I fancy that these sinews and bones would have been in the neighborhood of Megara or Boeotia long ago"), follows the Good for the polis and accepts his death penalty. But his defiant self-defense throughout his trial indicates that he did not simply equate the Good with public opinion, or with the obedience to the existing Athenian laws. As the *Apology* of Plato narrates, Socrates equated the Good with God's wisdom, and claimed to be following God's orders as a philosopher, even if this meant the destruction of his bodily existence. In this way, by following what he thought was the universal Good, Socrates put himself in opposition to the majority opinion in Athens, which reflected the spirit of its time. For this reason, concludes Hegel, "His accusation was . . . just" (426). For Hegel, what is just, or unjust, is a historical category. It coincides with the Spirit of a nation at a given time.

To wit, the subjective individualism of Socrates is based upon *objective*, universal thought, which is the universal Good. According to Hegel, "The objective produced through thought, is at the same time in and for itself, thus being raised above all particularity of interests and desires, and being the power over them." The subjective side of Socrates, and Plato, emanates from the fact that, with them, "the moment of subjective freedom is the directing of consciousness into itself," and, consequently, "coming out from particular subjectivity." In this dialectic, the "contingency of events is abolished, and man has this outside within him, as the spiritual universal." For Hegel, this is "the true, the unity of subjective and objective in modern terminology," as distinct from "the Kantian ideal," which is "only phenomenal and not objective in itself" (386–87).

We must, however, take Hegel's interpretation here with a grain of salt, especially his claim that "it is hereby implied that contingency of events is abolished." While some sense of the absence of contingency is implied in the *Apology* by Socrates, it is equally true that he thought reason does not always rule the world in the sense Hegel says it does. In Plato's *Republic*, for instance, it is questionable whether or not Socrates thinks the ideal, just city, one in which reason rules, is possible in reality. Indeed, Socrates asserts that he is constructing a "theoretical model of a good city." He further asserts that the possibility of this practical model depends on the rule of the philosophers, or on the coincidence of "political power and philosophy." Socrates himself finds this a very hard idea to sell, and fears that uttering it would produce "a wave of laughter that will drown me in ridicule."[7] Whether or not Socrates thought the *kallipolis* (the ideal polis) is practically possible is debatable. What is not debatable is that he did not see the ideal as an inevitable telos of reason, as did Hegel, for he clearly detected around him a flight from it.

Relatedly, in the Socrates of Plato, we find a critical attitude toward existence, which one would be hard-pressed to find in Hegel. The objectivity of thought puts itself in opposition to the existing order of things. In creating the *kallipolis*, thought raises itself above existence, and becomes a reference point with which the existing order of things can be evaluated. The malfunctioning of the society of Socrates-Plato is thus not taken as a kind of Hegelian "ruse of reason," but as irrationality, pure and simple. In this way, reason becomes the antithesis of existence. Perhaps, it is better to attribute to Socrates Kant's point that the Good entailed in reason designates how things "ought to happen," with an eye on "the conditions under which what ought to happen frequently does not."[8] In this sense, the moral imperative becomes a duty for the individual to follow the universal Good. Here, ethics enters into philosophy.

Hegel is not necessarily against this interpretation of Socrates. He states that Socrates was the first to add "ethics as a new conception to Philosophy, which formerly only took nature into consideration" (387). He goes on to say that "the Athenians before Socrates were objectively, and not subjectively, moral, for they acted rationally in their relations without knowing that they were particularly excellent." In this, the pre-Socratic Athenians practiced morality dogmatically, and thus lacked "reflective morality," which "adds to natural morality the reflection that this is the good and not that." In other words, the reflective morality of Socrates is not simply a moralized philosophy but a philosophy of morality, of what moral action ought to entail.

---

7. Plato, *Republic*, trans. G.M.A Grube, ed. C.D.C. Reeve (Indianapolis: Hackett, 1992), 147 (472e), 148 (473d-e).
8. Immanuel Kant, *Grounding for the Metaphysics of Morals*, trans. James W. Ellington (Indianapolis: Hackett, 1993), 1.

Socrates thus anticipates "the Kantian philosophy," which is also "reflectively moral," and is so on the basis of showing "the difference," not only between the laws of nature and morality, but also between universal and non-universal morality (388). The distinction between universal and non-universal morality reflects the awareness of the contradiction between *ought* and *is*. There is nothing in Socrates's words to suggest that *ought* always triumphs, or will inevitably triumph, over what *is*, however. Hence, his morality is related to duty, to the imperative that one must lead a just life, regardless of the given mores or expected outcomes. In this way, Socrates's thought is not altogether different than the Confucian position on moral duty.

For this reason, his philosophical principle became Socrates's "religion." The Good to Socrates, is "not only the essential point to which men have to direct their thoughts, but it is that exclusively. We see him showing how from every individual this universal, this absolute in consciousness may be found as his [true] reality. Here we see law, the true and good, what was formerly present as an existent, return into consciousness." This returning into consciousness, this "reflective morality," represents the beginning of a new "universal consciousness in the spirit of the people to which [Socrates] belongs." Socrates heralds this beginning, and "stands above as the consciousness of this change. The spirit of the world here begins to change, a change which was later on carried to its completion." What this beginning brings forth is the reflection that self-consciousness "is real existence." Before Socrates, the Good took the shape of "the law of the State; it has authority as the law of the gods, and thus it is universal destiny which has the form of an existent, and is recognized as such by all." Beginning with Socrates, "moral consciousness asks if this is actually law in itself . . ." and proceeds to find such a law in individual consciousness, therefore accepting and justifying the law on the grounds consciousness gives to itself (407–8).

According to Hegel, ". . . what Socrates develops in the consciousness, is nothing but the good in as far as it is brought forth from consciousness through knowledge—it is the eternal, in and for itself universal, what is called the Idea, the true, which just in so far as it is end, is the Good," or "the Good . . . as end in itself." The affirmative, or positive, that emerges from Socrates's dialectic is precisely what distinguishes him from the Sophists. Here, Hegel returns to Protagoras's famous proposition in order to further bring out this distinction. The Sophist "proposition that man is the measure of all things" is linked to the "particular ends" of "man," whereas, to

Socrates, the proposition means bringing forth the implicit "universal" through "free thought... in [an] objective fashion" (406).

But Hegel finds an ambiguity in Socrates's principle. He says, Socrates's "philosophy, which asserts that real existence is in consciousness as a universal, is still not a properly speculative philosophy, but remained individual; yet the aim of his philosophy was that it should have a universal significance" (392). The ambiguity, then, is between what Socrates was able to deliver and intended to deliver. Because of the ambiguity, Socrates's principle remains abstract and individualized. "It now seems as if we had not yet shown forth much of the Socratic philosophy, for we have merely kept to the [abstract] principle; but the main point with Socrates is that his knowledge for the first time reached this abstraction." This is also to say it remained as a mere principle. To qualify this further, the Good in Socrates, says Hegel, "is nevertheless no longer as abstract as the *nous* of Anaxagoras, but is the universal which determines itself in itself, realizes itself, and has to be realized as the end of the world and of the individual. It is a principle, concrete within itself, which, however, is not yet manifested in its development, and in this abstract attitude we find what is wanting in the Socratic standpoint, of which nothing that is affirmative can, beyond this, be adduced" (406–7). Consequently, "the Socratic principle... [is] still merely formal," and simply expresses "that consciousness creates and has to create out of itself what is the true" (407). Hegel calls this Socratic principle "return into itself" of the *nous*, and says it represents "the highest point reached by the mind of Greece" yet.

> Consciousness and Being have here exactly the same value and rank; what *is*, is consciousness; neither is powerful above another. The authority of [the existing] law is no oppressive bond to consciousness, and all reality is likewise no obstacle to it, for it is secure in itself. But this return is just on the point of abandoning the content, and indeed of positing itself as abstract consciousness, without the content, and, as existent, opposed to it. From this equilibrium of consciousness and Being, consciousness takes up its position as independent. This aspect of separation is an independent conception, because consciousness, in the perception of its independence, no longer immediately acknowledges what is put before it, but requires that this should first justify itself to it, i.e. it must comprehend itself therein (409).

At the same time, this newfound morality suggests the advance of virtue in private life, as Socrates brought forward the idea that "in these times every one has to look after his own morality, and thus he looked after his through consciousness and reflection regarding himself; for he sought the universal spirit which had disappeared from reality, in his own consciousness" (ibid.). Even though he does not explicitly or clearly explain it, what Hegel seems to mean in this context is that Socrates, like Anaxagoras, also failed to establish the modality of the universal reason in his peculiar reality. In the Socratic sense, reason only rules, or ought to rule, the moral individual. If contingency disappears, it disappears only in the consciousness and actions of the moral individual. On the other hand, the world-at-large remains contingent.

4. The Shortcomings of Socrates's Dialectic

Hegel has told us several times above that Socrates's principle remained abstract. This issue relates to the "content" of his teachings and the "point reached" by Socrates "in the development of thought." In terms of addressing these issues, Hegel argues, Plato's depiction of Socrates is not very accurate. For the "content of his teaching and the point reached by him in the development of thought," we have to mainly rely upon Xenophon's *Memorabilia*, "a work which [also] aims at justifying Socrates." We should note in passim that Hegel thinks Xenophon's defense of Socrates against the accusations of blasphemy turn Socrates into a simpleton incapable of offending anybody. Hegel finds this aspect of Xenophon's depiction of Socrates unsatisfactory. What we more usefully find in Xenophon's *Memorabilia* is the unity of both "a positive and a negative side," of the Socratic universal (414).

In this work, "as regards the positive side," that is, the Good, Xenophon describes how Socrates, after refuting the particularity of the purely subjective Good, taught the youth "the good in the clearest and most open way. That is, he showed them the good and true [the universal] in what is determined [the particular]." But, he always went back into the particular "because he did not wish to remain in mere abstraction" by relying solely on the pure principle of the Good. However, says Hegel, Socrates creates inconsistencies when he attempts to demonstrate the universal, the absolute, in the particular cases. This is because Socrates wounds up reducing the former to the latter at times (415).

This inconsistency comes across in the dialogue Xenophon creates between "the Sophist Hippias" and Socrates. Socrates asserts in this dialogue, as Hegel summarizes it, that

> the just man is he who obeys the law, and that these laws are divine. Xenophon makes Hippias reply by asking how Socrates could declare it to be an absolute duty to obey the laws, for the people and the governors themselves often condemn them by changing them, which is allowing that they are not absolute. But Socrates answers by demanding if those who conduct war do not again make peace, which is not, any more than in the other case, to condemn war, for each was just in its turn.

Socrates implies here that the opposite actions may have the same universal Good as their end. The example of war and peace presumably helps illustrate the point that the changing particular conditions, or actions, do not obliterate the absolute contained in the law. It follows that the just man remains the same because being just means obeying the law regardless of its specific manifestation. "Socrates thus says, in a word, that the best and happiest State is that in which the citizens are of one mind and obedient to law." Hegel does not find this to be a satisfactory answer. Socrates simply "looks away from the contradiction" between the absolute and particular, and ends up making "laws and justice, as they are accepted by each individually . . . , the affirmative content. But if we here ask what these laws are, they are, we find, just those which have a value at some one time, as they happen to be present in the State and in the idea; at another time they [negate] themselves as determined, and are not held to be absolute" (415–16).

Generally speaking, argues Hegel, when perception "positively acknowledges as law that which was held to be law (for the positive subsists through having recourse to laws), this acknowledgment of [the law] always passes through the negative mode, and no longer has the form of absolute being-in-itself." Perception thus is incapable of producing "a Platonic Republic," which can only be produced speculatively on the basis of the cognition of the "absolute being-in-itself." Thus, the existing concrete determinations of the law are dissolved in the Absolute Notion; "only the purely implicit universal Good is the true." "But since this [purely implicit universal] is empty and without reality, we demand . . . that again a movement should be made towards the extension of the determination of the universal."

Socrates does not make this demand: "Now because Socrates remains at the indeterminateness of the good," that is, takes it as purely implicit universal, "its determination means for him simply the expression of the particular good. Then it comes to pass that the universal results only from the negation of the particular good; and since this last is just the existing laws of Greek morality, we have here the doubtlessly right, but dangerous element in perception, the showing in all that is particular only its deficiencies." This produces the "inconsistency of making what is limited [that is, the existing laws] into an absolute . . ." Because this "demand" is not made, the inconsistency here arises from equating the particular, the limited, with the absolute. "But" once the demand is made, "the dialectic sublates the particular" and brings it to bear the universal. This more developed dialectic is not found in Socrates (414–15). Such dialectic is found in Plato, as we will see below.

Next, Hegel proceeds to demonstrate the "negative side" of Socrates's dialectic, as it is found in Xenophon's account. The "negative side" here refers to the dismantling of what is taken as the universal by his opponents, which really is a particular determination. Hegel quotes several different exchanges between Socrates and Euthydemus to illustrate this negative side. The basic premise of these exchanges is that Socrates now tries to get Euthydemus to accept that what is just and unjust can be distinguished from each other in the sense that they are mutually exclusive terms. With the approval of Euthydemus, Socrates places "'. . . lies, deceit, robbery, making a slave of a free man'" under the category of unjust, and the opposites of these determinations under the category of just. Then, Socrates introduces a series of scenarios to show "'that the same qualities come under the determination both of justice and of injustice.'" To illustrate this, in one of these scenarios, which, by the way, is also found in Plato's *Republic*, Socrates asks, "'Is anyone wrong who takes arms from his friend secretly or by force, when he sees him in despair, and in the act of taking his own life?' Euthydemus has to admit that this is not wrong." However, under a different scenario, when one's friend is not in despair, taking what belongs to him would be wrong. Once again, it is shown here that "the same determinations" may be perceived as both justice and injustice. As Hegel concludes, "Here we see that abstention from lying, deceit, and robbery, that which we naturally hold to be established [as just actions], contradicts itself by being put into connection with something different, and something which holds equally good. This example further explains how through thought, which would lay hold of the universal in the form of the universal only, the particular becomes uncertain" (416–

17). For Hegel, the particular is always uncertain, and this is what Socrates also attempts to demonstrate here.

In the first argument against Hippias, as noted above, Socrates reduces the universal to a specific determination, namely that justice is the obedience to law. However, the problem is that there is no absolute particular action which could be readily equated with the general standard. In the second, he demonstrates that the particular determinations are necessarily contradictory. He thus unwittingly denies the conclusion of the first argument. Consequently, says Hegel, the "positive, which Socrates sets in the place of what was fixed" in the first argument, "has now become vacillating" in the second. The aim in the first was to "give a content to the universal" which was expressed as "the obedience to law." But this content falls into contradiction when it faces specific determinations. Such determinations thus fall into the realm of perception, since they "do not hold good [valid] for the Notion." In order to make them consistent with the Notion, perception has now "to justify itself as a determination proceeding out of the constitution of the whole . . . [W]e do not find this perception present in Socrates, for it remains in its content undetermined." But, as Hegel sees the matter at hand, in reality perception alone is always "a contingent" (418).

The general problem that emerges from these considerations can be illustrated with the following example, says Hegel. Universal commands, such as the Socratic "obedience to the law," or the biblical maxim "'Thou shalt not kill,' are connected with a particular content which is conditioned." This maxim thus ties the universal to a specific command, and thus conditions it with a particularity. "Now whether the universal maxim in this particular case has value or not, depends first on the circumstances; and it is the perception which discovers the conditions and circumstances whereby exceptions to this law of unconditioned validity arise . . . [T]hrough this contingency in the instances, the fixed nature of the universal principle disappears, since it, too, appears as a particular only." Because Socrates does this in the argument with Euthydemus, his consciousness "arrives at pure freedom in each particular content." "This freedom, which does not leave the content as it is in its dissipated determination to the natural consciousness [perception], but makes it to be penetrated by the universal, is the real mind which, as unity of the universal content and of freedom, is the veritable truth. Thus if we here consider further what is the true in this consciousness, we pass on to the mode in which the realization of the universal appeared to Socrates himself" (ibid.).

We may thus call what appeared to Socrates's consciousness "the mind which thinks at the right time," first of the universal, and then of the particular. This makes his consciousness "spirit, but an unspiritual consciousness." What is meant here is further clarified when Hegel tells us that the "first step towards reaching a spiritual consciousness is the negative one of acquiring freedom for one's consciousness." This acquisition of freedom requires putting perception under the scrutiny of dialectic, which Socrates does. This is the negative step. The reason given for this is that, "since perception attempts to prove individual laws, it proceeds from a determination to which, as a universal basis, particular duty is submitted; but this basis is itself not absolute, and falls under the same dialectic [of negation]." For example, "were moderation commanded as a duty on the ground that intemperance undermined the health, health is the ultimate which is here considered as absolute; but it is at the same time not absolute, for there are other duties which ordain that health, and even life itself, should be risked and sacrificed." Yet, this contradiction between the absolute duty and particular manifestations of duty does not obliterate the absolute: "The so-called conflict of duties is nothing but duty, which is expressed as absolute, showing itself as not absolute." In this "constant contradiction" of the absolute with its specific appearances, nevertheless, the given, determinate "morals become unsettled." Thus, "the positive truth has not yet become known in its determination," since its appearance in the particular has negated it. "To know the universal in its determination . . . is only possible in connection with the whole system of actuality" (419). To account for this knowledge, the truth that is, requires showing the inner connections of all the particular determinations. The truth after all, as Hegel tells elsewhere, is the whole. What Hegel recommends here is not the same approach as the demonstration of the Absolute in many separate determinations, which Socrates seems to be doing. The manifold manifestation of the Absolute, which constitutes the whole, must be understood on the basis of the true ground, which is the "universal spirit." The individual must be shown to be connected "with this real universal spirit" of inextricable necessity (419–20). It is Plato who first makes a significant advance in this regard.

Elsewhere, Hegel explains what this means more clearly: "Among the Ancients, Plato is called the inventor of dialectic." This statement, of course, is historically inaccurate for, as Hegel also noted when dealing with Zeno, the ancients credited Zeno with this invention. Hegel, however, seems to mean that Plato invented the first truly scientific dialectic. "With Socrates, dialectical thinking still has a predominantly subjective shape." In contrast, with Plato "dialectic first occurs in a form which is freely scientific, and hence also objective." Plato, "by means of a dialectical treatment . . . , shows in his strictly scientific dialogues the general finitude of all fixed determinations of the understanding. Thus, for example, in the *Parmenides*, he deduces the Many (determinations) from the One, and, notwithstanding that, he shows that the nature of the Many is simply to determine itself as the One."[9]

Still, Socrates was instrumental in the commencement of this scientific dialectic, which placed him in opposition to his times. In this sense, Socrates was a tragic hero.

> In general history we find that this is the position of the heroes through whom a new world commences, and whose principle stands in contradiction to what has gone before and disintegrates it: [These heroes] appear to be violently destroying the laws. Hence individually they are vanquished, but it is only the individual, and not the principle, which is negated in punishment, and the spirit of the Athenian people did not in the removal of the individual [Socrates], recover its old position. The [Socratic] individuality is taken away . . . in a violent way by punishment; but the principle itself will penetrate later, if in another form, and elevate itself into a form of the world-spirit. This universal mode in which the principle comes forth and permeates the present is the true one; what was wrong was the fact that the principle came forth only as the peculiar possession of one individual. His own world could not comprehend Socrates, but posterity can, in as far as it stands above both (444).

The universal Spirit marches on, finds more tragic heroes and uses them for its own purposes. This inevitable march forward is the development of Reason, and is transmitted to us through the minds of philosophers. Socrates was one necessary step in this development, and a very significant one at that.

---

9. Hegel, *The Encyclopaedia Logic*, 129.

CHAPTER 8

First Greek Period, Second Division - Part III: The Socratics

1. Introduction

Hegel calls *Socratic* "those schools and methods . . . in which we find nothing but the one-sided understanding of Socratic culture." An exception to this one-sidedness is Plato. Apart from Plato, the Socratics divide into four schools of thought. One branch of the Socratics "kept quite faithfully to the direct methods of Socrates, without going any further." This branch includes Xenophon, Aeschines, Phaedo, and the "shoemaker, Simon." They merely transcribed Socrates's dialogues, either from what they directly heard from him, or by copying the transcriptions of others, or by "working out similar dialogues in [the fashion of] his method." With the works of these Socratics, Hegel finds "only a literary interest," and does not consider them any further in his lectures (449–50).

Apart from this imitative school, and not counting Plato, three other Socratic schools emerge in the post-Socrates period: "the Megaric . . . , Cyrenaic and Cynic Schools." What makes these diverse schools Socratic is that, as is the case with Socrates, they held "the true and good" as the "end" in the "determination of the subject." These three Socratic schools all share the "saying that the subject itself is end," and the subject "reaches its subjective end through the cultivation of its knowledge." In this manner, they reproduce subjective individualism by declaring the Good to be the end of each individual subject. While the universal seems to vanish in this sort of subjective individualism, at least in the philosophies of some Socratics, Hegel maintains that "the form of determination in them is still the universal, and it is also so that it does not remain abstract, for the development of the determinations of the universal gives real knowledge." The Socratics declared that true knowledge "requires that men should be able to tell what the good and true really are" (452). For some Socratics, this meant knowing how to live well in accordance with the subjectively determined Good, which they defined as pleasure or the absence of pain.

However, the Socratics did not agree on the proper means and ends of happiness. They even disagreed on whether or not happiness is possible. Some of them did not even consider the question at all, and focused, instead, on the sophistical ways of disputing the logic of truth claims. The fact that these schools, and their principles, are actually diverse and contradictory, and that each seems to borrow something from Socrates's thought, suggests to some that Socrates's philosophy itself was incoherent. Hegel, however, argues that this diversification is due to the "indefiniteness and abstraction of [Socrates'] principle" (449). This "indefiniteness," in turn, is a "function of the dialectical approach" of Socrates, which negates everything definite. According to Hegel, the Socratic schools attempted to give the Socratic principle of the Good "more definite forms," and this attempt, in turn, produced diversity.[1]

Even though the Socratics did not make this transition from the indefinite to definite forms of the Good sufficiently, what Hegel sees here is a necessary development in the historical dialectic of philosophy, which is the transition from the abstract Notion of the Good to its more concrete manifestations, that is, from *being-in-itself* to *being-for-itself*. Because the Socratics were mainly concerned with the philosophy of good-life, this transition comes across, one-sidedly, as the transition from the individual person *in-itself* to individual *for-itself*, instead of the Notional transition demanded by truly speculative philosophy. As we will discover later, what is lacking in this transition is the objectively moral, or substantive, individuality, which thinks and wills in accordance with the Absolute Spirit. Thus, *for-itself* becomes in this context merely what is good "for me." In this sense, the end of living well is to live *for-myself*.

Hegel, in reformulating Socrates's thought, now maintains that "subjectively, Socrates had the formal effect of bringing about a discord in the individual; the content was subsequently left to the free-will and liking of each person, because the principle was subjective consciousness and not objective thought. Socrates himself only came so far as to express for consciousness generally the simple existence of one's own thought as the Good, but as to whether the particular conceptions of the Good really properly defined . . . the essence [of *being*], he did not inquire." In this way, "Socrates made the Good the end of the living man." But, because he did not make the transition from the Idea of the Good to real existence, he "made the whole world of idea" exist apart from the "objective existence in general." In other words, he did not seek to "find a passage from the Good," which is the ideational essence, to objective existence. He thus failed to recognize the "real essence as the essence of things" (449).

---

1. Hegel, *Lectures on the History of Philosophy 1825–6*, 157.

Hegel clarifies that "the true and essence are not the same; the true is essence as [explicit] thought, but essence [when it is contemplated by itself] is the simply implicit [thought]." Thus, the simply implicit is, "indeed, thought, and is in thought." The true, on the other hand, is the unity of the implicit thought and the object which thought contemplates. Before the Socratic period, essence appeared either as the simply implicit or as the simply objective. Philosophy after Socrates no longer contemplates "essence as left to itself," or "as purely objective," but as in "unity with the certainty of itself." This definition of essence assumes "the unity of Being and Thought" in consciousness, and is the "definition of absolute essence" (450–51).

Since Hegel has now produced overdrawn conclusions that cannot be found in the Socratics, he takes a step back and says the Socratics had no such knowledge of the absolute essence. "It is rather the case that the philosophers in this period could no longer speak of essence and actuality without this element of self-certainty." This is to say, this "middle period" in the first Greek period, represents the "movement of knowledge, and considers knowledge as the science of essence, which first brings about that unity," of the essence and *being*, if not the "content and definition of the absolute essence" (451–52). If not a complete system, the possibility of such a system arises in this period because simple essence and existence, thought and *being*, are brought into a direct relation.

However, we must qualify Hegel's evaluation above of the Socratic period. The Socratics did not explicitly identify the Good, which is the universal, with essence. The language of essence is entirely missing in their arguments, not to mention the fact that some of the Socratics did not even engage with the terminology of the Good. The discussion of the category of essence in this context is the result of Hegel's forward looking interjection. Indeed, Hegel points out that, as a consequence of further development, "all present speculative philosophy expresses the universal as essence . . . ," though this presentation, "as it first appears," still "has the semblance of being a single determination, beside which there are a number of others." By this, Hegel means that the present speculative philosophy identifies the universal with essence, and makes the requisite transition from essence to existence. The transition is "speculative" because essence can be grasped only super-sensuously. But, since this form of speculative philosophy treats existence as many independently subsisting finite determinations, it assigns a definite and independent, and thus a finite, essence to each determination. In this way, it contemplates an essence for each existent thing in the atomistic tradition. "It is the complete movement of knowledge," says Hegel, "that first removes this semblance, and the system of the universe then shows forth its essence as Notion, as a connected whole" (ibid.). This point suggests that, for Hegel, there is one infinite essence which holds all the particular existents together, and organizes them as the internally connected moments of the whole.

As he explains elsewhere, "We speak . . . about *finite* essences, and [for instance] we call man a finite essence. But, in speaking of essence, we have strictly speaking, gone beyond finitude, so that to designate man as a finite essence is inaccurate." This is because the essence of "man," like all other finite essences, derives from the universal essence, and cannot be conceived adequately without it. This universal essence is God.[2] Even though God is declared to be the infinite essence in this context, in strictly philosophical terms, the universal Notion plays the same role. The Notion is the infinite essence, and the finite essences, or finite universals, are its manifestations within the particular determinations in existence. If the Good is taken to represent the Notion, then it must be shown that it is the essence and the truth of all that is particular.

Now, in some sense, it is true that the question of essence arises during this Socratic period. Plato was a contemporary of the founders of the Socratic schools. It was Plato who first explicitly discussed the category of essence, and more satisfactorily made the transition from essence to existence. This transition is the crux of Plato's dialectic. To repeat, Plato, "by means of a dialectical treatment . . . , shows in his strictly scientific dialogues the general finitude of all fixed determinations of the understanding. Thus, for example, in the *Parmenides*, he deduces the Many (determinations) from the One, and, notwithstanding that, he shows that the nature of the Many is simply to determine itself as the One."[3] The Platonic One thus is the infinite essence of the many. We must remember that the One in Plato is the Form (the Idea) of the Good, and all the other particular Forms partake in it. St. Augustine later equated the Form of the Good, which he learned from the Platonists, with the Christian God. Consequently, St. Augustine declared that "There are none who come nearer to us than the Platonists."[4] We also frequently find this identification of the Idea, or the Absolute essence, with God in Hegel.

With the above introductory remarks, Hegel once again begins a new period in philosophy with somewhat exaggerated enthusiasm.

---

2. Hegel, *The Encyclopaedia Logic*, 177.
3. Ibid., 129.
4. St. Augustine, *City of God* (London: Penguin Books, 1984), 304.

Perhaps, this has to do with Hegel's thesis that the history of philosophy entails development. If so, development has to be demonstrated. For this reason, Hegel attributes ideas to the Socratics that they had not themselves contemplated. Another problem with Hegel's introductory comments is that, because he places the Megaric, Cyrenaic, and Stoic schools under the same philosophical category, that is, *the Socratics*, he ends up somewhat conflating their otherwise diverse ideas. This conflation is centered on the Socratic principle of the Good as the end of the individual, which, presumably, all the Socratics share in common. When he begins to deal with the specific Socratic philosophers in the ensuing sections, Hegel retreats from this conflation, though he still attributes his own ideas to the Socratics. On the one hand, this strategy makes it difficult for us to sort out what belongs to Hegel and what belongs to each Socratic philosopher discussed below. On the other hand, it creates a valuable opportunity to understand some of the key tenets of Hegel's own philosophy.

2. The Megarics

One interpretation of the Megarics posits that they were bent upon negating the universal essence along with particular determinations. According to Hegel, the Megarics tried to achieve the universal by casting doubt on all that is particular. This is consistent with their negative dialectic through which the universal is to be established in its pure and simple form, as the simple essence. For this reason, "The Megarics were most abstract, because they held to the [simple] determination of the good" as their principle. Here, the simplicity of the Good acquires a new meaning. The Megaric Good is no longer the implicit, infinite, abstract essence, but, rather, a simple determination. With these thoughts, Hegel creates some confusion when he adds that the Megaric school attached this "simplicity of the good" to "the dialectic" of negation, namely, "that all that was defined and limited is not true" (452–53).

If the latter point is the case, then the Megarics cannot at the same time hold on to a determinate definition of the Good. It would be more plausible to say that the Megarics took the Good in the abstract, infinite, and undetermined sense. This interpretation is more consistent with Hegel's claim above that "the Megarics were" the "most abstract" among the Socratic schools. It is also more consistent with what Diogenes Laërtius says of their principle: Anything that "is contradictory of the good," which is necessarily in unity within itself, has "no existence."[5] Attached to this proposition is the Megaric claim that everything determinate is contradictory of the Good. If so, we cannot say that the Megarics made the transition from the simple essence to determinate existence, or gave the Good a simple, determinate form, as Hegel suggested above. Hegel is about to admit as much. The identification of the Good with particular determinations of thought or sensation is the business of the Cyrenaics, and not of the Megarics.

As for their dialectic, "because with the Megarics the principal point was to know the universal, and this universal was to them the Absolute which had to be retained in this [simple] form of the universal, this thought, as Notion, which holds a negative position in relation to all determinateness and thus to the [determinateness] of Notion also, was equally turned against knowledge and perception" (453). According to Hegel, this is because true knowledge requires the unity of the universal Notion with finite determinations. The unity of the particular and the universal is to be achieved through the sublation of what is first perceived as a particular determination, and not through the latter's elimination. This sublation requires "going back" from the determinate *this-ness* of the existents to the universal, as Plato had done. Said differently, the implicit essence, as thought, has to penetrate the objectivity of the determinate *being*, and thus see itself as the *prius* of the latter. The Megarics failed to make the transition from the universal, and simply put the universal in opposition to the particular. Indeed, in order to prove the nonexistence of the particular determinations, they thrived in creating contradictions.

2.1 Euclides

Euclides of Megara (a.k.a. Euclid, or Eucleides) "is regarded as the founder of the Megaric way of thinking." Because he and his followers "held to the forms of universality, and, above all, sought, with success, to show forth the contradictions contained in all particular conceptions, they were reproached with having a rage for disputation, and hence the name of Eristics was given them." They used dialectic as an instrument to bring "all that is particular into confusion [contradiction]," and thus annulled the truth of the particular determinations. In doing this, they tried to extract the universal form the dissolution of the particular. "With a dialectic thus

---

5. Diogenes Laërtius, *Lives of the Eminent Philosophers*, Vol. 1, 122.

constituted, we find them taking the place of the Eleatic School and of the Sophists; and it *seems* as though the Eleatic School had merely been reproduced, since [the Megarics] were essentially identical with it" (454).

However, Hegel says, there are differences between the Megarics and the Eleatics, and between the Megarics and the Sophists. While "the Eleatic dialecticians maintained Being as the one existence in relation to which nothing particular is a truth," the Megarics "considered Being as the Good." This difference suggests the Socratic streak in the Megaric thought, though it does not make the Megaric dialectic any different than the Eleatic dialectic. The Sophists, on the other hand, "did not seek their impulse in simple universality as fixed and as enduring," as did the Megarics and the Eleatics (454–55). More accurately stated, Euclides is the Megaric who is closer to the Eleatics, especially Parmenides, and Eubulides is the Megaric whose dialectic resembles that of the Sophists, and to some extent of Zeno.

In the tradition of the Eleatic Parmenides, "it was Euclides who said that 'the Good is one,' and it alone is, 'though passing under many names; sometimes it is called Understanding, sometimes God; at another time Thought (*nous*), and so on. But what is opposed to the good does not exist.'" Obviously, the Megaric principle enunciated by Euclides here combines the Eleatic principle of the One with that of Socrates by identifying the One with the Good. "Since the Megarics make the Good, as the simple identity of the true, into a principle, it is clearly seen that they expressed the Good as the absolute existence in a universal sense, as did Socrates." However, they did so with a different aim in mind. Socrates looked at all the particular determinations, or conceptions, as approximations of the Good that are "indifferent to the interests of man." The Megarics simply denied the existence of these particulars "for they asserted definitely that they were nothing at all." Like the Eleatics, they tried to show that "only Being [the Good] is, and that all else, as negative, does not exist" (455–56).

2.2 Eubulides

Like Zeno, Eubulides attempted to prove the nonexistence of the contradictory particulars, without trying to positively induce the universal from his proofs. In this sense, the dialectic of Eubulides relates to Euclides's principle in the same way Zeno's dialectic relates to the principle of Parmenides. Whereas Parmenides and Euclides asserted the truth of One, Zeno and Eubulides attempted to disprove the existence of many. However, we should add, there is no evidence for us to believe that Eubulides held the One to be the true *being*, as did Zeno or Euclides. For this reason, Eubulides is closer to the Sophists.

Eubulides, a pupil of Euclides, is famous for the paradoxes he created to refute ordinary truth claims. The Greeks, notes Hegel, "were quite enamored of discovering contradictions" found "in speech and in ordinary ideas." For Hegel, ordinary ideas necessarily fall into contradictions. It is important to note here that Hegel uses the term *contradiction* more liberally than we do today. Contradiction in the Hegelian usage does not simply signify an irreconcilable opposition, or inconsistency among the elements of a proposition, or a situation, or between two different propositions. Among its many specific meanings, contradiction may also refer to the difference between subject and its predicate, which is what Hegel has in mind when he says: "Subject and predicate, of which every proposition consists, are different, but in the ordinary idea we signify their unity; this simple unity, which does not contradict itself, is to ordinary ideas the truth. But in fact, the simple self-identical proposition is an unmeaning tautology; for in any affirmation, differences are present, and because their diversity comes to consciousness, there is contradiction." If I say A=A, which is the law of identity, I produce a "meaningless tautology." If I say *this table is brown*, I necessarily posit a contradiction, that is, a difference between the subject and the predicate, even though I assume the identity of *this* table and brown. Being brown may be a particular attribute of *this* table, but *brown* and *table* are not the same, and hence their assumed identity is contradictory. The "ordinary" conception, which is formal logic in this context, does not immediately realize this contradiction. Consequently, its dialectic of cognition comes to "an end" when the contradiction is pointed out. According to Hegel, "only where there is a contradiction is there the solution," and the solution comes from the self-negation of the subject. "Ordinary consciousness has not the conception that only the unity of opposites is the truth—that in every statement there is truth and falsehood, if truth is to be taken in the sense of the simple, and falsehood in the sense of the opposed and contradictory; in it the positive, the first unity, and the negative, this last opposition, fall asunder" (458).

What Hegel says above is extremely important to his philosophy. Elsewhere, he says that "the insight that the very nature of thinking is the dialectic, that, as understanding, it must fall into the negative of itself, into contradictions, is an aspect of capital importance in the

Logic."[6] Hegel credits Kant for discovering this necessary connection between thinking and the dialectic of contradiction: "For Kant... it lies in the very nature of thinking to lapse into contradictions ('antinomies') when it aims at the cognition of the infinite." Hegel considers this Kantian intervention to be a great advance in modern philosophical thinking, especially against "the older metaphysics," which assume that "where cognition falls into contradictions, this is just an accidental aberration and rests on a subjective error in inferring an arguing."[7]

Eubulides takes advantage of the weakness of "ordinary" consciousness (the understanding), though in his own terms and without the recognition that contradiction is a necessary component of thinking and a necessary step in the knowledge of truth. "In Eubulides' propositions, the main point was that because the truth is simple, a simple answer is required." One has to be able to answer yes or no if one purports to know the truth. One thus should not "have regard to certain special considerations." (Such considerations are allowed in Aristotle.) Eubulides's principle demands simplicity, which, after all "is really the demand of the understanding... The simplicity of the truth is thus grasped as the principle" (458–59).

We must clarify here that attributing to Eubulides the proposition that "the truth is simple," which Hegel does, is misleading. He demands simple answers to his questions with the explicit purpose of casting doubt on all truth claims by illustrating their inherent contradictions. He demands simple answers because the understanding claims that the truth is simple, that is, devoid of contradiction. Hegel conflates Eubulides's position with that of the formal logic in this context, and this conflation comes across more vividly when he says, "With us," by which he means the formal logic in his own time—this simplicity "appears in the form of making such statements as that one of opposites is true, the other false; that a statement is either true or not true; that an object cannot have two opposite predicates. That is the first principle of the understanding, the *principium exclusi tertii* [excluded third, or the middle]." Accordingly, "the true is the universal; which is abstractly the identity of understanding, according to which what is said to be true cannot contradict itself." This principle is expressed most clearly by the Megaric Stilpo, says Hegel (see below). "The Megarics thus kept to this principle of our logic of the understanding, in demanding the form of identity for the Truth." However, in the examples they

---

6. Hegel, *The Encyclopaedia Logic*, 35.
7. Ibid., 92–93.

produced, they did not identify the universal, but, rather, "sought examples in ordinary conception, by means of which they perplexed people" (458–59). Hegel's last point shows awareness of the fact that the Megarics, especially Eubulides, was not after the proof of the proposition that "the truth is simple," but, rather, that all truth claims entail contradictions. His aim in showing this, furthermore, is to leave people "perplexed," and only that. This makes him a kind of sophist.

The sophistical examples of bringing about perplexity are called *elench*, which are usually given specific names. One *elench*, proposed by Eubulides, is called the Liar. It goes as follows: "'If a man acknowledges that he lies, does he lie or speak the truth?' A simple answer is demanded, for the simple whereby the other is excluded, is held to be the true." Thus, "If it is said that he tells the truth, this contradicts the content of his utterance, for he confesses that he lies. But if it is asserted that he lies, it may be objected that his confession is the truth." According to Hegel, it is obvious that "he thus both lies and does not lie." Thus, in this example, "we have a union of two opposites, lying and truth, and their immediate contradiction." In general, simple answers cannot be demanded when "the content is contradictory," though, as Hegel tells us elsewhere, we may demand simple answers to such questions as When was Ceasar born? The proper answer to the above riddle should be that "he speaks the truth and lies at the same time, and the truth is this contradiction." But, "a contradiction is not the true," they say, "and cannot enter into our ordinary conceptions." Consequently, when ordinary thinking detects contradiction, it keeps "the contradictory sides apart," instead of incorporating them into synthetic truth. "These sophisms thus not only appear to be contradictory, but are so in truth: this choice between two opposites, which is set before us in the example, is itself a contradiction," which needs to be demonstrated as such (459–61).

Other sophisms attributed to Eubulides, which are named *the Concealed* and *the Electra*, "proceed from the contradiction of knowing and not knowing someone at the same time." In the former, "I ask someone 'Do you know your father?' He replies 'Yes.' I then ask 'Now if I show you someone hidden behind a screen, will you know him [as your father]?' 'No.' 'But it is your father, and thus you do not know your father.' It is the same in the Electra. 'Can it be said that she knows her brother Orestes who stands [too far away from] her or not?'" Hegel says these sophisms are more interesting than they first appear. They exploit the weaknesses of ordinary conception. To know in the ordinary conception means to perceive someone as "this" person. "The son thus knows his father when he sees him, i.e. when he is a 'this' for him." But, adds Hegel, when the father is hidden, he is no longer a "this" for him, but a negated "this." "The hidden one as a 'this' in ordinary conception, becomes a general, and loses his sensuous being, thereby is in fact not a true 'this.'" The hidden contradiction in this sophism is between the sensuous "this," the person I see here and now, and the universal *this-ness*, the implicit Notion of Father, which is beyond sense perception. "The contradiction that the son both knows and does not know his father thus becomes dissolved through the further qualification that the son knows the father as a sensuous 'this,' and not as a 'this' of the idea." "In this way," adds Hegel, "there enters into these histories the higher opposition of the universal and of the 'this,'" which is the particular. For Hegel, in contrast, the negated *this* "has its truth in the universal" (461–62).

In other words, the true knowledge of the particular father, that is, *this* father, is only possible if we recognize that the universal Notion of Father is its essence, and that all particular fathers, who are differentiations of the universal Notion, partake in this universal. Whether or not Eubulides wanted to express this dialectic is uncertain. It seems more to be the case that he simply, in a sophistical manner, wanted to create confusion. Indeed, perhaps sensing that his conclusions are overdrawn here, Hegel points out that "the consciousness of this" relationship of the universal and particular, "as we shall soon see, is indicated by Stilpo," and not directly by Eubulides (462). In this way, Hegel seems to be reading Eubulides's quibbles through the prism of Stilpo.

Other quibbles, such as *the Sorites* and *the Bald*, are more meaningful, says Hegel. They both are related to the contradiction between quantity and quality. What is posited by these is a "quantitative progression which can [seemingly] reach no qualitative opposite, and yet at the end finds itself at a qualitative absolute opposite." For instance, it is asked: "'Does one grain of corn make a heap, or does one hair less make a bald head?' The reply is 'No.' 'Nor one again?' 'No, it does not.'" The logic of this paradox relies on the premise that *one grain of corn does not make a heap*. It is not asked if 10,000 grains added together would make a heap. This addition process goes on, one grain being added each time, and the question remains, "does one grain make a heap"? Likewise with *the Bald*, though instead of adding, a single hair is plucked from the head each time. At some point, if we add up all the single grains and hairs added or plucked, we come to recognize "that there is a heap or a bald head." It is thus "found that the last added grain or last abstracted hair has made the heap or the baldness, and this was at first denied" (463). It appears from these examples that one grain both makes and does not make a heap, and one hair removed both makes and does not make a bald head. This indicates a contradiction between quantitative and qualitative change.

Hegel adds that "we always separate quality and quantity from one another, and only accept in the many [grains of corn, for instance] a quantitative difference; but this indifferent distinction of number or size here turns finally into qualitative distinction, just as an infinitely small or infinitely great [magnitude] is no longer [magnitude] at all. This characteristic of veering round is of the greatest importance, although it does not come directly before our consciousness." Such movements from quantity to quality occur everywhere in nature. For instance, water, if heated up to 100 Celsius, evaporates and becomes steam. "The dialectic of this passing into one another of quantity and quality is what our understanding does not recognize." By this, Hegel means that we do not ordinarily recognize the identity of quantity and quality. Thus, the ordinary conception, the understanding, "is certain that qualitative is not quantitative, and quantitative not qualitative." It is also the case that Eubulides did not recognize the identity of quantity and quality. However, in his above quibbles, there is still a "genuine reflection on the thought-determinations which are in question" (463–64). In other words, Eubulides demonstrates the contradiction between quantity and quality, though he does not reconcile it.

Hegel gives considerable attention to the relationship between quantity and quality in *Logic*. He explains that the transition from one to the other is the transition of the implicit essence. Qualities, says Hegel, "are conditioned by quantitative ratios between the substances they contain." A quality cannot have too much or too little of its substance, or else it becomes another quality, that is, another determinate *being* in existence. The unity of quantity and quality in a determinate *being* is called "measure." Thus, measure designates the becoming of the implicit *being* into a determinate *being*. "When we speak of being, it appears initially to be what is entirely abstract and lacking all determination; but being is essentially what determines itself, and it reaches its completed determinacy in measure."[8]

But, since every measure is involved in the process of self-negation, measure by itself proves inadequate to the task of comprehension. The process of measure is precisely the passing of quantity and quality into each other. But this continuous passing into each other suggests to the ordinary consciousness a "spurious infinity . . . in the shape of a perpetual overturning of quality into

---

8. Hegel, *The Encyclopaedia Logic*, 173.

quantity and of quantity into quality . . ." This is the limitation of the ordinary conception of measure: It does not account for "the true Infinity" also present in measure. The true Infinity "consists in the going together with one self in one's other." Hence, when quantity and quality pass into one another "each of them only becomes what it already is *in-itself*, and we now obtain the being that is negated in its determinations, in general terms the sublated being that is *Essence*." As it turns out, essence is all along "implicit within measure," that is, within the determinate being as a synthesis of quantity and quality. Without it, the process of moving from quantity to quality, and vice versa, is not possible. Without the cognition of *essence*, quantity and quality cannot be cognized as the unity of opposites. The measure "consists simply in its positing itself as what it is in-itself."[9] That is to say, measure is always the positing of the universal essence.

2.3 Stilpo

It is with Stilpo that the universal finds a more direct expression, says Hegel. Even though he took the universal mainly "in the sense of the formal abstract identity of the understanding," he still gave "prominence to the form of universality as opposed to the particular" (465). Once again, we see here, too, the opposition of the particular *this* to the universal Notion, and the negation of the particular's truth consequently.

For instance, Stilpo asserts that "'who ever speaks of any man, speaks of no-one, for he neither speaks of this . . . [man] nor that [man]. For why should it rather be [speaking] of this [man] than that [man]? Hence it is not of this one [man that is spoken of]'" (ibid.). Hegel adds to this that everyone readily acknowledges that "man is the universal, and that no one is specially indicated," when one speaks of *man* in general. However, "some one," a particular man, "still remains present to us in our conception." Even though Hegel does not say so explicitly here, for him the particular man comes to us through sense perception. Only through speculative reason, we come to see the universal *man* as the form in which all particular men partake. The universal is thus the essence of the particular, as it is the identity of all the men that are otherwise many individuals, or differences. In this case, the individual coincides with the human individual, though the term *individual* generally refers to a member of a *genus*.

---

9. Ibid., 176.

According to Hegel, what Stilpo means to say above is "that the 'this' does not exist at all, and cannot be expressed—that the universal only exists." Here, two issues are conflated: the ontological (the existence of the particular) and the epistemological (the ability to know, and express the particular). The assumption underlying this conflation is that whatever cannot be expressed also does not exist, and *vice-versa*. This, of course, is not a universally held position. Diogenes Laërtius and Tennemann, on the other hand, posit that "'Stilpo abolished distinction of genera'" (ibid.).

The word "genera" is obviously the plural of genus. A genus contains differentia (the individuals that belong to a genus). What counts as genus and differentia depends on what each thing is being related to. "Dog" can be both genus and differentia. It is the latter if we consider it as a member of the genus *animal*. It is the former if we have in mind the dog species as a whole. In the latter case, Fido is an individual dog, which belongs to the genus dog. When it is said that Stilpo "abolished distinction of genera," what is meant is that he did not uphold the distinctions of various genera to express the truth. However, in the above example, this seems to also mean that he not only denied the truth of *this* individual man, but also *man* as a general category (genus).

In his response to the interpretation of Stilpo by Diogenes Laërtius and Tennemann, Hegel says "from what is quoted from him the opposite may clearly be deduced—that *he* upheld the universal and did away with the individual." What the "universal" refers to here is clearly the genus *man*. Another statement from Stilpo, says Hegel, supports his own interpretation. In this statement, Stilpo says, "'The cabbage is not what is here shown [as this cabbage]. For the cabbage [genus] has existed for many thousand years, and hence this (what is seen) is not cabbage.'" It follows that "the universal [genus] only is, and this [particular] cabbage is not. If I say *this* cabbage, I say quite another thing from what I mean, for I say all other cabbages" (ibid.).

An important general lesson Hegel draws from Stilpo is that "the universal should in Philosophy be given a place of such importance," and "that only the universal can be expressed" as *the* truth. This does not mean that the sensible *this*, the cabbage here, cannot be expressed at all, or that it has no truth in it whatsoever, as Stilpo assumes. Rather, Hegel means that the latter mode of expression always falls into contradiction because it asserts the merely "immediate" as the true in opposition, or distinction, to the universal. Hegel defends this view clearly in the lengthy passage below, and adds that thought always contains the universal anyway:

For because the direct assertion that the immediate is the true is made, such statements only require to be taken with respect to what they say, and they will always be found to say something different from what they mean. What strikes us most is that they cannot say what they mean; for if they say the sensuous, this is a universal [category]; it is all that is sensuous, a negative of the "this," or "this" is all "these." Thought contains only the universal, the "this" is only in thought; if I say "this" it is the most universal of all. For example, here is that which I show; now I speak; but here and now is all here and now. Similarly when I say "I," I mean myself, this individual separated from all others. But I am even thus that which is thought of and cannot express the self which I mean at all. "I" is an absolute expression which excludes every other "I," but everyone says "I" of himself, for everyone is an "I." If we ask who is there, the answer "I" indicates [or implies] every "I." The individual also is thus the universal only, for in the word as an existence born of the mind, the individual, if it is meant, cannot find a place, since actually only the universal is expressed. If I would distinguish myself and establish my individuality by my age, my place of birth, through what I have done and where I have been or am at a particular time, it is the same thing. I am now so many years old, but this very now which I say is all now. If I count from a particular period such as the birth of Christ, this epoch is again only fixed by the "now" which is ever displaced. I am now thirty-five years old, and now is 1805 A.D.; each period is fixed only through the other, but the whole is undetermined. That "now" 1805 years have passed since Christ's birth, is a truth which soon will become empty sound, and the determinateness of the "now" has a before and after of determinations without beginning or end. Similarly everyone is at a "here"—this here, for everyone is in a "here." This is the nature of universality, which makes itself evident in speech. We hence help ourselves through names with which we define perfectly anything individual, but we allow that we have not expressed the thing in itself. The name as name, is no expression which contains what I am; it is a symbol, and indeed a contingent symbol, of the lively recollection (466–67).

The above explanation informs the core ideas Hegel expresses also in *Phenomenology*, especially in its first chapter.

Stilpo's philosophy, however, is not without its own shortcomings, according to Hegel. "Inasmuch as Stilpo expressed the universal as the independent, he disintegrated everything. Simplicius says 'Since the so-called Megarics took it as ascertained that what has different determinations is different, and that the diverse are separated one from the other, they seemed to prove that each thing is separated from itself. Hence since the musical Socrates is another determination from the wise Socrates, Socrates was separated from himself.'"

What this means is that "the qualities of things are determinations for themselves," that is, they are "fixed independently" in a thing that is otherwise an "aggregate of many independent universalities." Thus, Socrates is a particular person (a thing) with many universal qualities (wise, musical, etc.), and because he is all of these separate universals, him being musical Socrates and wise Socrates indicates that he is separated from himself, the universal Socrates. "Now because, according to [Stilpo], universal determinations are in their separation only the true reality, and the individual is the unseparated unity of different ideas, to him nothing individual [particular] has any truth" (467–68).

In this way, too, Stilpo fails to recognize not only that the universal entails the particulars, but also that the particular/individual is a many-sided manifestation of the universals, that is, it exists as a whole in its own right. The universal *man*, or "I," entails all individuals and individualities, such as Socrates, who are themselves the concrete of many universal qualities. Stilpo, on the other hand, "only wished to know propositions identically expressed." This comes across in his statement, quoted by Plutarch, which says,

> "A different predicate may in no case be attributed to any object. Thus we could not say that the man is good or the man is a general [in the military], but simply that man is only man, good is only good, the general is only the general. Nor could we say ten thousand knights, but knights are only knights, ten thousand are only ten thousand, &c. When we speak of a horse running, he says that the predicate is not identical with the object to which it is attributed. For the concept-determination man is different from the concept-determination good. Similarly horse and running are distinct: when we are asked for a definition of either, we do not give the same

for both. Hence those who say something different of what is different are wrong. For if man and good were the same, and likewise horse and running, how could good be used of bread and physic, and running of lions and dogs"?

Some, such as Colotes, "attack" Stilpo for ignoring the "common life" of man. In response, Plutarch remarks that this argument of Stilpo "'is an elaborate joke'" (468–69).

Hegel, for his part, weighs in on this particular debate with his silence. In the Hegelian scheme of things, be the above "an elaborate joke" or not, the reasoning indicated in it is one-sided. While it rightly emphasizes the truth of the universals in each instance, and also rightly highlights the necessary contradiction between the subject and the predicate, it does not recognize that the universal subject is sublated in the predicate. For Hegel, when "the dialectic has the negative as its result, then, precisely as a result, this negative is at the same time the positive, for it contains what it resulted from sublated within itself, and it cannot be without it."[10] Symbolically speaking, the contradiction ~A (non-or-not-A, indicated by a predicate) is in the very nature of A (the universal subject) as its implicit potentiality, and ~A contains A, and cannot be what it is without it. When any given *being* or proposition A is negated, it is negated as A, and not as something else. In its negation into ~A, A thus remains the internal relation of its own negation. In this way, the negative of A, that is, ~A, "cannot be" without A. Thus, the negative is at the same time positive, since ~A is the dialectical overcoming (sublation/negation) of A. In this overcoming, A has been negated into its own opposite, and therefore is not only retained but also further developed—for negation (sublation) implies precisely retaining and uplifting what has been negated. In this sense, negation is not complete obliteration ("nullity") of A, but rather its transcendence into something more concrete.[11]

It follows that, to use the above examples attributed to Stilpo in a Hegelian manner, the statement that this "man is a general" appears to entail a difference between man and general. But being a general is a possibility inherent in the "man" in question, and the "general" is the sublation, and explicit manifestation of this inherent possibility within the subject. Likewise, the actual "running," which is the predicate here, is implied in the subject horse as one of its

---

10. Hegel, *The Encyclopaedia Logic*, 131.
11. Hegel, *Hegel's Science of Logic*, 107.

possibilities, though the universal Horse entails an infinite number of finite negative and positive possibilities. The abstract *being* of Horse implies running, standing still, eating, being of this or that color, reproducing, and so on.

It seems that the Megarics did not present a uniform philosophy, nor did they all rest their respective thoughts on the Socratic Good. Euclides is the one who directly identifies Good with the One. Eubulides seems to deny the One, and overlooks the concept of the Good altogether. Stilpo, to the limited extent that he mentions it, does not seem to think of the Good as the ultimate universal, but a specific universal which is independent of all the specific universals, such as "cabbage," "man," and a "horse." None of the Megarics have demonstrated any inclination to make the transition from the universal One, be this universal the Good or otherwise, to the particular determinations. Indeed, all three Megarics seem to deny this very possibility by denying the existence of the particular determinations altogether. The only transition of this kind we have witnessed above was induced by Hegel himself.

3. The Cyrenaic School

Hegel's account of the Cyrenaic philosophy, at least as it is given in the edition prepared by Michelet, is difficult to follow. In explaining how Hegel interprets this school, I find it more useful to provide a more extended summary found in Hegel's own main source, which is, *Lives of the Eminent Philosophers* by Diogenes Laërtius. It is with this school that the Socratic principle, the Good, finds more definite expression(s), though with Hegesias, for instance, the Good plunges back into indefinite uncertainty.

Diogenes Laërtius's summary goes as follows:[12] "[The Cyrenaics] laid down that there are two states, pleasure and pain, the former a smooth, the latter a rough motion, and that [one] pleasure does not differ from [another] pleasure nor is one pleasure more pleasant than another." (We will see below, however, that Theodorus, one of the influential Cyrenaics, held joy to be the highest and grief the lowest state of mind.) Pleasure, in short, is pleasure. Pleasure is not attached to any other universal moral standard. It is its own criterion. Pleasure

---

12. I have summarized this section and changed the order of some sentences to present the material in a less redundant and more coherent manner.

is good even if it is obtained from what society may consider "the most unseemly conduct . . ." Thus, they "held that nothing is just or honorable or base by nature, but only by convention and custom." There is thus no natural hierarchy or differentiation in the pleasures we receive. What makes something pleasurable is the approbation it produces in us, and painful when something produces disapprobation. In this principle of pleasure-pain, they differ from Epicurus. For the former, "the bodily pleasure, which is the end, is . . . not the settled pleasure following the removal of pains, or the sort of freedom from discomfort . . ." Unlike Epicurus, they hold that "both pleasure and pain" consists "in motion, whereas absence of pleasure like absence of pain is not motion, since painlessness is the condition of one who is, as it were, asleep." Pleasure and pain are thus linked to the activity of actual feeling. In other words, there is no such thing as negative pleasure or pain. For these reasons, "they gave the names of absence of pleasure and absence of pain to the intermediate conditions." These intermediate conditions are sensuously indeterminable.[13]

The Cyrenaics also distinguished "between 'end' and 'happiness.'" They assert that the *end* of individual impulses and actions is "particular pleasure, whereas happiness is the sum total of all particular pleasures, in which are included both past and future pleasures." In other words, we do not directly, or immediately, seek happiness. The Cyrenaics posit that "particular pleasure is desirable for its own sake, whereas happiness is desirable not for its own sake but for the sake of particular pleasures." The proof of this, they assert, is to be found in the fact that "from our youth up we are instinctively attracted to specific pleasures, and, when we obtain it, seek for nothing more . . ." This is not to say that all individuals seek pleasure all the time. But this limitation does not take away the universality of pleasure as the immediate end of the individual life because abstaining from pleasure results from the perversion of the mind, and not from its natural functioning.[14]

The Cyrenaics also held "bodily pleasures" higher than "mental pleasures," and "paid more attention to the body than to the mind." Here, the Cyrenaic intention is not to completely dismiss the role the mind can play in obtaining pleasure, since they also hold that, "although pleasure is in itself desirable," what produces "certain pleasures are often of a painful nature . . ." For this reason, "to accumulate the pleasures which are productive of happiness appears to them a most irksome business." It is possible that they thought, as

---

13. Diogenes Laërtius, *Lives of the Eminent Philosophers*, 114.
14. Ibid.

Hegel will suggest below, mindful, cultured "reflection" is necessary to avoid pain and obtain pleasure. The issue of the mind comes into play from another angle as well. Even though they do not hold that "wise man" *always* "lives pleasantly," and the "fool" *always* "painfully," they still hold that this is "true for the most part . . ." For this reason, "they say that prudence is a good, though desirable not in itself but on account of its consequences." Likewise, "we make friends from interested motives" in order to obtain pleasurable ends. The virtue in prudence and friendship lies in the end these two serve, and these two virtues, especially, may require the cultivation of reason. Even though "some of the virtues are found even in the foolish," ". . . training contributes to the acquisition of virtue." A sage, for instance, "will not give way to envy or love or superstition, since these weaknesses are due to mere empty opinion; he will, however, feel pain and fear, these being natural affections." In a similar manner, the virtuous, good person is not defined on the basis of some universal principle of virtue. She/he is not, in other words, defined by such virtues as *obedience to law*, as Socrates suggested. If a virtuous person obeys the law, it is because the consequences of not doing so can be too painful. Thus, "the good man will be deterred from wrong-doing by the penalties imposed and the prejudices that it would arouse . . ."[15] In other words, the good man obeys the law because it is wise to avoid pain, and not because obeying the law is a good in and of itself.

Furthermore, the Cyrenaics also "affirm that mental affections can be known, but not the objects from which they come." For this reason, "they abandoned the study of nature because of its apparent uncertainty, but fastened on logical inquiries because of their utility." In this, they promoted the learning of the "theory of good and evil" as the instrument with which to "be free from superstition, and to escape the fear of death." Theoretical knowledge thus instrumentally serves to avoid pain that comes from lack of knowledge. In this way, they anticipated Stoicism as well. In short, for the Cyrenaics, "the wise man really exists," and such "man" are those who know how to avoid pain and obtain pleasure. Knowledge, thus, does not eliminate pain, though its cultivation can be instrumental in the management of pain and obtainment of more pleasure.[16]

According to Hegel, the Cyrenaics treated the principle of the Good more explicitly then the Megarics. The former, as seen above, define the Good more precisely as pleasure. Hegel says that, on the

---

15. Ibid., 114–16.
16. Ibid., 115–16.

surface of things, this Cyrenaic principle appears "far removed from that of Socrates, since we at once think of the transient existence of feeling [which pleasure is] as directly in opposition to the Good." Hegel argues that this appearance is misleading. "The Cyrenaics likewise upheld the universal, for, if it is asked what the Good is, we find they certainly made pleasurable feeling, which presents the appearance of a determinate, to be its content, but seeing that a cultured mind is also requisite, enjoyment, as it is obtained through thought, is here indicated" (453). Hegel assumes here that thought is not transient, or is essentially universal. His defense of this view is at best sketchy for he does not show whether or not the Cyrenaics held thought to be a good in itself, nor does he indicate whether or not thought, or thinking, is the highest of all pleasures for them. Indeed, as we have seen, the Cyrenaics found merely instrumental value in reason, and did not treat its cultivation as an end in itself.

Hegel seems to recognize the inconsistency between the universality of thought and the contingency of pleasure in the Cyrenaic approach when he goes on to say, "Feeling is the indeterminate individual. But if thought, reflection, mental culture, are given a place in this principle, through the principle of the universality of thought that principle of contingency, individuality, mere subjectivity, disappears; and the only really remarkable thing in this school is that this greater consistency in the universal is therefore an inconsistency as regards the principle" (469–70). When dealing with the Cyrenaic Hegesias below, Hegel redefines the Cyrenaic "universality" as a negative principle, which emerges out of the pure contingency of pleasure, or happiness. His reasoning is that in determining something to be contingent, we necessarily assume the universal. This is similar to Hegel's argument, as we will see in the second volume of this work, that the Skeptical denial of all truth necessarily implies a universal truth claim. Thus, what is negated is implied in the negation.

The teaching of the Cyrenaics "is very simple," says Hegel. They took the "relation of consciousness to existence in its most superficial and its earliest form, and expressed existence [i.e., *being*] as it is immediately for consciousness, i.e. as feeling simply." For the Cyrenaics what determines "both the theoretic and practical truth" is feeling (sensation). Hence and more accurately stated, the Cyrenaic principle is "not the objective [sensible] itself, but the relation of consciousness to the objective." As Sextus Empiricus summarizes their view,

"Thus the Cyrenaics say, sensations form the real criterion; they alone can be known and are infallible, but what produces feeling [i.e., the objective] is neither knowable nor infallible. Thus when we perceive a white and sweet, we may assert this condition as ours with truth and certainty [hence their subjective individualism]. But that the causes of these feelings are themselves a white and sweet object we cannot with certainty affirm [hence their skepticism]. What these men say about ends is also in harmony with this, for sensations also extend to ends. The sensations are either pleasant or unpleasant or neither of the two. Now they call the unpleasant feelings the bad, the end of which is pain; the pleasant is the good, whose invariable end is happiness. Thus feelings are the criteria of knowledge and the ends for action. We live because we follow them from testimony received and satisfaction experienced, the former in accordance with theoretic intuitions, and the latter with what gives us pleasure."

To this summary, Hegel adds, "That is to say, as end, feeling is no longer a promiscuous variety of sensuous affections, but the setting up of the Notion as the positive or negative relation to the object of action, which is just the pleasant or the unpleasant" (473–74).

Hegel further points out that "two kinds of determinations," found in the Cyrenaic doctrine, "constitute the chief points of [philosophical] interest." These determinations are taken up later, especially by "the Stoics, the new Academy, &c." The first kind is the determination itself in general, that is, "the criterion" we use to make a determination. The "second is what determination for the subject is." From these the "idea of the wise man results—what the wise do, who the wise are, &c." In determining what the good is in general, "the main interest is to find a content [criterion] for the good, for else men may talk about it for years" without obtaining any results. Secondly, "the interest of the subject appears, and that is the result of the revolution in the Greek mind made by Socrates." Here, the criterion for the good is determined by the individual "on his account." This latter wisdom, so to speak, arises from the discord between the individual and the spirit of his times/society. Thus,

> When the religion, constitution, laws of a people, are held in esteem, and when the individual members of a people are one with them, the question of what the individual has to do on his own account, will not be put. In a moralized, religious condition of things we are likely to find the end of man in what is present, and these morals, religion and laws are also present in him. When, on the contrary, the individual exists no longer in the morality of his people, no longer has his substantial being in the religion, laws, &c., of his land, he no longer finds what he desires, and no longer satisfies himself in his present. But if this discord has arisen, the individual must immerse himself in himself, and there seek his end.

This is what Socrates had done. The question after this individual self-immersion becomes: "After what end must he form himself and after what [must he] strive?"

> Thus an ideal for the individual is set up, and this is the wise man: what was called the ideal of the wise man is the individuality of self-consciousness which is conceived of as universal essence. The point of view is the same when we now ask, What can I know? What should I believe? What ought I to hope? What is the highest interest of the subject? It is not what is truth, right, the universal end of the world, for instead of asking about the science of the implicitly and explicitly objective, the question is what is true and right in as far as it is the insight and conviction of the individual, his end and a mode of his existence? This talk about wise men is [common] amongst the Stoics, Epicureans, &c., but is devoid of meaning. For the wise man is not in question, but the wisdom of the universe, real reason (475).[17]

Such wisdom is not sought for in the Cyrenaic philosophy, or in its offshoots, such as Stoicism and Epicureanism.

---

17. Elsewhere, Hegel refers to Socrates as the "wise man," and gives a similar description of this expression. Hegel, *The Phenomenology of Mind*, 418–19.

Here, it would be useful to reiterate what is a significant Cyrenaic contribution, and what this contribution lacks in relation to "real reason." The free thinking of the individual, the thinking with which the individual understands and accepts the grounds of the truth, is an advance over the dogmatic obedience to the universal given externally to the individual by society. Such dogmatic obedience establishes what the individual has to do as her/his *duty*. However, this Cyrenaic advance plunges into too much individualism, so to speak. The "wisdom of the universe," the "universal end of the world" as what is "implicitly and explicitly . . . true and right," disappears in the Cyrenaic mode of thinking. Duty here, if it exists at all, is the duty to achieve the individual's ends, which are identified with pleasure. The real universality resembles the dogmatic view of duty in some sense for both are beyond individual subjectivity. However, "real reason," which dogmatism lacks, achieves the real universal through the freedom of thought. The individual reason thus becomes the universal Spirit through its free activity by partaking in this Spirit's life in thought and society.

This convergence of free individuality, of free will, and moral-ethical duty emerges in the modern society, and the demonstration of this convergence is one of the cornerstones of Hegel's philosophy of right. In *Philosophy of Mind*, Hegel points out that,

> the free individual, who, in mere law, counts only as a *person*, is now characterized as a *subject*—a will reflected into itself so that, be its affection what it may, it is distinguished (as existing in it) as *its own* from the existence of freedom in an external thing. Because the affection of the will is thus inwardized, the will is at the same time made a particular, and there arise further particularizations of it and relations of these to one another. This affection is partly the essential and implicit will, the reason of the will, the essential basis of law and moral life; partly it is the existent volition, which is before us and throws itself into actual deeds, and thus comes into relationship with the former. The subjective will is *morally* free, so far as these features are its inward institution, its own, and willed by it. Its utterance in deed with this freedom is an *action*, in the externality of which it only admits as its own, and allows to be imputed to it, so much as it has consciously willed.

This coincides with the "subjective of 'moral' freedom" of the modern individual. Here, "In virtue of the right thereto a man must possess a personal knowledge of the distinction between good and evil in general: ethical and religious principles shall not merely lay their claim on him as external laws and precepts of authority to be obeyed, but have [the individuals'] assent, recognition, or even justification in his heart, sentiment, conscience, intelligence, etc. The subjectivity of the will in itself is its supreme aim and absolutely essential to it."[18] Clearly, this modern individual Hegel describes here is not the self-interested individual of liberalism.

Hegel, In *Elements of the Philosophy of Right*, further explains this convergence of the subjective and objective freedom; of the free will and duty; this disappearance of the arbitrariness and contingency of the subjective will, as follows:

> A binding duty can appear as a *limitation* only in relation to indeterminate subjectivity or abstract freedom, and to the drives of the natural will or of the moral will which arbitrarily determines its indeterminate good [as the Cyrenaics do.] The individual, however, finds his *liberation* in duty. On the one hand, he is liberated from his dependence on mere natural drives, and from the burden he labors under as a particular subject in his moral reflections on obligation and desire; and, on the other hand, he is liberated from that indeterminate subjectivity which does not attain existence or the objective determinacy of action, but remains *within itself* and has no actuality. In duty, the individual liberates himself so as to obtain substantial freedom.[19]

Again, this liberation, that is, the "substantial freedom of the individual" only becomes possible in modern times—in Hegel's Germany to be more precise. The Greeks, up to the point of the Cyrenaics, remained at the level of subjective freedom. As Hegel told us at the end of his treatment of "Oriental Philosophy," "the true, objective ground of thought finds its basis in the real freedom of the subject; the universal or substantial must itself have objectivity." This can only occur when the individual becomes the medium of universal thought and gives it concrete, "immediate existence and actual presence" (146). Hegel also promised in the same context that we

---

18. Hegel, *The Phenomenology of Mind*, 249.
19. Hegel, *Elements of the Philosophy of Right*, 192.

would find this "principle ... in the Greek world" (147), which does not seem to be the case up to this point.

3.1 Aristippus

Aristippus is the founder of the Cyrenaic philosophy. As organized by Michelet, in this section Hegel provides a general discussion of the Cyrenaic thought, most of which I have already discussed above. Naturally, Hegel says very little directly on Aristippus's philosophy, if he had one, for very little remains of his sayings/writings that can be considered philosophical. Because of the principle of pleasure he had introduced, and his lifestyle, he has been linked to hedonism throughout the succeeding ages. He is known also as a Sophist and the first follower of Socrates to charge money for his lectures. Most of what is directly attributed to him consists of witty statements. All of them seem to justify the point that his principle was based on the following: "'it is not abstinence from pleasures that is best, but mastery over them without ever being worsted.'"[20]

Hegel says that Aristippus treated "enjoyment as the only thing [with] . . . which man had rationally to concern himself." Hegel repeats that the principle of enjoyment alone "may well be said to be a principle in opposition to Philosophy; but when it is considered in such a way that the cultivation of thought is made the only condition under which enjoyment can be attained, perfect freedom of spirit is retained, since [the cultivation of thought] is inseparable from culture [i.e., higher learning, or philosophy]." Aristippus, says Hegel, proceeds from the standpoint that "culture at its highest" should be esteemed. Thus, he did not treat what is pleasant as known "immediately," or a priori, but sought to find it by cultivated "reflection," which, as such, he placed among (perhaps above) of all that is pleasurable (471). Perhaps, Hegel's evidence, a flimsy one at that, for this conclusion is Aristippus's point that "mastery" over pleasures is necessary. Beyond this point, the more philosophical aspects of the Cyrenaic thought are to be found in Aristippus's followers.

---

20. Aristippus, quoted in Diogenes Laërtius, *Lives of the Eminent Philosophers*, 108.

3.2 Theodorus

Diogenes Laërtius says of him that "Theodorus was a man who utterly rejected the current belief in the gods. And I have come across a book of his entitled *Of the Gods* which is not contemptible. From that book, they say, Epicurus borrowed most of what he wrote on the subject."[21] As Hegel adds, Theodorus was "banished from Athens" because he denied the "existence of the gods, and being." What he denied, says Hegel, has "no further interest or speculative significance, for the positive gods which Theodorus denied, are themselves not any object of speculative reason." Theodorus's philosophical, speculative significance stems from the fact that he introduced "the universal . . . into the idea of that which was existence for consciousness . . ." In doing this, as Hegel quotes from Diogenes Laërtius, "'he made joy and sorrow the end, but in such a way that the former pertained to the understanding and the latter to want of understanding'" (475–76).

Theodorus "defined the good as . . . justice and the bad as the opposite" (476). He also distinguished joy and grief from pleasure and pain. He held joy to be higher in value than pleasure. Joy, or happiness, comes from understanding, as does justice, and the unpleasant from lack of understanding. It follows from Theodorus's principle that the "individual sensuous feeling, as it is immediately," has no real existence for its existence depends on understanding. Thus, "the sensuous generally, as sensation, theoretic or practical, is something quite indeterminate." Nothing in the realm of senses is inherently pleasant or unpleasant. The universal comes to us negatively through the criticism of each unit of sensation by the understanding. "But this advance on individuality is culture [higher learning], which, through the limitation of individual feelings and enjoyments, tries to make these [units of feeling] harmonious [with the individual], even though it first of all only calculates" which sensation of all produces "the greater pleasure." Thus, the question becomes: Among many types of sensation I am capable of enjoying, which specific type of enjoyment is the most harmonious with me? To this, "it must be replied that the completest harmony with me is only found in the accordance of my particular existence and consciousness with my actual substantial Being." Theodorus identified this answer with "understanding and justice, in which we know where to seek enjoyment" through reflection. Thus, understanding what enjoyment is, which some call practical wisdom,

---

21. Ibid., 117.

becomes the end of the individual. Hegel points out that this mode of thinking makes understanding incongruous with sensation/feeling, "For the feeling in which felicity is contained, is in its conception the individual, self-changing, without universality and subsistence. Thus the universal, [that is,] understanding, as an empty form, adheres to a content [feeling] quite incongruous with it" (475–77). What Hegel means by this incongruity between sensation and universality becomes clearer with Hegesias.

3.3 Hegesias

According to Diogenes Laërtius, while "the school of Hegesias . . . adopted the same ends, namely pleasure and pain," as the other Cyrenaics, it also tied everything to self-interested skepticism. About virtues, they held that "there is no such thing as gratitude or friendship or beneficence, because it is not for themselves that we choose to do these things but simply from motives of interest." Without self-interest, "such [virtuous] conduct is nowhere found."[22]

As for happiness, Hegesias holds that ". . . the body is infected with much suffering, while the soul shares in the sufferings of the body and is a prey to disturbance, and fortune often disappoints. From all this it follows that happiness cannot be realized." It seems that the principle with Hegesias and his followers is not so much seeking happiness through pleasure, but leading a life in which we try to avoid pain as much as possible. The ability to avoid pain distinguishes the wise from the fool: "The wise man will not have so much advantage over others in the choice of goods as in the avoidance of evils, making it his end to live without pain of body or mind. This then, they say, is the advantage accruing to those who make no distinction between any of the objects which produce pleasure." Furthermore, "The wise man will be guided in all he does by his own interests, for there is none other whom he regards as equally deserving. For supposing him to reap the greatest advantages from another, they would not be equal to what he contributes himself."[23]

However, it does not appear to be the case that Hegesias and his followers totally denied the possibility of pleasure. Rather, they thought of it as a sensation without any objective, certain basis. The

---

22. Ibid., 116–17.
23. Ibid.

same objects of experience can produce different sensations, as much as different objects and experiences can produce the same sensations in both the fool and the wise alike. For instance, both "life and death" can be "desirable." Thus, they deny that "there is anything naturally pleasant or unpleasant." They add that "when some men are pleased and others pained by the same objects, this is owing to the lack or rarity or surfeit of such objects." Here, a standard creeps in to the calculus of pleasure and pain. The standard seems to have something to do with scarcity or abundance of the objects of one's desire, the former being linked to pain ant the latter to pleasure. But this standard, suggested by the above claim that "rarity or surfeit" of the objects of desire play a role in determining pleasure and pain, is undermined when Diogenes Laërtius attributes to them the claim that "Poverty and riches have *no relevance* to pleasure; for neither the rich nor the poor as such have any special share in pleasure" (italics added). Likewise, they say, "slavery and freedom, nobility and low birth, honor and dishonor, are alike indifferent in a calculation of pleasure."[24] Diogenes Laërtius does not provide enough information or reflection for us to determine the status of this standard in more precise terms. Perhaps their point was that none of the external conditions and objects has any determinate bearing on pleasure and pain.

In addition, "They also disallow the claims of the senses, because they do not lead to accurate knowledge. Whatever appears rational should be done."[25] Again, for want of information, what Diogenes Laërtius means here is uncertain. It seems that Hegesias disallowed the absolute self-certainty of senses, that is, of sense-perception inducing "accurate knowledge," and not that he disallowed "the claims of the senses" altogether. At the same time, it does not appear to be the case that Hegesias established reason as an absolute beacon for choices one ought to make in life. Indeed, he says above that whatever "appears" rational, "should be done." This is not the same as saying this or that is the rational course of action. Thus, we have with Hegesias the uncertainty of both sense-perception and reason, and, consequently, what appears to be a resolute rejection of a subjective and objective universal standard. However, Hegel is about to find some notion of universality even in Hegesias.

The section on Hegesias in Hegel's *Lectures* begins with the statement that "it is remarkable that another Cyrenaic, Hegesias,

---

24. Ibid.
25. Ibid.

recognized this incongruity between sensation and universality . . ." The universal, Hegel says, "is opposed to the individual," and has "what is agreeable as well as disagreeable within itself." The universal is thus a standard which makes possible the determination of pleasure and pain possible for it knows in certain terms what these are. Consequently, "because, on the whole, he took a firmer grasp of the universal and gave it a larger place, there passed from him all determination of individuality, and with it really the Cyrenaic principle." Hegesias realized, unlike the other Cyrenaics, that "individual sensation is in-itself nothing; and, as he nevertheless made enjoyment his end, it became to him the universal." But "if enjoyment is the [universal] end, we must ask about the content [which is sensation]; if this content is investigated, we find every content [to be] a particular which is not in conformity with the universal, and thus falls into dialectic [of negation]." It falls into dialectic because the particularity of the content is negated due to its indeterminacy. "Hegesias followed the Cyrenaic principle as far as to this consequence of thought" (477).

However, the universal is posited negatively in Hegesias's teachings. Instead of positing positively that *enjoyment/happiness is X*, he expresses it as "'There is no perfect happiness. The body is troubled with manifold pains, and the soul suffers along with it; it is hence a matter of indifference whether we choose life or death. In itself nothing is pleasant or unpleasant.'" In other words, as Hegel interprets this passage, "the criterion of being pleasant or unpleasant, because its *universality is removed*, is thus itself made quite indeterminate; and because it has no objective determinateness in itself, it has become unmeaning" (italics added). Still, Hegel goes through some of the passages Diogenes Laërtius provides, which I have summarized above, to support his claim of universality in Hegesias. This universality is paradoxical, according to Hegel. What is removed becomes a new principle. Because senses and life-conditions are indeterminate, the individual is freed of all such influences. "This universality, . . . proceeds from the principle of the freedom of the individual self-consciousness" (478). This is infinite subjective universality *par excellence*. It is the pursuit of, we should add, complete self-interest on the basis of what the individual thinks is rational or pleasurable. Thus, universal comes to mean not so much a maxim, such as *thou shall not kill*, but an infinite possibility, or unrestrained freedom, of the individual subjectivity.

The ambiguities found in Diogenes Laërtius's account lead to ambiguities in Hegel's final words on Hegesias. Hegel now says "Hegesias expressed" this subjective universality "as the condition of the perfect indifference of the wise men . . ." I think this "perfect indifference" should not be taken to mean complete apathy, since he allows for the avoidance of pain, if not the pursuit of enjoyment. Indeed, Hegel says above that "he nevertheless made enjoyment his end." The kind of indifference we can find more certainly in Hegesias is precisely the means and methods with which one seeks to avoid pain or obtain enjoyment, and not indifference toward such ends. This infinite indifference toward the means includes life and death. Either option can be as desirable or undesirable as the other. Consequently, "it is told that Hegesias, who lived in Alexandria, was not allowed to teach the Ptolemies of the time, because he inspired many of his hearers with such indifference to life that they took their own." Hegel adds that this "indifference to everything" influences later "philosophic systems of the kind." What comes forth in such systems is "a surrendering of all reality, the complete withdrawal of life into itself" (ibid.).

3.4 Anniceris

Most of what Diogenes Laërtius says of Anniceris and his followers revolves around the question of friendship. Anniceris disagreed with Theodorus's belief that meaningful pleasure had to be above and beyond mere sensual enjoyment, and included understanding and mental states of happiness, such as joy. He also differed from Hegesias's indifferentism by allowing that some pleasures, such as friendship, are goods worth pursuing.

In brief, what is said of him and his school is the following: "The school of Anniceris in other respects agreed with [Hegesias], but admitted that friendship and gratitude and respect for parents do exist in real life, and that a good man will sometimes act out of patriotic motives." It is not uncommon for scholars to attribute to Anniceris the view that these virtues are goods in themselves, as opposed to being mere means toward other ends, such as pleasure. However, Diogenes Laërtius's account is ambivalent on this issue. On the one hand, he says that, for Anniceris, "the happiness of a friend is not in itself desirable, for it is not [necessarily] felt by his neighbor." On the other hand, "A friend should be cherished not merely for his utility . . . but for the good feeling for the sake of which we shall even endure hardships." Likewise, "though we make pleasure the end and are annoyed when deprived of it, we shall nevertheless cheerfully endure [displeasure stemming from friendship] because of our love to our friend." Consequently, Anniceris's "wise man" is not someone who tries to maximize happiness as much as possible: ". . . the wise man . . . will be . . . happy even if few pleasures accrue to him." It is possible to conclude that Anniceris held friendship above pleasure for pleasure's sake, and made it the basis of happiness.[26]

Hegel offers a very brief interpretation of Anniceris's philosophy. Anniceris and his followers, notes Hegel, ". . . departed from the distinctive character of the principle of the Cyrenaic school, and thereby gave philosophic culture quite another direction." In this new direction, "the universal, the theoretically speculative element in the [Cyrenaic] school, is thus lost; it sinks more into what is popular." With this sinking, "a method of philosophizing in morals arises, which later on prevailed with Cicero and the Peripatetics of his time, but the interest has disappeared, so far as any consistent system of thought is concerned" (479).

4. The Cynic School

Hegel says "the Cynics . . . further defined the principle of the Good, but in another way from the Cyrenaics." We are to assume here that the Cyrenaics defined it as pleasure and/or as avoidance of pain. For the Cynics, the content of the Good is "man's keeping to what is in conformity with nature," which principle translates into the mere satisfaction of basic, natural needs. The Cynics also held the development of learning to be necessary and important. Hegel says "culture through the knowledge of the universal is [their] principle." The aim of the "knowledge of the universal" is the attainment of "the individual end." The Cynic principle is thus "abstract universality," which requires that the individual "should keep himself . . . in freedom and independence, and be indifferent to all he formerly esteemed" (453–54). However, Hegel tells us below that the Cynics also disregarded all thought, which does not quite fit with what he says here. Indeed, when we arrive at Diogenes of Sinope, we realize that some Cynics took a flight from culture also. Basically, the Cynics sought to acquire their liberty from luxury beyond the basic, natural needs. Beginning with Diogenes of Sinope, and extending into later Cynics, who were called "dogs" for their lack of shame, independence was also sought from all social convention and mores. The most important philosophical lessons Hegel draws from the Cynics revolves around the issue of individual freedom from the realm of necessity.

---

26. Ibid., 117.

Like the Cyrenaics, "the Cynics had also only to do with themselves, and the individual self-consciousness was likewise principle." However, unlike the earlier Cyrenaics and perhaps much like Hegesias, the Cynics proposed "the principle of freedom and indifference, both in regard to thought and actual life" as the guide for individual life. This required them to stand in opposition to all "external individuality, particular ends, needs, and enjoyments; so that culture not only sought after indifference to these and independence within itself, as with the Cyrenaics, but for express privation, and for the limitation of needs to what is necessary and what nature demands." In short, the Cynics "maintained as the content of the good, the greatest independence of nature, i.e. the slightest possible necessities; this meant a rebound from enjoyment, and from the pleasures of feeling." Thus, the principle of enjoyment is posited negatively as withdrawal from enjoyment. Consequently, concludes Hegel, Cynic philosophy "had no scientific weight," even though it "constitutes an element which must necessarily appear in the knowledge of the universal." This necessary element is that "consciousness must know itself in its individuality, as free from all dependence on things and on enjoyment." But, again, this is abstract universality. It is true that "to him who relies upon riches or enjoyment such dependence is in fact real consciousness, or his individuality is real [material] existence," and is thus also limited. But the Cynics went to the extreme opposite by enforcing that "negative moment" so much so that "they placed freedom in actual renunciation of so-called superfluities." In this manner, "they only recognized this abstract unmoving independence, which did not concern itself with enjoyment or the interests of an ordinary life." Anticipating his *Elements of the Philosophy of Right*, Hegel insists contra the Cynics that "true freedom does not consist in flying from enjoyment and the occupations which have as their concern other men and other ends in life; but in the fact that consciousness, though involved in all reality, stands above it and is free from it" (480).[27]

What Hegel means here is explained in more detail as follows:

> The freedom and independence of the Cynics, however, which consists only in lessening to the utmost the burden imposed by wants, is abstract, because it, as negative in character, has really to be a mere

---

27. This thought runs throughout Hegel's *Elements of the Philosophy of Right*. For a concentrated discussion on this subject, see the section called "The System of Needs," 227–39.

renunciation. Concrete freedom consists in maintaining an indifferent attitude towards necessities, not avoiding them, but in their satisfaction remaining free, and abiding in morality and in participation in the moral life of man. Abstract freedom, on the contrary, surrenders its morality, because the individual withdraws into his subjectivity, and is consequently an element of immorality (482).

Also:

> That on which they placed highest value was the simplification of their needs; it seems very plausible to say that this produces freedom. For needs are certainly dependence upon nature, and this is antagonistic to freedom of spirit; the reduction of that dependence to a minimum is thus an idea which commends itself. But at the same time this minimum is itself undetermined, and if such stress is laid on thus merely following nature, it follows that too great a value is set on the needs of nature and on the renunciation of others. This is what is also evident in the monastic principle. The negative likewise contains an affirmative bias towards what is renounced; and the renunciation and the importance of what is renounced is thus made too marked.

Thus, there is something ironic in the withdrawal from what seem to be luxurious needs. This negative attitude turns into too much emphasis on nature and need. This irony comes across clearly when, in order to demonstrate his simplicity, "'Antisthenes turned outside a hole in his cloak, Socrates said to him, I see thy vanity through the hole in thy cloak'" (483).

On the whole, Hegel thinks too much emphasis on needs, one way or another, has little philosophical value. Needs have a natural way of development in history, and vary in different times and circumstances—an idea that Karl Marx found to be of great significance. For instance, says Hegel,

> Clothing is not a thing of rational import, but is regulated through needs that arise of themselves. In the North the clothing must be different from that in Central Africa; and in winter we do not wear cotton garments. Anything further is meaningless, and is left to

chance and to opinion; in modern times, for instance, old-fashioned clothing had a meaning in relation to patriotism. The cut of my coat is decided by fashion, and the tailor sees to this; it is not my business to invent it, for mercifully others have done so for me. This dependence on custom and opinion [and the work of others] is certainly better than were it to be on nature. But it is not essential that men should direct their understanding to this (484).

Antisthenes is the founder of the Cynic school. As Hegel notes, "Antisthenes bears a high place in this Cynical philosophy." Most of what Diogenes Laërtius says of him consists of witty comments and aphorisms. Hegel's brief account of his main teachings below is sufficient enough. However, it seems too harsh to say, as Hegel does, that "the attitude he adopted comes very near to that of rudeness, vulgarity of conduct and shamelessness," which the later Cynicism adopted (482–83). For instance, in the account of Diogenes Laërtius, this description does not come across. In one passage, the following saying is attributed to him:

> To the wise man nothing is foreign or impracticable. A good man deserves to be loved. Men of worth are friends. Make allies of men who are at once brave and just. Virtue is a weapon that cannot be taken away. It is better to be with a handful of good men fighting against all the bad, than with hosts of bad men against a handful of good men. Pay attention to your enemies, for they are the first to discover your mistakes. Esteem an honest man above a kinsman. Virtue is the same for women as for men. Good actions are fair and evil actions foul. Count all wickedness foreign and alien.[28]

Hegel's own account of Antisthenes in fact does not overlook the importance of virtue in Antisthenes:

> Antisthenes' principles are simple, because the content of his teaching remains general; . . . He gives general rules, which consist of such excellent maxims as that "virtue is self-sufficing, and requires nothing more than

---

28. Diogenes Laërtius, *Lives of the Eminent Philosophers*, Vol. 2, trans. Robert Drew Hicks (London: Loeb Classical Library, 1925), 13.

a Socratic strength of character. The good is excellent, the bad discreditable. Virtue consists of works, and does not require many reasons or theories. The end of man is a virtuous life. The wise man is contented with himself, for he possesses everything that others seem to possess. His own virtue satisfies him; he is at home all over the world. If he lacks fame, this is not to be regarded as an evil, but as a good," &c.

Hegel's problem with these maxims is that they reproduce "the tedious talk about the wise man, which by the Stoics, as also by the Epicureans, was even more spun out and made more tedious" then before. More philosophically speaking, Hegel also complains that "when Antisthenes says that virtue does not require reasons and theories, he forgets that he himself acquired, through the cultivation of mind, its independence and the power of renouncing all that men desire." In this irony of downplaying and cultivating the power of independent thought, virtue acquires "another signification." In this signification,

> It no longer is unconscious virtue, like the simple virtue of a citizen of a free people, who fulfills his duties to fatherland, place, and family, as these relationships immediately require. The consciousness which has gone beyond itself must, in order to become Mind, now lay hold of and comprehend all reality, i.e. be conscious of it as its own. But conditions such as are called by names like innocence or beauty of soul, are childish conditions, which are certainly to be praised in their own place, but from which man, because he is rational, must come forth, in order to recreate himself from the sublated immediacy (483).

Diogenes of Sinope seems to have taken the simplicity of needs proposed by Antisthenes to the extremes. For the latter, the required simplicity of life was based on self-reliance and minimization of bodily needs. Such a life did not exclude various virtues and compliance to social conventions. The epithet of "rude" Hegel uses above seems more appropriate for the description of Diogenes. He slept in the streets of Athens much of his life, and took physical and mental abuse from the youth and adults alike. Hegel does not find much philosophical value in his witty sayings. He says of this Diogenes that he "is only famed for his manner of life; with him, as with the moderns, Cynicism came to signify more a mode of living than a philosophy. He confined himself to the barest necessities, and tried to make fun of others who did not think as he, and who laughed at his ways" (484).

In dealing with the later Cynics very briefly, Hegel says of them that they

> are not any the less conspicuous by their exceeding shamelessness, but they were, generally speaking, nothing more than swinish beggars, who found their satisfaction in the insolence which they showed to others. They are worthy of no further consideration in Philosophy, and they deserve in its full the name of dogs, which was early given to them; for the dog is a shameless animal. Crates, of Thebes, and Hipparchia, a Cynic, celebrated their nuptials in the public market. This independence of which the Cynics boasted, is really Subjection, for while every other sphere of active life contains the affirmative element of free intelligence, this means the denying oneself the sphere in which the element of freedom can be enjoyed (486–87).

5. A Brief Evaluation of the Progress of Philosophy

Hegel's account of the Socratic period thus ends on a very anticlimactic note. It seems that, especially with the Cynics, reason in the history of philosophy retreats instead of developing further. This, in one sense, challenges Hegel's main thesis regarding the history of philosophy; in three other senses, it does not. First, Hegel himself acknowledged in the introduction that the historical development of philosophy is not a smooth process. It has its ups and downs.

Second, the overall result of the history of philosophy up to this point represents general development. This development was made possible through many different and significant contributions by most, if not all, philosophers up to this point in history. Generally stated, this development represents both the intensification and diversification of the Notion. The Notion is freed from the sensuous limitations imposed on it during its initial conceptions, and has become not only purer but also self-determining during the time of Anaxagoras. During this time, the One, if not sufficiently, is at least properly identified with *nous*. The question that remains to be settled is how *nous* rules the world, or manifests itself in Nature and human affairs. Socrates makes an important intervention in this regard, though more in terms of human affairs than in terms of nature-logic. With him, thus, philosophy branches out into a new territory, that of morality. This comes in addition to the ontological and epistemological diversifications, which, of course, are intermingled in many philosophical traditions. After Socrates, the universal Notion, which is now identified with the Good, acquires more definite forms in the hands of the Socratics. In the meanwhile, a streak of skepticism had begun to develop before Socrates. The Sophists gave skepticism its initial, but solid, foundation. Some of the Socratics, if not Socrates himself, continued this tradition, and some intertwined it with the question of the good life. In Hegel's view, philosophy has not suffered from these interventions, but has become richer, and more concrete because of them.

Third, the Socratic period we have discussed above runs concomitantly with the life and philosophical development of another philosopher, who also belongs to the Socratic school. This philosopher is Plato. On Hegel's scale, Plato's philosophy represents a very significant advance in philosophy. Due to space constraints, Hegel's lecture on Plato will be examined in the next volume of the present work. In order to give a glimpse of Plato's contribution, I offer the following comment by Hegel from the second volume:

> Plato, who must be numbered among the Socratics, was the most renowned of the friends and disciples of Socrates, and he it was who grasped in all its truth Socrates' great principle that ultimate reality lies in consciousness, since, according to him, the absolute is in thought, and all reality is Thought. He does not understand by this a one-sided thought, nor what is understood by the false idealism which makes thought once more step aside and contemplate itself as conscious thought, and as in opposition to reality; it is the thought which embraces in an absolute unity reality as well as thinking, the Notion and its reality in the movement of science, as the Idea of a scientific whole. While Socrates had comprehended the thought which is existent in and for itself, only as an object for self-conscious will, Plato forsook this narrow point of view, and brought the merely abstract right of self-conscious thought, which Socrates had raised to a principle, into the sphere of science. By so doing he rendered it possible to interpret and apply the principle, though his

manner of representation may not be altogether scientific (II, 1–2).

If not entirely scientifically construed, with Plato, "the Idea of a scientific whole" becomes possible. This is a giant step toward the formation of a philosophical system, which is even more concretely contemplated by Aristotle. A philosophical system only becomes possible with the contemplation of the Idea, or Thought, which "embraces in an absolute unity reality, as well as thinking," that is "the Notion and its reality in the movement of science, as the Idea of a scientific whole."

Bibliography

Works by G. W. F. Hegel

Hegel, G. W. F. *Lectures on the History of Philosophy*, Vol. 1. Translated by. E. S. Haldane. London: Kegan Paul, Trench, Trubner & Co., 1892.
———. *Lectures on the History of Philosophy*, Vol. 2. Translated by E. S. Haldane. London: Kegan Paul, Trench, Trubner & Co., 1894.
———. *Lectures on the History of Philosophy*, Vol. 3. Translated by E. S. Haldane. London: Kegan Paul, Trench, Trubner & Co., 1896.
———. *The Philosophy of History*. Translated by J. Sibree. New York: Dover Publications Inc., 1956.
———. *Lectures on the Philosophy of Religion*, Vol. 2. Translated by Rev. E. B. Spiers and J. Burdon Sanderson. New York: The Humanities Press Inc., 1962.
———. *Lectures on the Philosophy of Religion*, Vol. 3. Translated by Rev. E. B. Spiers and J. Burdon Sanderson. New York: The Humanities Press Inc., 1962.
———. *Philosophy of Mind: Part Three of the Encyclopaedia of the Philosophical Sciences*. Translated by A. V. Miller. Oxford: Clarendon Press, 1971.
———. *Hegel's Introduction to the Lectures on History of Philosophy*. Translated by T. M. Knox and A. V. Miller. Oxford: Oxford University Press, 1985.
———. *Hegel's Science of Logic*. Translated by A. V. Miller. New York: Humanity Books, 1989.
———. *Elements of the Philosophy of Right*. Translated by H. B. Nisbet. Cambridge, UK: Cambridge University Press, 1991.
———. *The Encyclopaedia Logic: Part I of the Encyclopaedia of Philosophical Science with the Zusatze*. Translated, with introduction and notes, by T. F. Geraets, W. A. Suchting, and H. S. Harris. Indianapolis: Hackett, 1991.
———. *The Phenomenology of Mind*. Translated, with introduction and notes, by J. B. Baillie. Mineola: Dover Publications, 2003.
———. *Lectures on the History of Philosophy 1825–6: Greek Philosophy*. Edited by Robert F. Brown, Vol. 2. Oxford: Clarendon Press, 2006.

Other works

Aristotle. *De Anima*. Massachusetts Institute of Technology. "The Internet Classics Archive," http://classics.mit.edu/Aristotle/soul.1.i.html.

———. "Metaphysics." In *Aristotle: Selections*, translated by Terence Irwin and Gail Fine, 221–346. Indianapolis: Hackett Publishing, Inc., 1995.

———. "Physics." In *Aristotle: Selections*, translated by Terence Irwin and Gail Fine, 83–145. Indianapolis: Hackett Publishing, Inc., 1995.

———. *Politics*. Translated by C. D. C. Reeve. Indianapolis: Hackett, 1998.

Barnes, Jonathan, ed. *Early Greek Philosophy*. London: Penguin Books, 2001.

Bernaconi, Robert. "With What the History of Philosophy Begin? Hegel's Role in the Debate on the Place of India within the History of Philosophy." In *Hegel's History of Philosophy: New Interpretations*, edited by David A. Duquette, 35–50. New York: State University of New York, 2003.

Bernard, Theos. *Hindu Philosophy*. New Delhi: Motilal Banarsidass, 1999.

Colebrooke, Henry Thomas. *Essays on the Religion and Philosophy of the Hindus*. London: Williams & Norgate, 1858.

Confucius, *The Analects*. Translated by Raymond Dawson. Oxford: Oxford University Press, 2008.

Davey, Kevin. "Aristotle, Zeno, and the Stadium Paradox." *History of Philosophy Quarterly* 24, no. 2 (2007): 127–46.

Engels, Frederick. "Socialism: Utopian and Scientific." In *Karl Marx and Frederick Engels Collected Works*, Vol. 24, 281–325. New York: International Publishers, 1989.

———. "Ludwig Feuerbach and the End of Classical German Philosophy." In *Karl Marx and Frederick Engels Collected Works*, Vol. 26, 353–98. New York: International Publishers, 1990.

Findlay, J. N. *Hegel: A Re-Examination*. New York: Collier Books, 1958.

Fung Yu-Lan. *A Short History of Chinese Philosophy*. New York: The Free Press, 1966.

Gadamer, Hans-Georg. *Hegel's Dialectic: Five Hermeneutical Studies*. New Haven: Yale University Press, 1976.

Gorgias of Leontini, "On the Nonexistent." In Sextus Empiricus, *Against the Schoolmasters*, Vol. VII, 65–87. http://www.wfu.edu/~zulick/300/gorgias/negative.
Gotama, *Nyaya Sutras of Gotama*, edited by Satis Chandra Vidyabhusana, *The Sacred Books of the Hindus*, Vol. 3. Allababad: Sudhindranatha Vasu, 1913.
Hyppolite, Jean. *Genesis and Structure of Hegel's Phenomenology of Spirit*. Evanston: Northwestern University Press, 1974.
Ilyenkov, E. V. *The Dialectics of the Abstract and the Concrete in Marx's Capital*. Delhi: Aakar Books, 2008.
Immerwahr, John. "An Interpretation of Zeno's Stadium Paradox." *Phronesis: A Journal of Ancient Philosophy* 23, no. 1 (1978): 127–46.
Kant, Immanuel. *Grounding for the Metaphysics of Morals*. Translated by James W. Ellington. Indianapolis: Hackett, 1993.
Kierkegaard, Søren. *The Concept of Irony: With Constant Reference to Socrates*. Harper New York: Harper & Row, 1965.
Kirk G. S., J. E. Raven, and M. Schofield. *The Presocratic Philosophers: A Critical History with a Selection of Texts*, 2nd ed. Cambridge, UK: Cambridge University Press, 1983.
Kojéve, Alexandre. *Introduction to the Reading of Hegel: Lectures on the Phenomenology of Spirit*. Ithaca: Cornell University Press, 1969.
Laërtius, Diogenes. *Lives of the Eminent Philosophers*, Vol. 1. Translated by Robert Drew Hicks. London: Loeb Classical Library, 1925.
———. *Lives of the Eminent Philosophers*, Vol. 2. Translated by Robert Drew Hicks. London: Loeb Classical Library, 1925.
Lauer, Quentin, SJ. *Hegel's Idea of Philosophy*. With a translation of G. W. F. Hegel Introduction to History of Philosophy. New York: Fordham University Press, 1971.
———. *Essays in Hegelian Dialectic*. New York: Fordham University Press, 1977.
Marcuse, Herbert. *Reason and Revolution: Hegel and the Rise of Social Theory*. New York: Oxford University Press, 1960.
Marx, Karl. "Introduction" to *Outlines of the Critique of Political Economy*. In *Karl Marx and Frederick Engels Collected Works*, Vol. 28, translated by Ernst Wangermann, 17–48. New York: International Publishers, 1986.
———. "Marginal Notes on Adolph Wagner's Lehrbuch der politischen Oekonomie." In *Karl Marx and Frederick Engels Collected Works*, Vol. 24, translated by Barrie Selman, 531–59. New York: International Publishers, 1989.
McTaggart, John. *Studies in the Hegelian Dialectic*. Cambridge, 1896.

Plato. "Meno." In *Plato: The Collected Dialogues, Including the Letters*, edited by Edith Hamilton and Huntington Cairns, 353–84. Princeton: Princeton University Press, 1961.

———. "Phaedo." In *Plato: The Collected Dialogues, Including the Letters*, edited by Edith Hamilton and Huntington Cairns, 40–98. Princeton: Princeton University Press, 1961.

———. *Republic*. Translated by G.M.A Grube, and edited by C.D.C. Reeve. Indianapolis: Hackett, 1992.

Russell, Bertrand. *A History of Western Philosophy*. New York: Simon and Schuster Inc., 1945.

Samkhya Karika: with Gaudapadacarya Bhasya, commentator Brahmrishi Vishvatma Bawra. USA: Brahmrishi Yoga Publications, 2012.

Schwartz, Benjamin Isadore. *The World of Thought in Ancient China*. Cambridge, MA: Belknap Press, 1985.

Sharma, Chandradhar. *A Critical Survey of Indian Philosophy*. Delhi: Motilal Banarsidass, 1969.

St. Augustine. *City of God*. London: Penguin Books, 1984.

Tsung-I Dow, "Yin-Yang Dialectical Monism: A New Attempt to Explore the Symbiotic Relationship of Man and Nature through Reformulation of the Confucian-Taoist Metaphysical System." http://thomehfang.com/suncrates/7Dow.html.

Tzu Lao, *The Tao Te Ching of Lao Tzu*. Translated by Brian Browne Walker. New York: St. Martin's Press, 1995.

Viyagappa, Ignatius. *G.W.F. Hegel's Concept of Indian Philosophy*. Rome: Universita Gregoriana Editrice, 1980.

Watters, Thomas. *Lao-Tzu: A Study in Chinese Philosophy*. London: Williams & Norgate, 1870.

Young Kun Kim, "Hegel's Criticism of Chinese Philosophy." *Philosophy East and West* 28, no. 2 (1978): 173–80.

www.ingramcontent.com/pod-product-compliance
Lightning Source LLC
LaVergne TN
LVHW011416080426
835512LV00005B/81